The Risk Management Handbook

The Risk Management Handbook

A practical guide to managing the multiple dimensions of risk

Edited by David Hillson

LONDON PHILADELPHIA NEW DELHI

> **Publisher's note**
>
> Every possible effort has been made to ensure that the information contained in this book is accurate at the time of going to press, and the publisher and authors cannot accept responsibility for any errors or omissions, however caused. No responsibility for loss or damage occasioned to any person acting, or refraining from action, as a result of the material in this publication can be accepted by the editor, the publisher or any of the authors.

First published in Great Britain and the United States in 2016 by Kogan Page Limited

Apart from any fair dealing for the purposes of research or private study, or criticism or review, as permitted under the Copyright, Designs and Patents Act 1988, this publication may only be reproduced, stored or transmitted, in any form or by any means, with the prior permission in writing of the publishers, or in the case of reprographic reproduction in accordance with the terms and licences issued by the CLA. Enquiries concerning reproduction outside these terms should be sent to the publishers at the undermentioned addresses:

2nd Floor, 45 Gee Street	1518 Walnut Street,	4737/23 Ansari Road
London EC1V 3RS	Suite 900	Daryaganj
United Kingdom	Philadelphia PA 19102	New Delhi 110002
	USA	India

www.koganpage.com

© Kogan Page Limited, 2016

The right of David Hillson to be identified as editor of this work and the contributors to be identified as authors of their contributions has been asserted by them in accordance with the Copyright, Designs and Patents Act 1988.

ISBN   978 0 7494 7882 7
E-ISBN 978 0 7494 7883 4

British Library Cataloguing-in-Publication Data

A CIP record for this book is available from the British Library.

Library of Congress Cataloging-in-Publication Data

Names: Hillson, David, 1955– editor.
Title: The risk management handbook : a practical guide to managing the multiple dimensions of risk / edited by David Hillson.
Description: London ; Philadelphia : Kogan Page, 2016. | Includes bibliographical references and index.
Identifiers: LCCN 2016012811 (print) | LCCN 2016019637 (ebook) | ISBN 9780749478827 (paperback) | ISBN 9780749478834 (ebook)
Subjects: LCSH: Risk management. | BISAC: BUSINESS & ECONOMICS / Insurance / Risk Assessment & Management. | BUSINESS & ECONOMICS / Management.
Classification: LCC HD61 .R51974 2016 (print) | LCC HD61 (ebook) | DDC 658.15/5–dc23
LC record available at https://urldefense.proofpoint.com/v2/url?u=https-3A__lccn.loc.gov_2016012811&d=BQIFAg&c=euGZstcaTDllvimEN8b7jXrwqOf-v5A_CdpgnVfiiMM&r=x3f92h9vpKKMXZvIinxurwyf7NpH8IGAe1dbh3Zq7oc&m=4hCkP3IS2vqAvH4O8HNFgnoF7PCtThcK_b1556C5x4Q&s=7mqgt2nzAIs4NU8H6dTtuM_Yd9I38ZUwqsXcGn2et5Y&e=

Typeset by SPi Global
Print production managed by Jellyfish
Printed and bound by Ashford Colour Press Ltd.

CONTENTS

About the authors xii

01 Introducing risk 1

Dr David Hillson

What do you do? 1
What is risk? 2
What is risk management? 5
Why does it matter? 9
And finally... 10
References 10

PART ONE: Multidimensional risk management 13

02 Enterprise Risk Management 15

Liz Taylor

Why does Enterprise Risk Management matter? 15
What is Enterprise Risk Management? 19
What is risk in this context? 22
How is enterprise risk managed? 23
How does Enterprise Risk Management fit? 29
What's next? 29
Find out more 32

03 Governance, Risk and Compliance 34

Robert Toogood

Why does GRC matter? 34
What is Governance, Risk and Compliance (GRC)? 35

What is risk in this context? 36
How is GRC managed? 40
How does GRC fit? 45
What's next? 47
Find out more 48

04   Operational Risk Management 50

Edward Sankey, with Dr Ariane Chapelle

Why does Operational Risk Management matter? 50
What is Operational Risk Management? 51
What is risk in this context? 54
How is operational risk managed? 56
How does Operational Risk Management fit? 67
What's next? 68
Find out more 70

05   Project, programme and portfolio risk management 72

Dr Dale F Cooper

Why does project, programme and portfolio risk management matter? 72
What is project, programme and portfolio risk management? 75
What is risk in this context? 76
How is risk managed in projects, programmes and portfolios? 77
How does project, programme and portfolio risk management fit? 89
What's next? 90
Find out more 93

06   Political risk management 94

Robert McKellar

Why does political risk management matter? 94
What is political risk management? 95

What is risk in this context? 97
How is political risk managed? 100
How does political risk management fit? 105
What's next? 106
Find out more 107

07 Reputational risk 109

Arif Zaman

Why does reputational risk matter? 109
What is reputational risk management? 112
What is risk in this context? 114
How is reputational risk managed? 118
How does reputational risk management fit? 119
What's next? 120
Find out more 121

08 Supply chain risk management 122

Linda Conrad

Why does supply chain risk management matter? 122
What is supply chain risk management? 126
What is risk in this context? 128
How is supply chain risk managed? 131
How does supply chain risk management fit? 133
What's next? 134
Find out more 138

09 Business Continuity Management 141

Ian Clark

Why does business continuity matter? 141
What is Business Continuity Management? 142
What is business continuity in this context? 143
How is business continuity managed? 144
How does Business Continuity Management fit? 158
What's next? 158
Find out more 162

10   Managing stakeholder risk 164

Dr Lynda Bourne and Patrick Weaver

Why does stakeholder risk management matter? 164
What is stakeholder risk management? 166
What is risk in this context? 166
How is stakeholder risk managed? 171
How does stakeholder risk management fit? 177
What's next? 178
Find out more 179

11   Ethics in risk management 180

Giusi Meloni

Why do ethics matter in risk management? 180
What is ethical risk management? 183
What is risk in this context? 185
How is ethical risk managed? 187
How does ethical risk management fit? 190
What's next? 190
Find out more 192

12   Cyber risk management 194

Ben Rendle

Why does cyber risk management matter? 194
What is cyber risk management? 197
What is risk in this context? 200
How is cyber risk managed? 203
How does cyber risk management fit? 208
What's next? 210
Find out more 212

PART TWO: Emerging trends 215

13   Country risk management 219

Daniel Wagner

The importance of anticipation 219
A sound cross-border risk management platform 220

Best practices 221
Why every manager needs to be a country risk manager 222
Summary: staying ahead of the curve 224
References and further reading 224

14 Communicating uncertainty 225

Dr Veronica Bowman

Background 225
An effective communication strategy 226
Summary: case study 231
References 235

15 Risk-based decision making 236

Dr Keith Smith

Introduction 236
The decision maker's conundrum 236
Understanding how decisions are made 237
Dual processing 239
Clockspeed vs velocity 240
Situation awareness and decision making 241
Decision controls 241
Summary 243
References 243

16 Risk leadership in complex organizations 246

Dr Richard Barber

Introduction 246
Getting the assumptions right 246
Useful principles for leaders working in and on uncertainty 249
Systemic risk leadership in practice 251
Summary: what this means for leaders of organizations 253
References 254

17   Resilience   255

Dr Erica Seville

What is a resilience approach?   255
Resilience and risk management   256
Summary: proactive ways to develop resilience   258
References   260

18   Organizational change management and risk   262

Dr Ruth Murray-Webster

Why is change risky?   262
Why is risk analysis and management vital during change?   265
Critical success factors if risk management is to help change management   266
Summary   267
References   268

19   Risk culture   269

Alex Hindson

What is risk culture and why is it important?   269
How to approach risk culture   272
Diagnosing risk culture   272
Risk awareness   272
Changing or influencing risk culture   275
Case study   275
Summary   277
References   278

20   Social media risk   279

Dr Greg Ker-Fox

Introduction   279
The social media business model   279
Opportunities created by social media for business   280
Threats associated with social media for business   281
Exploiting social media opportunities   285

Mitigating social media threats 286
Summary 288
References and further reading 289

21 Risk in development aid practice 290

Magda Stepanyan

Risk as an external danger 291
Risk as an accident associated with human fault 292
Risk as a social phenomenon 293
Risk as a global 'grand challenge' or mega risks 295
Summary 296
References 296

Epilogue: The future of risk management 298

Dr David Hillson

Risk is everywhere 298
Risk management is everywhere 299
What next? 300
Where now? 302
References and further reading 302

Index 304

ABOUT THE AUTHORS

The editor

Dr David Hillson

Known globally as The Risk Doctor, David Hillson is an award-winning thought leader and expert practitioner who consults and writes widely on risk management, with 10 major books on the topic. David leads The Risk Doctor Partnership (www.risk-doctor.com), a global consultancy offering specialist risk services across the world.

His groundbreaking work in risk management has been recognized with many professional awards, including being named inaugural 'Risk Personality of the Year' by the Institute of Risk Management (IRM) in 2010–11. In recent years David has specialized in strategic risk management, with a focus on risk culture, risk appetite and risk attitudes.

Chapter authors: Multidimensional risk management

Liz Taylor

Liz is a Chartered Insurance Practitioner. A varied career has given her multinational and multi-industry hands-on experience at operational and board level, specializing in encouraging organizations to take managed risk in order to innovate, grow and thrive. Liz was Europe-wide Risk Manager of the Year in 1993, chaired AIRMIC, bringing it to corporate membership, and initiated the set up of Pool Re.

Previously Chief Executive of ALARM and then Senior Vice President at Marsh, she now works with many sectors including Financial Services, Petrochemical and Nuclear, Utilities and Government providing ERM solutions.

Robert Toogood

Robert Toogood is a project and systems expert, who helps senior executives solve their project-related system challenges. His real-world project management experience spans many decades, based on a solid and successful systems background. Since forming his own consultancy, Project Systems Support, Robert has shared and developed his expertise with many consulting clients. He is interested in the business benefits of a more co-ordinated approach to Governance, Risk and Compliance (GRC) activities. This interest led him to launch a Special Interest Group (SIG) within the Institute of Risk Management (IRM) focused on GRC, and he also researched the topic as part of his recent MSc in Risk Management studies.

Dr Ariane Chapelle

Dr Chapelle holds a PhD in Economics and two Masters in Finance and Econometrics. She has been active in Operational Risk Management (ORM) since 2000, with experience acquired in managerial functions in ING Group and Lloyds Banking Group. Ariane Chapelle has been running her own training and consulting practice in risk management since 2006, her clients consisting of top-tier financial organizations. She is Honorary Reader in Operational Risk at the University College London and Fellow of the Institute of Operational Risk, for which she chairs the Sound Practice Guidance Committee. She is a columnist for *Operational Risk and Regulation* magazine.

Edward Sankey

Edward Sankey is Director at Larocourt Risk, and past Chairman of the Council of the Institute of Operational Risk. Edward consults in strategic and operational risk. He recently completed a long assignment as Interim Director and CF28, Operational Risk, and member of the Risk Committee at Santander UK. Edward has led risk activities in Marsh Europe, City Practitioners, AEA Technology/Risk Solutions and KPMG. His projects have been in wholesale markets, retail and corporate banking, insurance, investment management, full range major banks, and for a regulator/supervisor. He has worked in Russia, Europe and elsewhere, and is a member of the City Values Forum founded by the Lord Mayor, focusing on cultures and behaviours in firms. Edward is a Fellow at the IOR and Honorary Life Member of the Institute of Risk Management.

Dr Dale F Cooper

Dale Cooper is the Director of Broadleaf Capital International and has over 35 years' experience as a senior line manager and an international consultant. Broadleaf Capital International, established in 1991, provides high-level assistance and advice on all aspects of risk management, including the development and implementation of enterprise and project risk management processes for large public and private sector clients.

Dale Cooper has been an independent Chairman and member of several Audit and Risk Committees, and is a contributor to national and international standards. He is a Fellow of the Australian Institute of Company Directors, a Fellow of the Financial Services Institute of Australasia, a member of the Society of Petroleum Engineers and a member of the Society for Risk Analysis. He has written many professional papers and several books, most recently *Project Risk Management Guidelines: Managing Risk with ISO 31000 and IEC 62198*, written with colleagues from Broadleaf and published by John Wiley in March 2014.

Robert McKellar

Robert McKellar is a political risk management consultant and Director of Harmattan Risk, an independent risk advisory. He works with companies and development organizations to assess risk and plan risk management approaches in complex emerging markets, as well as to develop relevant in-house capabilities. His overseas work has mainly focused on North Africa and the Middle East. Robert studied Arabic in Tunis for a year, and holds an MA in Political Science from Canada and a Master of International Business from France. Robert is author of *A Short Guide to Political Risk*, published by Gower Publishing in 2010.

Arif Zaman

Arif Zaman, FRSA, is Executive Director of the Commonwealth Businesswomen's Network, the only organization focused on women's economic empowerment recognized by 53 Commonwealth governments. He is CEO of Riscaire, providing training and advisory services on governance and reputational risk with leading firms in related areas in emerging markets, and he is also on the faculty at Henley Business School, University of Reading. Arif authored the bestselling book *Reputational Risk* (Financial Times, 2004 and published in Russian, 2008), still the only international research-based book on reputational risk from a major business publisher and *Made in Japan: Converging Trends in Corporate Responsibility and Corporate Governance* (Chatham House, 2003). He was Global Market and Industry Analyst at British Airways (1996–2005) and previously at HSBC. Arif is also Executive Secretary, Commonwealth Research Network on International Business (CRN-IB).

Linda Conrad

Linda Conrad is Head of Strategic Business Risk for Zurich Insurance, Global Corporate in North America. She leads a global team responsible for delivering tactical solutions to Zurich and to customers on strategic issues such as business resilience, cyber and supply chain risk, Enterprise Risk Management (ERM), risk culture and Total Risk Profiling. Linda also addresses enterprise resiliency issues in print and television appearances, including CNBC, Fox Business News and the *Financial Times*, and is featured in a *Wall Street Journal* micro-site at www.SupplyChainRiskInsights.com.

Linda holds a Specialist designation in ERM, and serves on the global Education Advisory Board of the Institute of Risk Management in London. She is deputy member of the ERM Committee of RIMS, sits on the Supply Chain Risk Leadership Council, and was Chairwoman of the Asian Risk Management Conference. She taught at University of Delaware Captive programme and in the Master's on Supply Chain Management programme at University of Michigan's Ross School of Business, where she serves on the Corporate Advisory Council. Linda studied at the Graduate Institute of International Studies in Geneva, Switzerland and Fox Business School.

Ian Clark

Ian Clark is a highly motivated and experienced Business Continuity Management (BCM) practitioner with extensive practical experience of the disciplines and roles essential in developing and delivering holistic BCM programmes.

He has global experience in providing consultancy services to many business sectors and at all levels within organizations, ranging from multinational businesses and governments to small or medium-sized organizations. Ian is a proponent of the active integration of Risk Management and BCM techniques throughout the organizational ecosystem, in order to develop a resilient and balanced continuity programme that is effective, easily maintained, and suited to the organization's needs and culture.

He is the Principal of 4Thought Associates, and the incumbent chair of the Business Continuity Institute's Global Membership Council.

Dr Lynda Bourne

Dr Lynda Bourne FAIM, FACS, PMP is a senior management consultant, professional speaker and trainer with over 30 years of professional industry experience.

Dr Bourne is a recognized international author, seminar leader and speaker on the topic of stakeholder engagement and the Stakeholder Circle® visualization tool. She has presented at conferences and seminars in Europe, Russia, Asia, Australasia, South America and the Middle East to audiences in the IT, construction, defence and mining industries.

She is a member of the Core Committee for *PMBOK* 6th edition due for release in 2016; her focus is on the stakeholder and communications knowledge areas.

Patrick Weaver

Patrick is the Managing Director of Mosaic Project Services Pty Ltd and the business manager of Stakeholder Management Pty Ltd where he is responsible for managing the worldwide launch of the Stakeholder Circle® methodology and software tool. He is a senior consultant and project management trainer.

His interest is in improving project governance and controls, and in addition to his work on ISO 21500 and 21505, he has contributed to a range of standards developments with PMI, CIOB and AIPM and presented many papers, at conferences worldwide.

Giusi Meloni

With a degree in languages and a specialization in intercultural relations, Giusi combines her humanities background with a long experience in project management. She is currently a partner of The Project Management Lab, a consulting and training company based in Milan, Italy.

Giusi holds a certification in Guidance and Counselling, is certified as a Project Management Professional (PMP®) and is a PMI Leadership Institute Master Class Alumnus.

She has been an active volunteer in PMI for several years, both locally and at global level, and until recently she was team leader of the PMI Ethics Member Advisory Group.

Ben Rendle

Ben Rendle is managing director of risk consultancy Riosca Limited (www.rioscaconsulting.co.uk). He has worked in risk management and project consulting for the past 10 years with BAE Systems, Deloitte and HVR Consulting Services. Ben has provided cyber risk management and business change consulting for the UK government Department of Energy and Climate Change and other associated industry organizations.

Ben co-authored the Cabinet Office 'Cost of Cybercrime' report in 2011, which gathered considerable interest across academic and national media. He has also presented on this report to a number of professional bodies, including the Association for Project Management (APM) and the UK Fraud Advisory Panel.

Chapter authors: Emerging trends

Daniel Wagner

Daniel Wagner is CEO of Country Risk Solutions, a country risk consulting firm based in Connecticut (United States). He has more than a quarter century of experience managing country risk, including 15 years of underwriting experience with AIG, GE, the Asian Development Bank, and the World Bank Group.

Daniel has published three books on country risk – *Political Risk Insurance Guide* (International Risk Management Institute, 1999), *Managing Country Risk* (CRC Press, 2012) and *Global Risk Agility and Decision Making* (Macmillan, 2016) – and has published hundreds of articles on current affairs and risk management in a plethora of platforms. He holds master's degrees in International Relations from the University of Chicago and in International Business from Thunderbird.

Dr Veronica Bowman

Dr Veronica Bowman is a statistician at the UK government's Defence Science and Technology Laboratory. She specializes in uncertainty calculation and communication and Bayesian inference, and is internationally recognized as the lead technical expert for Chemical, Biological and Radiological (CBR) knowledge management. Veronica was the chair of the Calculating and Communicating Uncertainty Conference (CCU 2015), which brought together leading researchers from the field of uncertainty. She has a BSc with First Class Honours and a PhD in Statistical Modelling, both from the University of Southampton. She is a fellow of the Institute of Mathematics and its Applications and is a chartered mathematician.

Dr Keith Smith

As an engineer, Keith project managed a number of high-tech projects in telecommunications where he owned and managed many risks. His interest in practical risk management continued to grow with the development of his first risk tool in 1995. In 2000 Keith launched RiskCovered, winning a government-sponsored industry award for his novel approach to risk management with techniques that have since become mainstream in the field. More recently he engaged in further research, gaining a doctorate for his work on Risk Clockspeed. Through RiskCovered, Keith also delivers practical consultancy, training and coaching in both risk and decision making.

Dr Richard Barber

Richard leads RiskIQ, a consulting business with a focus on maximizing the performance of organizations in the face of change and uncertainty. He works with senior leaders on their most difficult challenges, getting below symptoms to find effective points of leverage in complex systems.

Richard is the architect of the Risk Leadership Framework, a systems approach to risk management that integrates the management of uncertainty into routine work practices and governance. He is on several governance boards and lectures at the Queensland University of Technology. He has extensive experience in the public and private sectors, including as an engineer, logistician, project leader and chief executive.

Dr Erica Seville

Dr Erica Seville co-leads Resilient Organisations, which involves more than 35 researchers around New Zealand, striving to make organizations more resilient. Erica has authored over 100 research articles and is regularly invited to speak on the topic of resilience. Erica is a member of the Resilience Expert Advisory Group, providing advice and support to the Australian Federal Government. Erica is also a member of the BCI 2020 think tank, to re-envision what business continuity practice might look like in 2020. Erica is an Adjunct Senior Fellow with the Department of Civil and Natural Resources Engineering at the University of Canterbury and she has a PhD in risk management.

Dr Ruth Murray-Webster

Dr Ruth Murray-Webster is Director of the Change Portfolio for Associated British Ports Ltd. Prior to taking up this role in 2015, Ruth has had 30 years of experience in a series of roles to enable organizations in most sectors to deliver change objectives. Along this journey, Ruth researched organizational change from the perspective of the recipients of change for an Executive Doctorate at Cranfield School of Management. She has also taken a keen interest in risk management along the way, co-authoring four books on the people aspects of risk management with David Hillson (*Understanding and Managing Risk Attitude*, 2007; *Managing Group Risk Attitude*, 2008; *A Short Guide to Risk Appetite*, 2012), and Penny Pullan (*A Short Guide to Facilitating Risk Management*, 2011). She was awarded an Honorary Fellowship of the Association for Project Management in 2013 for her services to risk and change.

Alex Hindson

Alex Hindson is Chief Risk Officer at Argo Group where he is responsible for the implementation of Enterprise Risk Management across the Group as well as the Compliance function, adoption of the Internal Capital Model and purchasing of corporate insurances. Alex has extensive experience of working on the topic of Risk Culture having led the Institute of Risk Management programme in this area in 2011. Previous roles included Chief Risk Officer of Amlin AG, Head of Group Risk at Amlin plc and Head of ERM at Aon Global Risk Consulting. Alex is a Certified Fellow of the IRM as well as being a past Chairman.

Dr Greg Ker-Fox

Dr Greg Ker-Fox qualified from Stellenbosch University in South Africa with a BEng, MEng (cum laude) and PhD in Civil Engineering. He researched quantitative methods for modelling project risk. Greg joined global engineering and construction contractor Murray & Roberts in 2002. He was seconded to the Pebble Bed Modular Reactor project for three years as their Project Risk Manager, before moving to Murray & Roberts Head Office where he served eight years as the Group Risk Executive. In 2013 Greg founded FoxCo Risk, a specialist risk consultancy based in South Africa. Greg is a member of the Risk Doctor Partnership and serves as the Executive Advisor: Education and Training to the Engineering and Construction Risk Institute.

Magda Stepanyan

Magda Stepanyan is founder and CEO of the Risk Society consultancy (www.risk-society.com). She holds an MA in Sociology from Yerevan State

University, Armenia, an MSc in Public Administration from Leiden University, the Netherlands, and the International Certificate in Risk Management from the Institute of Risk Management (IRM).

Magda's expertise is in resilience programming, integrated risk management (IRM), risk-informed strategy planning and implementation, disaster and climate risk management, horizon scanning for strategy and policy development, monitoring and evaluation. She has more than 15 years' management and consultancy experience, working with organizations such as the EC, UN, WB, Red Cross, and others. In 2012 Magda authored a UNDP Technical Paper titled 'Risk Management for Capacity Development Facilities'.

Introducing risk   01

DR DAVID HILLSON

What do you do?

Many risk professionals and practitioners will be familiar with this conversation in a bar or over dinner:

'So, what do you do?'
    'I'm a risk practitioner.'
'Oh, you're in insurance.'
    'No, I'm not.'
'Then I guess you must be a health & safety person, preventing slips and trips?'
    'Actually no, I'm not that either.'
'So, what do you actually do?'
    'Well…'

And this is where the problem starts. For those of us who work in the risk management field, what exactly do we do, and how do we explain it to non-specialists? How do we justify our existence in a way that avoids jargon or boredom, and that reflects the value of our contribution to business, society and the general good?

This book seeks to offer an answer, drawing on the experience and expertise of leading risk practitioners, each with their own area of specialist knowledge and practice. For those unfamiliar with the risk management domain, the result may be surprising. Why do we need a whole book to explain what risk management is all about? And those who are already active in this area may find inspiration for the next time they encounter the bar or dinner-table challenge.

It's important to start at the beginning, with some basic concepts and principles, before going on to explore the richness of the risk management subject area. This introductory chapter provides a context for what follows, outlining the basics of risk management in a straightforward and simple manner, and providing a firm foundation on which later chapters build. Here we start by defining what we mean by 'risk', what steps are needed if we want to do 'risk management', and why it matters to organizations and businesses around the world.

What is risk?

A favourite saying of a colleague is this: 'Risk is risk is risk.' I think I understand what she means, but I only partly agree.

It is possible to define the word 'risk' in generic terms with broad applicability. But like many universal concepts, some tailoring may be necessary to make the general fit the specific. These more nuanced and particular definitions of risk are discussed in the chapters that follow, but first we need to understand the underlying idea.

Risk and uncertainty

The first consideration to explore is the relationship between risk and uncertainty. These are clearly related, since all risks are uncertain. But not all uncertainties are risks. There are billions of uncertainties in the world around us, but a much smaller subset are identified as risks, recorded in risk registers, addressed through risk responses, or discussed in risk reports. We need to apply some filter to the uncertain world in order to determine which uncertainties we need to know about, think about, prepare for and communicate.

Theoretical approaches to this distinction began with Knight (1921) in the field of economics, who sought to separate insurable risk from true uncertainty. His approach drew on basic mathematical theory, that 'risk' arises from randomness with knowable probabilities, whereas 'uncertainty' reflects randomness with unknowable probabilities. Put more simply, according to Knight, risk is measurable uncertainty.

In theory this distinction may seem useful and clear, but in reality probabilities are rarely known with any precision or certainty. Throwing unbiased dice or flipping fair coins are idealized cases of risky situations, but any real-world example will not behave in so straightforward a manner.

If we are to find a clear role for risk management in relation to meeting the challenge of uncertainty, mathematical theory is unlikely to yield usable solutions. A more pragmatic approach is required, which is useful in practice, and which supports effective risk management and good decision making when conditions are not certain. Perhaps 'risk' can be seen as a subset or special case of 'uncertainty'.

Reviewing the world around us confirms that it is characterized by uncertainty in many forms arising from a variety of sources. However, the task of risk management is quite specific. It is to enable individuals, groups and organizations to make appropriate decisions in the light of the uncertainties that surround them. The key word here is 'appropriate'. How can we determine what response is appropriate for any particular uncertainty? One way is to separate the various uncertainties into two groups: those that matter to us, and those that do not matter. There are perhaps an infinite number of uncertainties in the universe but they do not matter equally; indeed some do not matter at all, while others are literally vital. As we seek to make sense of our uncertain environment and decide what to do in order to move forward, we need to know which uncertainties matter, and then respond appropriately to those. Any uncertainties which do not matter can be ignored, or perhaps reviewed from time to time to see whether they or our circumstances have changed to the point where they might now matter.

This leads us to a proto-definition of 'risk' which offers a useful distinction to guide our thinking and practice (Hillson 2004, 2009): **risk is 'uncertainty that matters'.**

While this may not be a fully-formed definition, it does point us in the right direction. Not every uncertainty is a risk, though risk is always uncertain. Risk is a subset of uncertainty, filtered on whether or not it matters. If risk management focuses on identifying and managing those uncertainties that matter, it will help us to respond appropriately.

Risk and objectives

So how can we decide whether a particular uncertainty matters or not? The key is to focus on **objectives**. These define what matters to any individual, group or organization. Objective setting is the process of describing our desired goal and the end point that represents success. To concentrate on what matters means to link everything to achievement of agreed objectives. By defining 'risk' as the subset of uncertainties that matter, we are tightly coupling risk management to achievement of objectives, since the goal is to identify and manage any uncertainty that could affect our desired outcome. This provides a clear link between risk management and success, delivery, value and benefits. Where risks are effectively managed, the chances of achieving objectives will be optimized. Conversely, poor risk management will reduce the likelihood of success.

Making the link between risk and objectives moves us closer to a usable definition of risk. Risk is a type of uncertainty, but not every uncertainty is a risk. Instead risk is that subset of uncertainty that matters, and we determine whether a particular uncertainty matters by considering the possibility that objectives might be affected. Of course the uncertainty will only actually matter in practice if it occurs and becomes reality. So our proto-definition of risk as 'uncertainty that matters' can be expanded: **risk is 'uncertainty that, if it occurs, will affect achievement of objectives'**.

The essential link between risk and objectives has a number of implications. The typical organization has a range of objectives at many levels. There are strategic objectives at the highest level, which are translated into increasing detail for implementation through the delivery elements of the organization. Subsidiary objectives exist at financial, safety, regulatory, programme and project levels, among others. If risk is defined as 'uncertainty that, if it occurs, will affect achievement of objectives', then it applies wherever there are objectives. This allows us to define various levels of risk management. Strategic risks are uncertainties that, if they occurred, would affect strategic objectives, and strategic risk management addresses these risks. Project risk management tackles risks that could affect project objectives, reputation risk management deals with risks to reputation, and so on. Risk management is not just relevant to technical or delivery disciplines, but affects every part of an organization from top to bottom. Successful identification and management of uncertainties that matter is essential for success across the business at every level. This is why risk management deserves such wide attention. The left-hand side of Figure 1.1 illustrates the hierarchical nature of both objectives and risks in the typical organization.

This leads to a further important consideration for the management of risk. If an organization has a hierarchy of objectives, and each level is affected by risk, then it follows that the people responsible for managing each level of risk should be those who own the objectives that would be affected. This is shown in the right-hand side of Figure 1.1.

Risk, threat and opportunity

One further key concept arises from the idea that risk is 'uncertainty that matters'. Not everything that matters is bad. In recent years there has been an increasing realization that risk is a double-sided concept, with upside and downside risks, positive and negative impacts, adverse and beneficial outcomes (Hillson, 2004). An uncertainty that, if it occurs, will have a negative effect on objectives is known as a **threat**. Conversely, an uncertainty that, if

FIGURE 1.1 Hierarchies of objectives, risks, and risk management

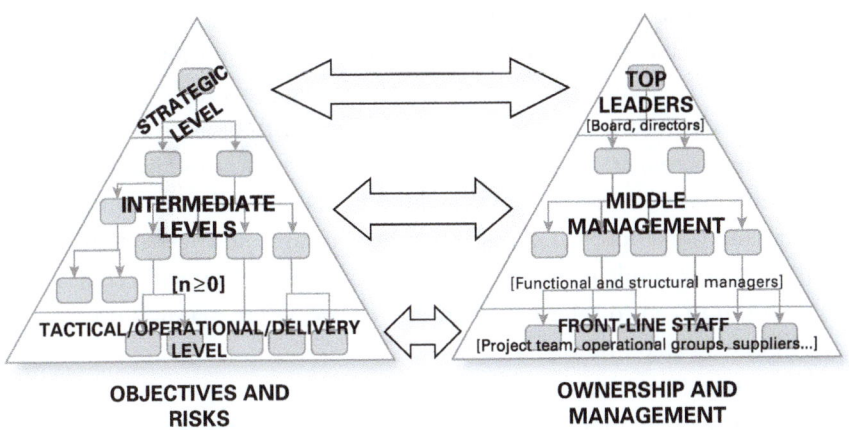

it occurs, will have a positive effect on objectives is an opportunity. Both threats and opportunities are 'uncertainties that matter', so both are encompassed within the term 'risk', and both can be proactively managed through the risk management process.

This leads to a final refinement to our evolving definition of risk: risk is 'uncertainty that, if it occurs, will have a positive or negative effect on achievement of objectives'.

This broad definition of risk, including the two key characteristics of being uncertain and potentially affecting objectives, and recognizing the possibility of either positive or negative outcomes, is reflected in most current risk management standards (IRM/ALARM/AIRMIC, 2002; ISO, 2009a, 2009b; OGC, 2010; APM, 2012; PMI, 2013; IEC, 2013; ICE/IFA, 2014). It is also being increasingly adopted by organizations around the world in a variety of industry sectors as the basis for their risk management practice.

What is risk management?

My colleague with the circular definition of risk has a second equally insightful saying: 'Risk management is risk management is risk management.' As before, she is definitely on to something, emphasizing that the universal nature of risk means that we can adopt a generic approach to managing it. But, also as before, the variety of settings where we encounter risk means that there is no one-size-fits-all methodology for risk management, and a degree of tailoring is needed.

Later chapters describe how risk might be managed in different domain areas, but in each case the underlying process follows remarkably similar steps. Fortunately, these steps are intuitively obvious, enabling the thoughtful practitioner to implement a risk management approach naturally and effectively.

The intuitive nature of risk management is demonstrated by representing the process as a series of questions. These form a thinking framework that any leader, manager or responsible professional will recognize. Each question leads naturally to the next, making it easy to follow the process. By structuring our approach to risk management around these questions, we make it easy to implement, without having to worry about what comes next, and with no need to refer to a textbook or procedure manual to work out the following step in the process.

Eight basic questions underlie the risk management process, as outlined in the following paragraphs, and each question corresponds to a step in the generic risk management process (named in brackets).

1. **What are we trying to achieve?** (Establishing the Context.) The definition of risk discussed above makes it clear that risks only exist in relation to defined objectives. This means we cannot start any risky venture without first clearly defining its scope and clarifying the objectives that are at risk. We also need to know how much risk key stakeholders are prepared to accept, since this gives us the target threshold for risk exposure. We must address these factors as the first step of the risk process.

2. **What could affect us achieving these objectives?** (Risk Identification.) Once objectives and risk thresholds are agreed, we can start identifying risks, which are uncertainties that could affect achievement of objectives (including both threats and opportunities). There are a variety of risk identification techniques, each of which has strengths and weaknesses, so we should use more than one approach.

3. **Which of those things are most important?** (Risk Assessment.) Not all risks are equally important, so we need to filter and prioritize them, to find the worst threats and the best opportunities. This will help us decide how to respond. When prioritizing risks, we could use various characteristics, such as how likely they are to happen, what they might do to our objectives, how easily we can influence them, when they might happen, etc.

4. **What shall we do about them?** (Plan Risk Responses.) Now we can start to think about what actions are appropriate to deal with

individual risks. We might consider radical action (avoid threats or exploit opportunities), or attempt to influence the level of risk exposure (reduce threats or enhance opportunities), or decide to do nothing (accept the risk). We might also involve other parties in responding appropriately to the risks (transfer threats or share opportunities).

5 **Having taken action, did it work?** (Implement Risk Responses.) We can plan to address risks, but nothing will change unless we actually do something. Planned responses must be implemented in order to tackle individual risks and change overall risk exposure, and the results of these responses should be monitored to ensure that they are having the desired effect. Our actions may also introduce new risks for us to address.

6 **Who shall we tell?** (Risk Communication.) We are now in a position where we know what the risks are and how they would affect the objectives, and we understand which ones are particularly significant. We have also developed and implemented targeted responses to tackle our risk exposure, with the help of others. It is important to tell people with an interest in the objectives about the risks we have found and how we are addressing them.

7 **What has changed?** (Review Risk.) The risk process cannot end at this point, because risk is dynamic and changing. So we have to look again at risk on a regular basis, to see whether existing risks have been managed as expected, and to discover new risks that now require our attention.

8 **What did we learn?** (Risk Lessons Learned.) There is one more important step in the risk process, which is often forgotten. As responsible professionals we should take advantage of our experience with this risky situation to benefit future similar ventures. This means we will spend time thinking about what worked well and what needs improvement, and recording our conclusions in a way that can be reused by ourselves and others.

The eight questions outlined here can easily be formed into a generic risk management process, since each question leads logically and naturally to the next. Indeed, the processes contained in leading risk management standards and guidelines map well to this question set (although no one standard seems to address them all). Table 1.1 maps the questions to a number of leading standards, and as a detailed example, Figure 1.2 presents the process

TABLE 1.1 Mapping generic questions to risk management standards

Question	ISO 31000 (ISO, 2009a)	OGC M_o_R (OGC, 2010)	IRM Risk Standard (IRM/ALARM/AIRMIC, 2002)
What are we trying to achieve?	Establishing the context	Identify context	–
What could affect us?	Risk identification	Identify risks	Risk identification Risk description
Which are most important?	Risk analysis Risk evaluation	Assess	Risk estimation Risk evaluation
What shall we do about them? Did it work?	Risk treatment	Plan Implement	Risk treatment
Who shall we tell?	Communication and consultation	Communicate	Risk reporting
What has changed?	Monitoring and review	Embed and review	Monitoring and review
What did we learn?	–	–	–

from the international risk standard ISO 31000:2009, indicating which questions are answered by each stage.

One notable fact is evident from Table 1.1: most risk management standards do not include a formal step in the risk process to learn risk-related lessons from previous experience. This reflects the apparent reluctance of many organizations to undertake a lessons-learned review after making a key risk-based decision or at the end of a completed project. For some reason it seems that the effort to perform such a review is too much for most, despite the obvious benefits that can accrue. Perhaps this is because those benefits come too late to affect what has already occurred, or staff

FIGURE 1.2 Mapping generic questions to ISO 31000:2009 risk process

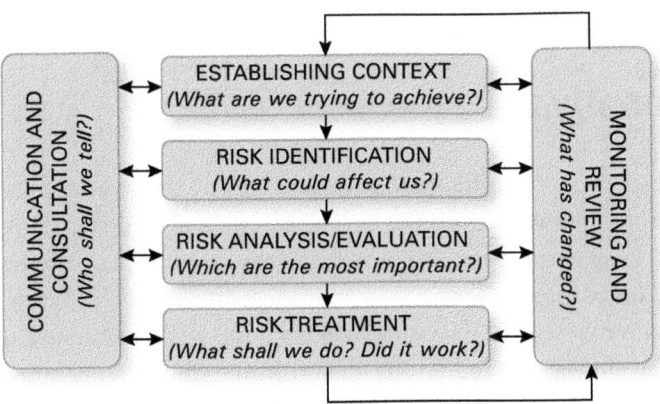

may lack the necessary altruism to help those who come after them. Or maybe it is simply a practical matter of people moving on to the next challenge before they have time to capture the lessons that could be derived from their recent experience. Whatever the reason, organizations that fail to conduct lessons-learned reviews are denying themselves the benefit of experience, and are increasing the chances of repeating the same mistakes in future. This applies to the risk process as much as to any other aspect of management.

Why does it matter?

Having defined the concept of risk and provided a framework for risk management, we need to understand why the typical organization or business should take notice. The reason that risk management matters derives directly from our definition of risk which links it to objectives. If risk matters because it has the potential to affect achievement of our objectives (either positively or negatively), then risk management matters equally. Our ability to manage those uncertainties that matter will have a direct bearing on our ability to succeed. Indeed risk management capability is a key competitive discriminator, since organizations that are able to recognize and manage risk effectively will have fewer problems and failures than their less competent rivals, as threats will have been avoided or minimized before they could impact the business. The competitive advantage is reinforced when the risk process is used to identify and capture opportunities proactively, creating additional benefits and more value than is available to more reactive organizations who are likely to miss the chance to operate faster, smarter or cheaper.

And finally...

As the reader explores the various dimensions of risk management in the chapters that follow, each with its own character and challenges, it would be helpful to keep in mind the generic principles and concepts described in this chapter. Comparing the specific risk management approach in each application domain to a common baseline will highlight what is unique and special about that dimension, and ensure that risk practitioners operating in that area will be on the same wavelength. It might also help them to answer the 'What do you do?' question!

References

Association for Project Management (APM) (2012) *Body of Knowledge*, 6th edn, Association for Project Management, Princes Risborough, Bucks, UK

Hillson, D A (2004) *Effective Opportunity Management for Projects: Exploiting positive risk*, Taylor & Francis, Boca Raton, USA

Hillson, D A (2009) *Managing Risk in Projects*, Gower, Farnham, UK

Institute of Risk Management, the Public Risk Management Association, and Association of Insurance and Risk Managers (IRM/ALARM/AIRMIC) (2002) *A Risk Management Standard*, IRM/ALARM/AIRMIC, London UK

Institution of Civil Engineers, Institute and Faculty of Actuaries (ICE/IFA) (2014) *Risk Analysis and Management for Projects (RAMP)*, 3rd edn, ICE Publishing, London, UK

International Electrotechnical Commission (IEC) (2013) *IEC 62198:2013, Managing Risk in Projects: Application guidelines*, International Electrotechnical Commission, Geneva, Switzerland

International Organization for Standardization (ISO) (2009a) *ISO 31000:2009. Risk Management: Principles and Guidelines*, International Organization for Standardization, Geneva, Switzerland

International Organization for Standardization (ISO) (2009b) ISO/IEC 31010:2009, *Risk Management: Risk assessment techniques*, International Organization for Standardization, Geneva, Switzerland

Knight, F H (1921) *Risk, Uncertainty, and Profit*, Hart, Schaffner & Marx, Boston, MA, USA

Office of Government Commerce (OGC) (2010) *Management of Risk (M_o_R): Guidance for practitioners*, 3rd edn, The Stationery Office, London, UK

Project Management Institute (PMI) (2013) *A Guide to the Project Management Body of Knowledge (PMBOK® Guide) 5th edn*, Project Management Institute, Newtown Square, PA, USA

PART ONE
Multi-dimensional risk management

DR DAVID HILLSON

Chapter 1 emphasized the common features of both risk as a concept, and risk management as a process. There is something attractive about this 'pure' view, reducing the apparent complexity of the topic to a few simple principles. And it is surely important for anyone facing the challenge of risk in their organization or business to have a firm grasp of these basics.

But risk management is actually a complex subject, driven by the complexity of the nature of risk. Having laid a foundation, it is time to explore the matter in more detail. The remainder of this book acts like a prism to examine risk management in practice. Anyone looking at a shaft of sunlight will see a single beam of white radiance. But place a prism in the path of the beam and something amazing happens. The pure white light is split into multiple colours, each strong and vibrant, different from all the others yet coming from the same source.

The same is true for our pure concept of risk and our generic process for managing it. Seen through the prism of experience and application, we discover a wide range of specific interpretations of risk, matched by a set of tailored risk management processes. Although there is indeed a unitary view of risk management, the reality is multidimensional. Each dimension has its origin in the pure foundational concepts and principles outlined in Chapter 1, yet each is suited to a distinct part of the risk challenge.

The following chapters each explore a single dimension of risk management in detail. Like the spectrum produced by the prism, each type of risk management has its own attraction and value. But also like refracted light, there are many specific types of risk management. Part One of this book addresses the main application areas that will be encountered by many business readers, and in Part Two we look at some new and emerging dimensions of risk management that are still being discovered and explored.

The growing nature of risk management as a discipline and profession makes it impossible to include every established and emerging risk speciality in this book, and some may argue over whether a specific topic belongs in Part One or Part Two, but the topics we have chosen to cover in this opening part address applications of risk management that most will encounter in the context of their business or organization, namely:

- Enterprise Risk Management (ERM);
- Governance, Risk and Compliance (GRC);
- Operational Risk Management (ORM);
- project, programme and portfolio risk management;
- political risk management;
- reputation risk management;
- supply chain risk management;
- Business Continuity Management (BCM);
- stakeholder risk management;
- ethics in risk management;
- cyber risk management.

Enterprise Risk Management

02

LIZ TAYLOR

Why does Enterprise Risk Management matter?

The world of business and enterprise is going through an increasingly tumultuous state of uncertainty. This uncertainty brings risks of widening ranges of frequency and magnitude. Enterprise Risk Management (ERM) is an essential tool in helping to bring more understanding of those risks; it enables the organization to be more prepared, more resilient to change and more ready to minimize threats and to seize opportunities.

Survival and uncertainty

The primary objective for most organizations is survival. This might be couched in many different terms such as profit, earnings, shareholder value and so on, but it boils down to just one thing – long-term sustainability for the business; in other words, survival.

Yet survival of businesses is increasingly becoming more affected by uncertainty; today's global economy has been proven to be vulnerable to the interconnected globalization that joins businesses and service providers from one end of the world to another. Goods and services are more and more interdependent; reputations and brands can be destroyed in minutes; our reliance on technology opens businesses to greater dependence and vulnerability on the net; the addiction to diminishing supplies of fossil fuels and other vanishing finite natural resources causes unlikely friends and foes across the globe (Blackman and Baumol, 2008); climate change and resultant lack of land, food and water drive heavier burdens on the most vulnerable; and uncertain times for some economies cause disenfranchised people to form into cohesive and focused groups seeking to force their own ideology onto others using terrorism tactics.

ISO 31000, the international standard for risk management, says 'The effect this uncertainty has on an organization's objectives is "risk".' Each of these uncertainties can bring with them threats as well as opportunities; threats where the organization is unprepared for the changes that may come about and opportunities for those who can predict and exploit the results of the uncertainties.

For organizations across the world, strategic decision making in the context of all this turmoil is about making risk decisions – to expand or to contract, to sell or to buy, to engage or to release, to change or to stay the same. These decisions all need an understanding of a wide range of risks and of the capacity of the organization to sustain risk over time.

Level at which risk is managed

Despite a wide awareness of uncertainty, 'risk management' often happens so far down the organization that the business leaders rarely understand it; they do not think it applies to them, nor do they have mastery over the powerful risk management skills that they could apply to their everyday jobs. Many of the great failures in business and public services have happened and continue to happen because of a failure in senior management and boards to engage in and commit to risk management.

The NCSU 2015 report on the current state of ERM states: 'While 59 per cent believe that the volume and complexity of risks have changed "extensively" or "mostly" in the last five years, only 25 per cent believe their organization has a "complete formal enterprise risk management process in place".' (Beasley, Branson and Hancock, 2015).

Enterprise Risk Management needs to be a top-level concern with top management having ERM skills and risk professionals who are hard-wired into strategic decision making and planning, advising on the threats and opportunities to which the business is exposed and alerting top management when the aggregate or individual risk areas might be outside the stated risk appetite.

Senior management and board engagement requires very little in terms of time and effort once it is understood and embedded into the ethos of the organizational culture (the understanding, practice and assimilation, however, do require effort and time).

The practice of Enterprise Risk Management gives the organization a unique perspective of risks and opportunities and of the capacity of the organization to take more or less managed risk.

Yet risk management practitioners, in whatever guise, are rarely taught the skills and ability to excite and engage top-level business leaders in the powerful array of ERM techniques. This power is often only unleashed when organizations embrace the concept that risk is about threats and opportunities and linked to the appetite for managed risk taking in the entity. After all, if a CEO were to be given a technique by which he or she could make an opportunity twice as attractive using Enterprise Risk Management techniques, he or she would most certainly sit up and listen.

Beyond overview – risk management skills for top-level management

The usual definition of risk management, and indeed Enterprise Risk Management, calls for top-level management overview of the process and framework. It is now clear, from all the corporate failures, that this is no longer adequate.

Let's just look at one of the things that will cause turmoil and uncertainty in the years to come; diminishing natural resources. The case with fossil fuels is well known, but how aware are we that there are only a few years of silver left in reserves and in unmined resources (Vince, 2012; Silver Institute, 2014)? We are only just discovering the wonderful uses of silver in technology and in medicine.

Where precious silver was used mainly in coins and jewellery (and later in photography), its industrial uses now outstrip the decorative market. Silver has the highest electrical (and thermal) conductivity of any metal, so it is used in a range of electronics – including sensitive radio frequency antennae such as those found in televisions and mobile phones, and in radio frequency identification (RFID) devices. Silver is also found in many printed circuit boards, in hearing aids and in batteries.

The medicinal properties of silver bullets have been known since at least the times of Hippocrates and rely on its toxic effects on pathogens, including bacteria and fungi. Silver ions kill pathogens by binding to proteins in their cells, making silver compounds ideal for use in antiseptics and wound dressings. Nanoparticles of silver are even woven into socks and other clothing to reduce bacterial and fungal growth – and the odours that arise. Silver is also used in heart valves and catheters, and researchers are now investigating silver's potential in killing cancer cells.

What's happening to the balance of supply versus demand for silver is just one example of uncertainty that can affect a wide range of enterprises. As a commodity it has low value compared to gold, but if economically viable new sources of gold ran out completely the world would just continue as it was. If we ran out of new (economically viable) sources of silver, there would have to be a major rethink about electrical components such as circuitry, the use of silver in photovoltaic cells, in batteries and the new antibacterial uses for silver in an age where no new antibiotic has been produced for thirty years against the fact that antibiotics are becoming less and less effective (*Washington Post*, 2014).

The relevance of all this to Enterprise Risk Management is about ensuring business sustainability in the light of uncertainty. Business leaders and risk practitioners need to look into the short- and long-term threats and opportunities that the organization is faced with and engage with risk-based strategic decision making that will ensure the longevity of the business. If business is dependent on computers, or on people being well, or on batteries or on radio waves, then the mismatch between supply and demand for silver (or any other natural resource that has finite availability) over the next two decades will be important.

Enterprise risk appetite, capacity and tolerance

Risk has a different meaning to each organization or individual because each has a different perception of the opportunity and the threat depending on their propensity to take risk or to avoid it. Enterprise Risk Management will not be seen as an essential part of releasing innovation unless there is an overarching risk appetite framework that is scalable for each part of the organization, understood in the context of each business unit's goals and framed in a common language.

Within a risk appetite framework, an organization needs to take into consideration aspects of risk seeking versus risk avoidance, the broad principles of risk appetite frameworks and, critically, how risk appetite frameworks need to be linked to compensation and reward programmes. Risk appetite must be owned and driven by the board and senior management in order to be real, practical and pertinent to the business of taking managed threats and opportunities. Risk practitioners are responsible for implementing the process and enabling the decisions on risk appetite to be made by the board and senior management.

Innovation cannot be successfully undertaken unless there are two things in place: first, there needs to be a clear understanding of risk appetite, and second, performance against risk appetite metrics should be measured and responded to.

There also needs to be a clear distinction between capacity and tolerance – the former is about fact, the ultimate ability of the organization to bear risk, and the latter is about preference, the risks that an organization is prepared to take in order to pursue its goals.

What is Enterprise Risk Management?

Rather than sitting aside from other areas of risk management, ERM should be an overarching methodology that pulls together and creates intelligence for the organization in order to aid in strategic decision making.

All encompassing

Enterprise Risk Management is an all-encompassing methodology that allows the organization to pull together intelligence from all its various risk management practices as well as tackling those top-level strategic or enterprise-wide risks. It should include a process to evaluate and respond to the aggregate of risks against the capacity or tolerance of the organization to bear those risks.

Recently, the Association for Federal Enterprise Risk Management (AFERM) defined ERM as 'a discipline that addresses the full spectrum of an organization's risks, including challenges and opportunities, and integrates them into an enterprise-wide, strategically aligned portfolio view. ERM contributes to improved decision making and supports the achievement of an organization's mission, goals and objectives.'

Through ERM, the organization can gain an overarching vision of the risks and exposures to which it is exposed as well as the opportunities and capacity of the organization to engage in managed risk-taking activities.

COSO (the Committee of Sponsoring Organizations of the Treadway Commission) describes ERM as:

> a process, effected by an entity's board of directors, management and other personnel, applied in strategy setting and across the enterprise, designed to identify potential events that may affect the entity, and manage risk to be within its risk appetite, to provide reasonable assurance regarding the achievement of entity objectives.

Regulation

In the case of banks (through the Basel accords) and European insurance and reinsurance companies (through Solvency II) the process of understanding and measuring the aggregated risks that the organization is exposed to, is matched with a requirement to hold adequate capital of a certain quality against those risks and then test that the capital is indeed adequate.

These financial models are perhaps the most extreme iteration of ERM, but they perhaps shed an interesting light on the primary objective of survival. After all, if we all ran our businesses and enterprises with enough capital to see us through the worst of our nightmare threat scenarios then might there be fewer corporate mishaps?

What is also interesting about this 'new' approach for banks and insurers, of measuring and valuing the capital needed against the worst threats, is that there is a requirement to take a long-term view of those threats and to match that with stress and scenario testing. This two-fold approach is arguably one that could be useful for every organization.

There are many countries that have implemented codes of corporate governance for publicly listed companies and increasingly these codes demand a systematic approach towards Enterprise Risk Management. US public companies are subject to the Sarbanes-Oxley Act which was enacted in response to the Enron and WorldCom scandals.

Top-level engagement

The Enterprise Risk Management 'process' is just one part of a whole cycle of contextual issues starting with board and senior management commitment and engagement.

The requirement to understand the organization and its context (ISO 31000 para 4.3.1) is a clear top-level responsibility in that there should be a thorough understanding of the systems, capacity and capabilities of the organization. This would include governance, social and cultural, political, legal, regulatory, financial, technological, economic, natural and competitive environments; key drivers and trends having impact on the objectives of the organization; and relationships with, and perceptions and values of, internal and external stakeholders.

The Risk and Insurance Management Society has identified seven characteristics that give some insight into their definition of Enterprise Risk Management:

- Encompasses all areas of organizational exposure to risk (financial, operational, reporting, compliance, governance, strategic, reputational, etc.).

- Prioritizes and manages those exposures as an interrelated risk portfolio rather than as individual silos.

- Evaluates the risk portfolio in the context of all significant internal and external environments, systems, circumstances and stakeholders.
- Recognizes that individual risks across the organization are interrelated and can create a combined exposure that differs from the sum of the individual risks.
- Provides a structured process for the management of all risks, whether those risks are primarily quantitative or qualitative in nature.
- Views the effective management of risk as a competitive advantage.
- Seeks to embed risk management as a component in all critical decisions throughout the organization.

Managed risk taking

There are two other issues to consider; the definition of risk in quarters other than enterprise wide, which tend to think along lines of 'ability to control risk', and for the top management team to 'exercise oversight'. When we are looking at risk on an enterprise-wide basis, we are looking at the organization's ability to take managed risk as opposed to being able to exercise control (Taylor, 2014). Figure 2.1 shows this dynamic where the

FIGURE 2.1 Risk taking versus risk control

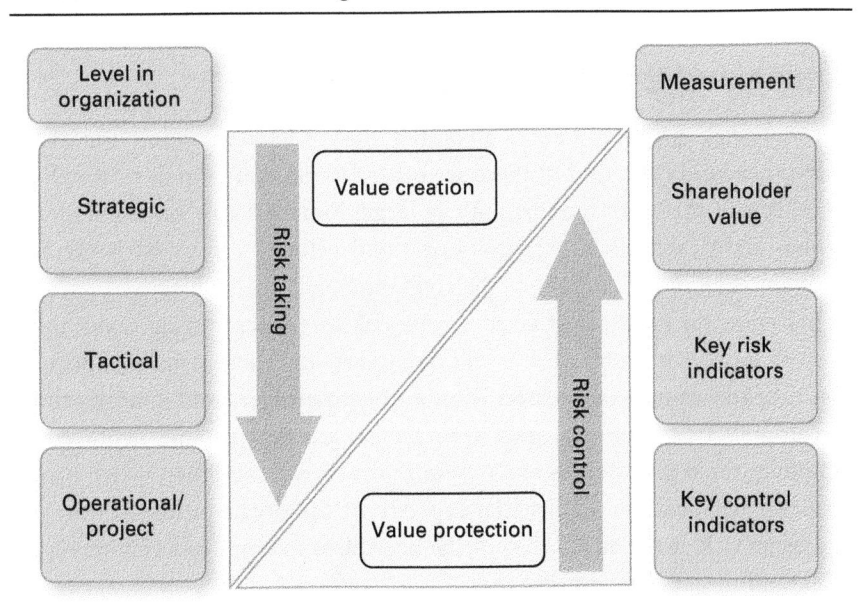

SOURCE: © Liz Taylor; *Practical Enterprise Risk Management*, adapted from IRM Risk Appetite and Tolerance Paper

top-down strategic use of Enterprise Risk Management is about value creation and the ability to engage (safely) in risk taking. This figure also shows the opposite position where bottom-up risk management is about risk control. This then implies that we should also be looking at the risk management skills of top management in exercising their risk-managed strategic decision making as opposed to merely having them as bystanders in an oversight role.

What is risk in this context?

Risks to the enterprise as a whole

If we accept that risk in the context of Enterprise Risk Management is about the effect of uncertainty on the goals of the organization, then this is no different from other aspects of risk (non-enterprise-wide) except that the focus is on those risks that could affect the whole organization.

Some call these strategic risks, but that is misleading, and can make us look at an organization's strategy and then focus on those risks. Enterprise-wide risks could come from a host of sources, whether internal or external, fast acting or slowly taking place, independently causing risk or needing to act in concert with other risks or risk factors.

Timing and speed of change of risk

Certainly risk in this context is a combination of likelihood and impact (as with other kinds of risk) but there are other factors that help us to weigh up whether the threat or opportunity is large, and that's to do with timing (when might the risk impact us most?) and velocity (how fast is the risk changing?) all in the context of the corporate plan/goals/objectives.

Let's take the example of an enterprise risk assessment on a possible takeover of another business. There will be threats, and there will be opportunities. The most important aspect is to be able to measure and quantify those threats and opportunities, look into the tactics that can be deployed to maximize the opportunities and minimize the threats, and then weigh up the resultant net position against the capacity of the organization to bear the aggregate risk at the end points of the possible outcomes (maximum versus minimum threat/opportunity).

That's all well and good on a linear scale, but when we are looking at adding timing and velocity of risk, that's when things get exciting and the probing needs to be much more detailed. One needs to look at why things have changed or could change over time, what are the variables that cause those changes, how things look when many variables happen at the same time, and what would be the effect of opportunity enhancement and threat treatment on those variables. In the real world of takeover, however, even in the most detailed due diligence processes, a prospective acquirer is unlikely to be able to gather enough data to give assurance to this level of inquiry. So assumptions and risk-based decisions need to be made so that the most important aspects that could skew the success of the takeover are given the full quantitative treatment, accompanied by scenario testing of the outlying ranges of possible risk effects against the risk appetite of the purchaser, taking timing and velocity into account when reviewing liquidity and capital exposure.

How is enterprise risk managed?

Value drivers

The starting point for managing enterprise risk is to work out what the context for the risk is. Many organizations start with their objectives or strategic goals, which is an approach that has merit. However, what often gets left out is the risk to the value drivers, which might not appear within the strategic goals or objectives. Intelligent organizations recognize the importance of value drivers and shape their corporate goals, both short and long term, around them. In that way the real threats and opportunities are constantly on the senior management agenda.

Here are some examples of value drivers: knowledge, capital, cash flow and liquidity, and reputation/goodwill.

Knowledge – people within the organization often hold key knowledge that makes the organization what it is. Retaining knowledge in the business is often overlooked; few businesses value 'handover' periods, or plan properly for succession. Many industries currently face a massive loss of knowledge as the 'baby boomers' born in the post-World War II 1950s era come up to retirement. In some industries this presents an industry-wide fault line. One such example is the nuclear industry where up to 20 per cent of the current senior management and nuclear experts across the world are approaching retirement. This was recognized in the industry in around 2006 and some effort is being made to rectify this gap with graduate recruitment, but many nuclear organizations are being faced with the prospect of hiring back their retirees as ongoing consultants.

Capital – this is commonly understood to be crucial to an organization's success and many organizations have good understanding of their capital position and the makeup of that capital. But is that matched against the capital requirement for the future state of the business? Are risks projected into the future, and stresses applied to those risks in order to calculate and plan the future capital requirement even if the threats are at their most extreme and the opportunities fail to transpire as planned?

To have enough capital to meet one's risks is all good logic but it misses the fundamental aspect of goodwill. When the US banks sold sub-prime mortgages, beginning in around 2004, and then sold the sub-prime book to each other, they gave no consideration to the long-term sustainability of this in terms of the effect on their customers and the future loss of goodwill. There was no concept of balancing future risk and capital at that time. The rise in mortgage delinquencies and foreclosures resulted in the reduction in securities that were backed by the mortgages.

This resulted in several major financial institutions collapsing in September 2008, with significant disruption in the flow of credit to businesses and consumers and the onset of a severe global recession.

Cash flow and liquidity – some banks, such as Morgan Stanley, did not get involved in the sub-prime business, but they took their eye off the ball with respect to cash flow and liquidity.

The New York-based bank ran out of cash because of a run on its prime brokerage, the unit that finances hedge funds' trades and holds their cash and securities. These loans also show the degree to which Morgan Stanley and other banks depended on such brokerage accounts for funding, even though clients could close them on short notice.

Goodwill, reputation and brand – some major organizations put a value on their balance sheet in terms of the brand. In many cases this is a tiny proportion of the true value of the brand and often the immense dependence on and power of the brand is only realized when it is gone.

Design

When designing an ERM programme, it is important to examine the internal and external context of the organization, including the requirements of various stakeholders. By establishing the context, the organization articulates its objectives, and defines the external and internal parameters to be taken into account when managing risk. These internal and external factors may be identified through a scan, which can be used to shape the design of the Enterprise Risk Management approach and process.

Regardless of the process used to design an ERM approach, there are several activities likely to occur at some point in the design process. Appropriate resources (people, partners, tools, etc.) need to be allocated for the design, implementation and maintenance of the ERM approach and process as well as for the ongoing conducting of ERM activities. With respect to resourcing, upfront investments could be necessary for the initial phases of design and implementation. Those organizations that have made substantial progress in implementing ERM will already have recognized the need for an initial investment of dedicated resources. Start-up costs (time, attention, training, systems, and communications) may be incurred until the practice becomes an integral part of organizational structures and processes.

In conducting an internal and external review, organizations may want to look at:

- results of audits, evaluations, reviews or other documentation that provides information regarding the organization's Enterprise Risk Management, strategic leadership, values and ethics, integrated performance information, stewardship, and accountability;
- strategic planning documents such as the corporate plan, business unit performance report, report on plans and priorities, capital assets, and functional plans;
- input from affected and interested parties including key partners and other stakeholders;
- key external factors (eg social, economic, etc.).

In addition to information collected during the review, it is important to develop an understanding of the organization's willingness to accept the possibility of negative events and its openness to opportunities in the pursuit of an objective or outcome.

An organization's appetite for threat and opportunity varies with its culture and with evolving conditions in its internal and external environments. Risk appetite and tolerance can be determined through consultation with affected parties, or by assessing stakeholders' response or reaction to varying levels of risk exposure. Consideration may be given to the following elements to get an understanding of the organization's risk appetite and tolerance level:

- the organization's overall risk culture;
- how risk appetite may have influenced the design of existing tools;
- how the organization has reacted to past risk events and issues;
- how stakeholders have reacted to past risk events and issues;

- the drivers and policies;
- other organizational information such as the organization's performance expectations and actual performance.

Implementation

The process of implementing Enterprise Risk Management is just the same as with all risk management processes (and indeed management processes) on a Plan/Do/Check/Act basis, as illustrated in Figure 2.2. There are, however, some elements that take the context to the broader, enterprise-wide, scale.

FIGURE 2.2 Enterprise Risk Management and Plan/Do/Check/Act

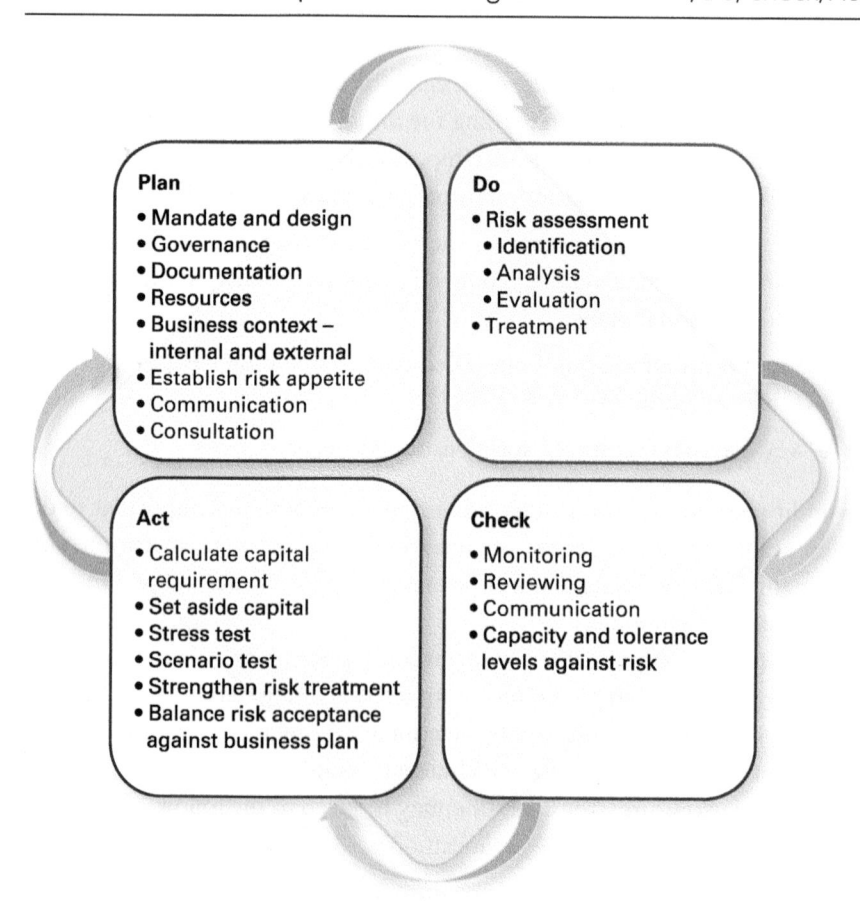

Plan
- Mandate and design
- Governance
- Documentation
- Resources
- Business context – internal and external
- Establish risk appetite
- Communication
- Consultation

Do
- Risk assessment
  - Identification
  - Analysis
  - Evaluation
  - Treatment

Act
- Calculate capital requirement
- Set aside capital
- Stress test
- Scenario test
- Strengthen risk treatment
- Balance risk acceptance against business plan

Check
- Monitoring
- Reviewing
- Communication
- Capacity and tolerance levels against risk

The central risk management techniques of risk identification, analysis, evaluation and risk treatment are the active elements of all risk management processes including ERM. These are illustrated in the 'Do' box in Figure 2.2.

Enterprise Risk Management takes the organization wider into a broader contextual analysis in the 'Plan' box, where the context includes the standard areas of mandate and design, governance, documentation, resources, communication and consultation. What is different about ERM is the requirement to establish the risk appetite for the organization. This isn't just the appetite on a risk-by-risk basis; this is the collective risk appetite for aggregated risk effects across the whole organization.

A further difference occurs at the point where the organization would 'Check' to see that what is happening is what was intended. This is where it would compare the risk outputs to its risk appetite and specifically check the individual and aggregated risks against the capacity or ability of the organization to take the risk as well as checking the risks against the tolerance or amount of risk that the organization is willing to take.

Once the organization has completed that 'check' process, it would then 'Act' upon the results. In some instances (such as for financial services organizations) it might calculate and set aside capital for the risks and test that the capital is adequate. In all circumstances organizations would look to strengthen the controls for those risks that take the organization beyond its stated tolerance levels and balance the risk acceptance levels against the business plan and future strategies – embracing more innovation in cases where more managed risk can be taken and adjusting the business where less risk should be experienced.

Embedding

Embedding Enterprise Risk Management requires more than a change of culture – it requires the right people to take ownership of their part in the process.

All management and staff should be provided with the training and other resources needed to ensure that they have the appropriate skills, competencies and experience to carry out their responsibilities.

It may take time and effort to gain momentum, train managers and specialists, and establish good tools and processes. Once fully implemented, initial start-up investments may be re-allocated as appropriate.

There is no standard size or allocation of resources for integrated ERM activities. In order to assess resource requirements for establishing and maintaining an ERM approach and process, it is important to identify the nature, adequacy, and usefulness of existing organizational tools, techniques, human resources skills, and expertise for managing risk to determine incremental requirements.

In the ongoing management of enterprise risks, specific attention should be given to the allocation of resources for risk response activities. While the identification and analysing of risks is much easier to embed into day-to-day decision-making activities, specific resources may need to be assigned to risk response action items. These resources should be at the appropriate level for the severity of the risk and should take into account any necessary trade-offs due to resource constraints.

It is important to note that resource allocations should be aligned with the level of risk to be managed, and focused not necessarily on every risk, but on the key risk areas as set out in the risk appetite statement.

Monitoring of the outputs of ERM is conducted in order to improve capabilities and to ensure that the objective for ERM is achieved. Key risk indicators are the focus for the tracking systems.

Communication

The communication of risk is only one factor in the monitoring of outputs but is a good driver for a focused and timely tracking process. Communications, consultations and reporting should involve external and internal stakeholders in order to successfully implement and conduct integrated ERM in an inclusive manner.

Establishing communications and reporting mechanisms provides a continuous means for keeping stakeholders informed of organizational ERM processes, practices, and risk responses. It helps maintain momentum to ensure that risk interest remains strong. It involves generating and sharing relevant information among the right people, anticipating and responding effectively to public concerns and expectations, achieving understanding of risks, getting action (voluntary or otherwise) and the reciprocal – receiving feedback.

In the interest of openness and transparency, an organization should be able to provide interested stakeholders with a snapshot of key threats and opportunities and what is being done to manage (and capitalize on) them at any time.

Many organizations do this through a form of monthly, bi-monthly or quarterly dashboard. This summarizes the main changes that have taken place on the risk list or risk register, and performance against the key risk indicators which in turn report on the performance against the risk appetite limits and thresholds.

As applicable, communications, consultations and reporting activities occur as an organization is establishing its approach and process and on an ongoing basis during all stages of the Enterprise Risk Management process when practising integrated ERM. However, to ensure that the mechanisms necessary to support these activities are in place, plans for communication, consultation and reporting should be developed at an early stage.

How does Enterprise Risk Management fit?

Enterprise Risk Management should, in an ideal world, be an integrated process that gathers all risk management activities in the organization together in one seamless and coherent whole. However, in practice, it often sits in a silo set away from such areas as Business Continuity Management, cyber risk and IT risk management, HR risk management, health and safety, treasury risk management, property and vehicle risk management, and so on.

As an overarching methodology it could be seen as the wheel of a ship (see Figure 2.3), where governance and audit provide the structure for the framework led by Enterprise Risk Management.

At best there is one risk list, or risk register, that collects all information from many areas on a common basis of measurement (in terms of impact and likelihood) under one framework or operating model; at worst there are separate risk registers and separate systems for measuring and evaluating risks.

It doesn't help that there are varying standards for each of these areas, varying statutory requirements, and varying guidance documents that detail different practices. The ISO 31000 standard is relatively young, but in this respect it is increasingly being referenced in other standards, which are aligning themselves with the language and guidance contained in the ERM standard (for example ISO 22301 for business continuity).

What's next?

Enterprise Risk Management is still struggling to become a useful tool for senior management. A 2015 report from NSU on the Current State of Enterprise Risk Oversight has reported the following (Beasley, Branson and Hancock, 2015):

- There appears to be a disconnect between the recognition of today's high-risk business environment and the decision to invest more in structured risk oversight.

Multidimensional Risk Management

FIGURE 2.3 The hub, spokes and wheel of types of risk management that make up the Enterprise Risk Management programme

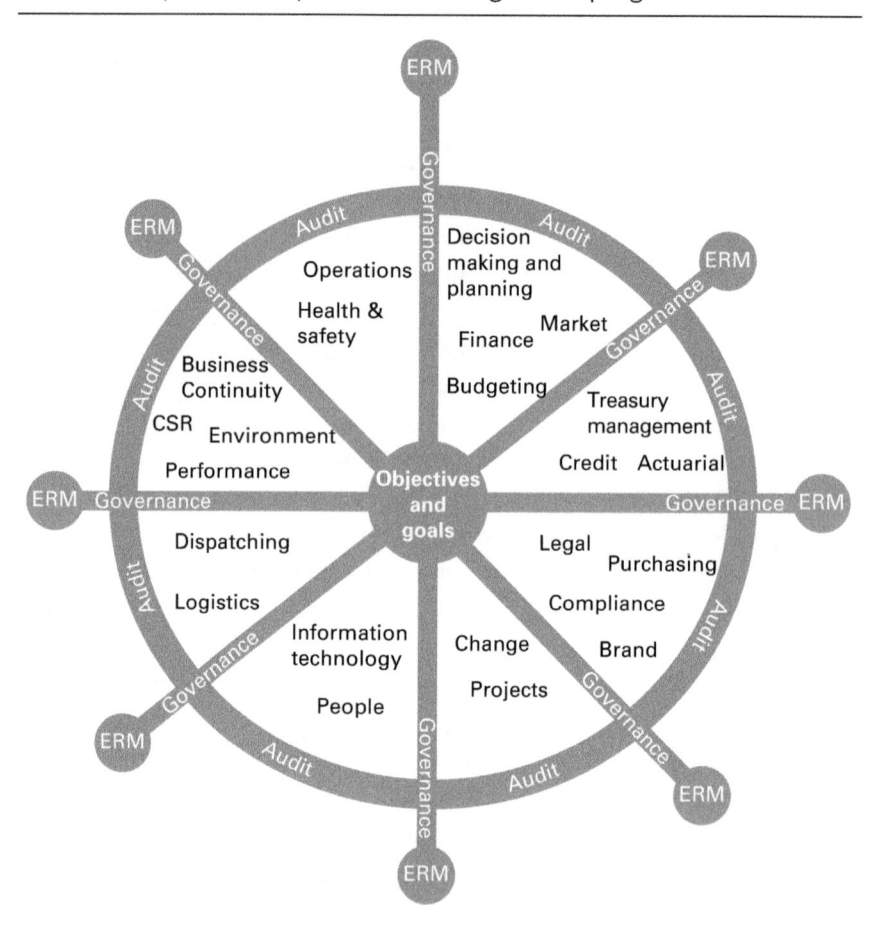

SOURCE: © Liz Taylor; *Practical Enterprise Risk Management* (2014)

- Few organizations have 'complete', 'mature/robust', or 'repeatable' ERM processes in place, even for the largest organizations and public companies.
- Executives indicate that they are receiving increased calls for greater engagement by executives in risk oversight.
- Organizations appear to be using management-level risk committees to lead the risk oversight effort. Few organizations, except for financial services firms, are creating new management-level risk leadership positions, such as chief risk officer or equivalent.

- Most organizations indicate they use written reports to communicate risk information to senior executives and most prepare a formal report of top risk exposures to the board at least annually. However, only about half of them (at best) maintain risk inventories at the enterprise level.
- About a third of the organizations update their understanding of risks annually while an additional 24 per cent update that understanding semi-annually or quarterly.
- Most organizations do not provide any guidelines or scales for management to assess risk probabilities or impacts.
- Organizations appear to be struggling to integrate their risk oversight with their strategy development and execution.
  - A majority indicates that their risk management activities are not important strategic tools.
  - Only about one-half of the organizations believe that existing risk exposures are considered when evaluating new strategic initiatives.
  - Boards are not extensively reviewing the top risk exposures when discussing the organization's strategic plan.
  - Most have not articulated the amount of risk they are willing to take in the pursuit of objectives.
  - Executives see risk management as a 'competing priority' despite the realities of the risk/return relationship.

As time goes on and our world becomes more and more uncertain, Enterprise Risk Management will become more important, more codified and more important to ratings agencies, although ratings agencies are currently only focusing on insurance companies (Towers Watson, 2010). Already, regulators in many countries, especially in the financial sector, are putting pressure on companies to manage risks more systematically and more codes of corporate governance are incorporating ERM requirements.

However, many of these regulations, Acts and areas of scrutiny are based on the requirement for 'internal controls'-based risk management. This has had the effect of making Enterprise Risk Management primarily focused on financial risks and is often accompanied by an audit-driven approach to the management of risk without taking into account a whole raft of important risk areas around the conduct of the business, the need for managed risk taking, risk appetite, strategic planning, balancing well-managed risk taking with appropriate remuneration, and the culture to support well managed risk taking.

For Enterprise Risk Management to be successful in adding value to the organization, it will have to embrace a wider approach than one that is driven based on an internal control culture – after all, how can you encourage well-managed risk taking under a culture of internal control?

Find out more

Association for Federal Enterprise Risk Management (no date), AFERM's Definition of ERM [online] http://www.aferm.org/resources.php [accessed Sept 2015]

Beasley, M, Branson, B and Hancock, B (2015) 2015 report on the current state of enterprise risk oversight: update on trends and opportunities [online] http://www.aicpa.org/interestareas/businessindustryandgovernment/resources/erm/downloadabledocuments/aicpa_erm_research_study_2015.pdf [accessed Sept 2015]

Blackman, S and Baumol, W J (2008) Natural Resources, *The Concise Encyclopaedia of Economics* [online] http://www.econlib.org/library/Enc/NaturalResources.html [accessed Sept 2015]

Chapman, R J (2011) *Simple Tools and Techniques for Enterprise Risk Management*, 2nd edn, J Wiley, Chichester, UK

COSO (2004) Enterprise Risk Management – integrated framework: executive summary [online] http://www.coso.org/documents/COSO_ERM_ExecutiveSummary.pdf. [accessed Sept 2015]

Institute of Risk Management (IRM), the Public Risk Management Association (ALARM) and Association of Insurance and Risk Managers (AIRMIC) (2010) *A Structured Approach to Enterprise Risk Management (ERM) and the Requirements of ISO 31000*, IRM/ALARM/AIRMIC, London UK

ISO 31000:2009, Risk management – principles and practices [online] http://www.iso.org/iso/home/standards/iso31000.htm [accessed Sept 2015]

ISO 22301:2012, Societal security – business continuity management systems – requirements [online] http://www.iso.org/iso/catalogue_detail?csnumber=50038 [accessed Sept 2015]

The Risk Management Society (no date) What is ERM? [online] https://www.rims.org/ERM/Pages/WhatisERM.aspx [accessed Sept 2015]

The Silver Institute (2014) Silver News, December 2014 [online] https://www.silverinstitute.org/site/wp-content/uploads/2015/01/SNDec2014.pdf [accessed Sept 2015]

Taylor, L (2014) *Practical Enterprise Risk Management: How to optimize business strategies through managed risk taking*, Kogan Page, London

Towers Watson (2010) S&P clarifies ERM treatment for nonfinancial companies [online] https://www.towerswatson.com/en/Insights/IC-Types/Survey-Research-Results/2010/07/SP-Clarifies-ERM-Treatment-for-Nonfinancial-Companies [accessed Sept 2015]

Vince, G (2012) Silver: The harsh realities behind diminishing supplies, *BBC* [online] http://www.bbc.com/future/story/20120418-no-silver-bullet [accessed Sept 2015]

Washington Post (2014) Antibiotics are becoming less effective, and their overuse is making them dangerous [online] http://www.washingtonpost.com/national/health-science/antibiotics-are-becoming-less-effective-and-their-overuse-is-making-them-dangerous/2014/07/28/9d78bc26-aad1-11e3-98f6-8e3c562f9996_story.html [accessed Sept 2015]

Governance, Risk and Compliance

03

ROBERT TOOGOOD

Why does GRC matter?

Some people claim that our recent economic challenges are due to a significant number of corporate failures which have then challenged the foundations of our global economic system. These failings could be viewed as evidence of an ineffective approach to managing Governance, Risk and Compliance activities within the modern-day corporation.

For over 12 years, the acronym GRC has been used to describe a coordinated approach to managing these components. During this period, the Open Compliance and Ethics Group (OCEG) has emerged as the only non-profit organization dedicated to promoting a framework to support this. OCEG describe themselves as 'a global non-profit think tank and community'. Together, they help organizations 'achieve Principled Performance by integrating governance, assurance and management of performance, risk, compliance and ethics (GRC)'.

So why are more organizations not using a GRC-based approach to improve their efficiency and effectiveness in the areas of Governance, Risk and Compliance?

The way in which the modern-day corporation has evolved in response to increasing commercial pressures has quite often resulted in a fragmented, inefficient and ineffective approach to managing Governance, Risk and Compliance activities.

Whilst this weakness may have been barely acceptable and tolerable in previous decades, recent corporate failures have highlighted the vulnerability and implications of such a silo-based approach. The interconnected world in which we all now live dictates a much more integrated way of handling the complex critical legal and regulatory activities associated with Governance, Risk and Compliance, but in doing so, the risks associated with getting this wrong significantly increase, as we have seen from recent global economic events.

The ever-increasing focus on globalization has resulted in a more tightly linked set of economic systems that in themselves present a higher level of risk to the economic stability of the world.

What is Governance, Risk and Compliance (GRC)?

GRC in itself is not a specific variant of risk management but instead is an approach for more tightly coordinating risk management with governance and compliance-related activities.

It is therefore important that some form of risk management should already be in place and operational; without it, any attempt to implement GRC would be severely compromised and therefore fail. However, the regulatory realities of the modern-day organization should ensure that there is at least some rudimentary form of Governance, Risk and Compliance activities already in place, although these could be at a very basic and potentially ineffective level.

So when we refer to GRC, we are meaning efforts to more effectively coordinate these three critically important pillars of modern-day business life.

Relationships

It is clear from life in the real world that activities associated with an integrated approach to Governance, Risk and Compliance can sometimes have an uneasy relationship with what is commonly known as enterprise-wide risk management (ERM). Some even go as far as suggesting that GRC is simply just another term for ERM.

As a starting point to understand whether this is true, OCEG defines a GRC capability as one that:

> Enables an organization to reliably achieve objectives while addressing uncertainty and acting with integrity; including the governance, assurance and management of performance, risk, and compliance (OCEG, 2015a).

In a LinkedIn Institute of Risk Management (IRM) GRC Special Interest Group (SIG) discussion thread, Norman Marks (IRM GRC SIG, 2013a) wholeheartedly endorses the OCEG definition and strongly urges the group to support it. He makes the additional point that 'we don't need the G in GRC if we are only considering ERM, but if we look at GRC in its entirety, then the OCEG definition provides the optimum way of understanding the bigger picture of how risk management should be positioned relative to governance and compliance'.

Culture

The author's experience in this area prompted a closer examination of the influence that risk culture has on being able to adopt an effective, coordinated approach to GRC.

In compliance there is frequent reference to 'tone from the top'. This statement attempts to emphasize the role-model-type power of the behaviour adopted by senior figures within an organization. However, real-life experience shows that there is much more to this statement than is immediately obvious from the simple phrase. It is critically important to ensure that this 'tone' is more than empty words and is backed up by consistent and rigorous reinforcing/supportive actions.

It is of particular interest to see that the Institute of Risk Management (IRM) has published a 10-point plan for implementing risk culture change (IRM, 2012a, p. 86) as well as a separate document specifically aimed at assisting board members (2012b). In this second document (p. 4) Richard Anderson, IRM Chairman at that time, made the point that 'Problems with risk culture are often blamed for organizational difficulties but, until now, there was very little practical advice around on what to do about it.'

IRM suggests a number of layers that contribute to risk culture, as shown in Figure 3.1, and defines risk culture as follows (2012a, p. 86):

> Risk culture is a term describing the values, beliefs, knowledge and understanding about risk shared by a group of people with a common purpose, in particular the employees of an organization or of teams or groups within an organization. This applies whether the organizations are private companies, public bodies or not-for-profits and wherever they are in the world.

What is risk in this context?

The Risk and Insurance Management Society, Inc. (RIMS) compares the OCEG view of GRC against risk management frameworks such as COSO and ISO 31000, and concludes that:

FIGURE 3.1 IRM Risk Culture Framework

- Risk culture
- Organizational culture
- Behaviours
- Personal ethics
- Personal predisposition to risk

SOURCE: © 2012 The Institute of Risk Management. Permission from IRM is required for reproduction and/or use of material

The major difference for the OCEG approach is the formal integration of the governance, risk and compliance processes, ideally supported by a common technology platform. In this framework, risk is given a limited role focused on identification and measurement. The primary directive for risk, though not exclusively, is to measure the likelihood of an event that has an adverse effect on objectives. The OCEG Capability Model relies heavily on an integrated technology platform as an enabling tool to identify and assess risk for prevention and/or remediation purposes (RIMS, 2011, p. 5).

Inconsistency

However, research conducted by Racz, Weippl and Seufert (2010, p. 1) has concluded that that there is no universally accepted definition of GRC. Their research (2010, p. 6) into a frame of reference for GRC showed that 'putting the complexity of GRC into a single phrase is provocative'. They claim (2010, p. 1) that their research '…provides a frame of reference for research of integrated GRC that was derived from the first scientifically grounded definition of the term'.

In addition, the outcome from their research (2010, p. 8) was the sharing of the following single-phrase definition:

> GRC is an integrated, holistic approach to organization-wide governance, risk and compliance ensuring that an organization acts ethically correct and in accordance with its risk appetite, internal policies and external regulations through the alignment of strategy, processes, technology and people, thereby improving efficiency and effectiveness.

But how do this and other definitions compare with what is referred to as ERM? It is interesting that COSO (2004, p. 2) defines Enterprise Risk Management as a:

> process, effected by an entity's board of directors, management and other personnel, applied in strategy setting and across the enterprise, designed to identify potential events that may affect the entity, and manage risk to be within its risk appetite, to provide reasonable assurance regarding the achievement of entity objectives.

By contrast, ISO 31000 (2009, pp. 1–3) includes the following definitions:

- Risk: 'Effect of uncertainty on objectives'.
- Risk Management: 'Coordinated activities to direct and control an organization with regard to risk'.
- Risk Management Process: 'Systematic application of management policies, procedures and practices to the tasks of communication, consultation, establishing the context, identifying, analysing, evaluating, treating, monitoring and reviewing risk'.

ISO 31000 was and remains controversial, and Leitch (2010, p. 892) points out that it:

> (1) is unclear; (2) leads to illogical decisions if followed; (3) is impossible to comply with; and (4) is not mathematically based, having little to say about probability, data, and models.

So what seems to emerge from a comparison of these definitions is that the main distinguishing feature of GRC is that it formally integrates governance and compliance with an associated risk management framework such as COSO or more recently, ISO 31000... but some of the components it is trying to integrate are unstable and subject to interpretation.

Perceptions

We are all products of our own experiences. It is because of our unique experiences, and therefore quite often perceptions, that when we look at something as complicated as GRC, it is easy to misunderstand or misinterpret what is actually going on. It just depends on how you and your organization are viewing things, and more importantly, what your expectations are.

Interestingly, Michael Rasmussen in a blog post entitled 'Rethinking GRC' (19 September 2012) makes the point that the time may have come for a rethink of what GRC means, with possibly more emphasis on the people and process aspects.

So although the use of the acronym GRC has been in use for over 12 years, there still remains much confusion and ambiguity surrounding the use of the term and what it really means. This may be one of the reasons why it is easy to have the perception that GRC has failed to deliver on its potential, and the global economy still suffers from significant corporate failures and misdemeanours which continue to threaten our future economic survival.

Disconnects

For some years now, the way in which organizations behave has been of great interest. Real-life experience demonstrates that so often there are major disconnects between the core functional activities of Governance, Risk and Compliance. Why is this, when on the surface, it is clear as to the significant benefits that can be derived from a more integrated approach as advocated by non-profit making bodies such as the Open Compliance and Ethics Group (OCEG)?

So how does OCEG define GRC? In OCEG's 3.0 Capability Model (2015a, p. 3), GRC is defined as a 'shorthand reference to the collection of critical capabilities that must work together to achieve Principled Performance'.

OCEG also state (2015a, p. 11) that the benefits of Principled Performance can be 'viewed through the lens of universal outcomes of high-performing GRC capabilities that every organization should seek to achieve'. These capabilities are defined by OCEG as:

1 Achieve Business Objectives. Ensure that all parts of the organization work together toward the achievement of enterprise objectives.
2 Ensure Risk-Aware Setting of Objectives and Strategic Planning. Provide timely, reliable and useful information about risks, rewards, and responsibilities to the governing authorities, strategic planners, and business managers responsible for execution at all levels.
3 Enhance Organizational Culture. Inspire and promote a culture of performance, accountability, integrity, trust, and communication.
4 Increase Stakeholder Confidence. Grow stakeholder trust in the organization.

5 Prepare and Protect the Organization. Prepare the organization to address risks and requirements while protecting it from adversity and surprise and enabling it to grasp opportunities.

6 Prevent, Detect, and Reduce Adversity and Weaknesses. Establish actions and controls to prevent negative outcomes, reduce impact, detect potential problems, and address issues as they arise.

7 Motivate and Inspire Desired Conduct. Provide incentives and rewards for desirable conduct, especially in the face of challenging circumstances.

8 Stay Ahead of the Game. Learn information necessary to support quick changes in strategic and tactical direction while avoiding obstacles and pitfalls.

9 Improve Responsiveness and Efficiency. Establish capabilities that make the organization as a whole more responsive and efficient so that it has a competitive advantage.

10 Optimize Economic Return and Values. Allocate human and financial resources in a way that maximizes the economic return generated for the organization while maximizing its values.

In a blog post entitled 'Why is GRC an Important Topic?' Marks comments that this definition can perhaps best be summarized as 'how an organization understands stakeholder expectations and then directs and manages activities to maximize performance against those expectations, while managing risks and complying with applicable laws, regulations and obligations' (Marks, 2010).

How is GRC managed?

Evidence relating to best practice in this area appears to be dominated by the activities of OCEG. Their latest 3.0 Capability Model (2015) provides a sound foundation for any organization wanting to benefit from a more integrated approach to Governance, Risk and Compliance activities (see Figure 3.2). Many organizations have used selected components from this framework to provide a springboard from which to launch more specific and localized initiatives such as those to be found in IT/IS. However, GRC remains a highly controversial and confusing area for many organizations and individuals.

FIGURE 3.2 GRC capability: model element view

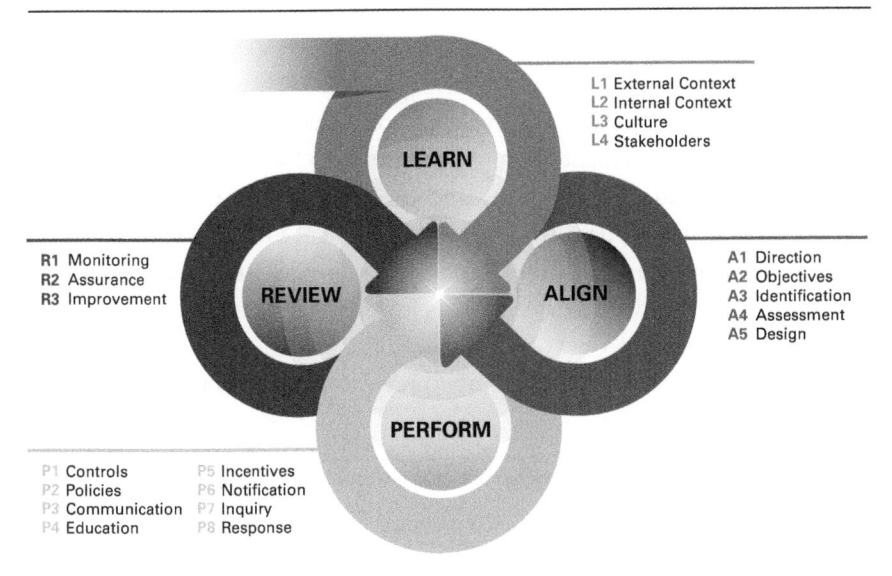

```
                    LEARN
                          L1 External Context
                          L2 Internal Context
                          L3 Culture
                          L4 Stakeholders

R1 Monitoring                           A1 Direction
R2 Assurance    REVIEW    ALIGN         A2 Objectives
R3 Improvement                          A3 Identification
                                        A4 Assessment
                                        A5 Design

                    PERFORM
P1 Controls     P5 Incentives
P2 Policies     P6 Notification
P3 Communication P7 Inquiry
P4 Education    P8 Response
```

SOURCE: © 2015 OCEG. Permission by OCEG is required for reproduction and/or use of material

Implementation of GRC cannot be driven by software alone, although it can sometimes help, depending on the maturity of the existing process and supporting systems infrastructure.

What GRC needs and demands is a top-down commitment to making it happen, which means board members have to understand and follow through on their individual actions and responsibilities. This quite often involves the need to work on much softer aspects of organizations such as attitudes, behaviour and, more importantly, culture.

Literature review

Based on an initial review of literature available, it is clear that previous formal academic-based research into this area is limited. There appears to be much written about the benefits of an integrated approach and how to justify such an investment, but less about the realities and challenges of implementation.

Pritchard (2000, p. 50) emphasizes the importance of an overall aim for organizations in managing risks, to ensure they are built into the fabric of corporate decision making. This is one of the reasons why GRC is attracting so much attention, because of the associated claims of being able to provide a more integrated and cost-effective way of managing all of these three key areas that are an integral part of management.

This way of more closely integrating governance with the associated areas of risk and compliance provides a potentially more powerful way of achieving risk management on an enterprise-wide basis in balance with the needs of stakeholder expectations and the associated activities needed to deliver these in a compliant way. Real-life experience has shown that all too often, risk is not managed holistically across an organization, but instead via functional silos that when viewed at this lower level present a fundamentally different and distorted view of the challenges ahead.

Frigo and Anderson (2009) identify three specific pitfalls to implementing an integrated approach:

1. The importance of establishing clear objectives.
2. The danger of opening up extensive discussion within the organization relating to a core rethinking of functional roles.
3. The potential pitfall of trying to implement an integrated approach within an organization that is at a lower level of maturity from a risk management perspective.

Further work from Anand (2010) takes a different view and identifies seven key requirements for integrated GRC success:

1. View Governance, Risk and Compliance (GRC) as a process, not a product.
2. Move information technology from the backroom to the boardroom.
3. Collaborate throughout (and outside) of the organization.
4. Stop pointing fingers.
5. Create benchmarks.
6. Nurture a culture of change.
7. Prioritize.

Using the work of both Frigo and Anderson (2009) and Anand (2010) it is possible to create an outline framework of some of the critical success factors needed for an effective integration of Governance, Risk and Compliance. However, real-life experience of working with the implementation and subsequent maintenance of Sarbanes-Oxley (SOX) compliance legislation has highlighted the critical importance of culture. None of these sources seem to correctly position the power and influence of culture when implementing an integrated approach.

Steinberg (2011, pp. 5–20) cites various examples, and explores what must be in place to prevent catastrophes and at the same time allow opportunities to be seized for sustained success. Moeller (2011) provides an additional dimension that leverages the power of the COSO Enterprise Risk Management framework to assist with establishing effective processes to support these activities.

So culture appears to be one, maybe the most significant, of the barriers to the implementation of a more coordinated approach. Real-life experience has also shown that there is a powerful relationship between organizational culture and the behaviour that is seen within that organization. However, the same real-life experience has shown that culture is difficult to objectively assess, analyse and influence, which might explain why it can result in the wrong behaviours being encouraged and/or rewarded.

Barriers to implementation

The author's research (Toogood, 2013) provides a deeper understanding of the barriers to implementing an integrated approach to governance, risk management and compliance (GRC) and what can be done to address them, in terms of best practice guidance. The following four barriers were identified.

Barrier 1: Realization/functional distortion

OCEG have developed a novel way of visualizing GRC using images in their 'Illustrated Series' guides (OCEG, 2015b). However, reaction from a range of informed stakeholders has been varied; on the surface, the majority responded positively but later demonstrated no real commitment to using the insights available from this visual representation. This highlights the importance of recognizing that we all have different ways of looking at situations based on our functional distortions and biases (a risk manager will look at a situation in a different way from a sales manager etc.), and this has to be factored into the way any dialogue relating to GRC is conducted.

Barrier 2: Common understanding

The research results emphasize the importance of getting clear understanding of how associated terms will be used and any associated assumptions being made, ie making sure people (key stakeholders) actually understand terms being used in the same way as others and in a form they can relate to.

Barrier 3: Leadership and implementation approach

The importance of a culture and implementation approach has been discussed above. Of particular importance is that any initiative of this type must be driven top down from board level and not bottom up. However, this seems to be different from the current status of GRC implementations worldwide, which possibly accounts for the relatively low take-up and success of the OCEG approach.

Barrier 4: Importance of people

Research results highlight that the real barriers are people related and not necessarily to do with methodology or software… and these people-related barriers can be directly linked back to some of the issues identified by the recent thought leadership work on risk culture from the Institute of Risk Management (2012a, b).

Given these four barriers to effective GRC implementation, four specific recommendations have been identified (Toogood, 2013), as follows.

Recommendation 1: Harness the power of risk culture management

Use risk culture management techniques to assist with more specific organizational aspects of creating the right environment for change. An analysis of barrier feedback clearly shows that cultural influences appear to have the biggest effect on the effectiveness of required changes. However, it is timely that IRM's recent focus on the impact of risk culture is available because there is now much useful best practice guidance available, particularly in the form of the publication 'Risk culture: resources for practitioners' (IRM, 2012a). Of particular relevance are Chapter 12, 'Practical guidance: a ten-point plan for implementing risk culture change' and Chapter 8, 'Implementation guidance: evaluating risk culture'.

Recommendation 2: Deploy NLP techniques to facilitate change

Adopt Neuro-Linguistic Programming (NLP) techniques to assist with softer people aspects of implementing required changes. NLP is defined by Molden (2007, p. 3) as a 'set of principles, models, and tools for learning, communication and change. It describes the workings of the mind and how verbal and non-verbal language is used to communicate our thoughts'. Whilst there has been a recent association between NLP and project management, the time has come to explore how it can be used with wider enterprise initiatives such as the implementation of a more integrated approach to Governance, Risk and Compliance activities.

Recommendation 3: Customize the approach to your organization

Ensure your approach has been properly tailored/designed to reflect your organization and its needs. As GRC already exists in the majority of organizations, it is just the degree of coordination and therefore effectiveness that is different. The level of integration or coordination, as Marks has emphasized, determines how effective the processes work together. So, as with any major change programme, organizational design work must be properly completed, and the initiative set up and treated like a formal change management programme, with clear and realistic expectations set. In addition, it is worth investigating the possibility of linking up with the ISO 31000 risk management approach, which provides many opportunities for tighter integration with governance and compliance activities.

Recommendation 4: Develop realistic expectations and stakeholder commitments

Be realistic about what can be achieved in the short, medium and longer term when embarking upon a GRC implementation programme. In some cases, the time may not be right to undertake this type of initiative. This is because a good risk management framework has to be in place first before embarking on an initiative to more tightly integrate governance, risk management and compliance activities. Where a robust risk management framework is lacking, this should be established as one of the first steps in the process.

How does GRC fit?

As we have seen, GRC represents a framework into which other types of risk management can be more effectively harnessed and directed, so potentially it has the capability to interact with all types of risk management, ERM, and all other business processes.

The IRM GRC SIG had a detailed, supportive and very useful interview session with Norman Marks in November 2012 which clarified the realities of the landscape relating to GRC (IRM GRC SIG, 2013a). In this session the importance of a coordinated – rather than just integrated – approach was emphasized. Another pivotal point was that GRC is already implemented in the majority of organizations and it is just the degree of effective coordination that differs. Figure 3.3 was developed during IRM GRC SIG activities to summarize the organizational context in which Governance, Risk and Compliance have to co-exist.

FIGURE 3.3 Organizational context

The discussion with Marks can be summarized into ten key points:

1 GRC already exists in the majority of, if not all, organizations, but not necessarily in an optimized/integrated (ie coordinated) form.

2 Coordinated GRC is what OCEG's Principled Performance is trying to achieve.

3 Coordinated GRC should be considered/evaluated based on what it is able to deliver... not on how it delivers it, ie benefits vs features.

4 Coordinated GRC is not a technology driven-solution, it is a different way of thinking, a way of driving improved performance, and this is an important way of selling it to senior management.

5 Coordinated GRC is a framework into which other industry-recognized frameworks/standards (eg ISO 31000) can and possibly should fit. This suggests that the risk aspects of OCEG's framework are not a viable alternative to ISO 31000, and one should not view OCEG as having all the answers or the best way of looking at things.

6 Coordinated GRC is a way of optimizing the way governance, risk management and compliance interact.

7 Coordinated GRC must be tailored (aka organizational design) to meet the specific needs of the target organization... without tailoring, any attempts to implement will almost certainly fail.

8 Coordinated GRC can be compared to the harmonizing role of a conductor in an orchestra – it ensures that delivery of all individual components is optimized and delivered in the most effective way.

9 Coordinated GRC is heavily dependent for success on a healthy implementation of ERM – if ERM is not operating efficiently, then this will constrain an integrated GRC implementation and eventually cause it to fail.

10 Coordinated GRC should be positioned as being all about achieving objectives more efficiently.

Finally, Marks (2014) has recently published a short and very useful guide which includes 12 simple questions to help understand GRC and assess its adequacy for your organization (see 'Find out more' section).

What's next?

We live in exciting but uncharted and dangerous times. Consequently, we must more effectively manage the dynamic and complex interrelationships between the areas of Governance, Risk and Compliance. A more integrated, coordinated approach to managing this complexity makes sound sense and in isolation, on paper, can be easily justified. However, the barriers to effective implementation are many and need to be better understood.

GRC has entered a critical phase – there are some industry pundits who claim that GRC has already peaked and passed away; others claim that it has mutated or been integrated into other initiatives that are not burdened by the historical controversy associated with the use of the GRC acronym. Initiatives such as Conduct Risk and Ethical Leadership also offer the potential for the original perceived benefits associated with GRC to be delivered, albeit using a less controversial approach.

From the author's own investigations into this area, it unfortunately seems that GRC should still be regarded as 'work in progress' as there are very few case studies of where it has been implemented top down into an organization and there is therefore little tangible evidence to support the business benefits of adopting such an integrated, coordinated approach. However, over the coming years this should change as longer-term GRC-related initiatives start to demonstrate tangible business benefits.

The harsh realities of the new world in which we all now live and work are such that we can no longer accommodate inefficiencies in our critical functions and processes. The time has come for us to look at our organizations and society in general in a different, more holistic, and sustainable way. An integrated and more coordinated approach to managing Governance, Risk and Compliance provides a way of achieving this, as long as we learn from the past and supply the correct environment for our efforts to succeed.

Find out more

Anand, S (2010) Technology and the integration of governance, risk management and compliance, *Financial Executive* (December), *EBSCO Host* [online] http://connection.ebscohost.com/c/articles/55699949/technology-integration-governance-risk-management-compliance [accessed 19 May 2012]

Committee of Sponsoring Organizations of the Treadway Commission (COSO) (2004) Enterprise risk management – integrated framework: executive summary *COSO* [online] http://www.coso.org/documents/coso_erm_executivesummary.pdf [accessed 2 February 2013]

Frigo, M L and Anderson, R J (2009) A strategic framework for governance, risk and compliance, *Strategic Finance*, February, *EBSCO Host* [online] http://connection.ebscohost.com/c/articles/36352824/strategic-framework-governance-risk-compliance [accessed 19 May 2012]

Institute of Risk Management (2012a) Risk culture: resources for practitioners, *IRM* [online] https://www.theirm.org/knowledge-and-resources/online-resource-centre/ [accessed 5 November 2012] (members' area of the website)

Institute of Risk Management (2012b) Risk culture: under the microscope, guidance for boards, *IRM* [online] https://www.theirm.org/media/885907/Risk_Culture_A5_WEB15_Oct_2012.pdf [accessed 5 November 2012]

Institute of Risk Management GRC Special Interest Group (IRM GRC SIG) (2013a), Quarterly Meeting, 31 January 2013 Presentation, unpublished internal document.

Institute of Risk Management GRC Special Interest Group (IRM GRC SIG) (2013b), GRC Q&A with Norman Marks, 30 May 2013, unpublished internal document.

Leitch, M (2010) ISO 31000:2009: the new international standard on risk management, *Risk Analysis: An International Journal* (June) **30** (6), pp. 887–92

Marks, N (2010, 7 July) Why is GRC an important topic? [blog post] http://www.cmswire.com/cms/enterprise-cms/why-is-grc-an-important-topic-007984.php [accessed 5 October 2015]

Marks, N (2014) *How Good is your GRC? Twelve questions to guide executives, boards, and practitioners*, CreateSpace Independent Publishing Platform

Moeller, R R (2011) *COSO Enterprise Risk Management: Establishing effective governance, risk and compliance processes*, 2nd edn, John Wiley & Sons Inc, New Jersey

Molden, D (2007) *NLP Business Masterclass: Driving peak performance with NLP*, 2nd edn, Pearson Education Limited, Harlow

Open Compliance and Ethics Group (OCEG) (2015a) GRC capability model, red book, 3.0 [online] http://www.oceg.org [accessed 10 October 2015]

Open Compliance and Ethics Group (OCEG) (2015b) GRC resources: illustrations [online] http://www.oceg.org/category/illustrations

Pritchard, P (2000) *Environmental Risk Management*, Earthscan Publications, London

Racz, N, Weippl, E and Seufert, A (2010) A frame of reference for research of integrated Governance, Risk & Compliance (GRC) in *Communications and Multimedia Security, 11th IFIP TC 6/TC 11 International Conference, CMS 2010 Proceedings*, ed. Bart De Decker and Ingrid Schaumüller-Bichl Springer, Berlin, pp. 106–17 [online] http://www.grc-resource.com/resources/racz_al_frame_reference_grc_cms2010.pdf [accessed 15 October 2015]

Rasmussen, M (2012, 19 September) Rethinking GRC [blog message] quoted at http://www.chaordicsolutions.co.uk/blog/from-our-grc-consultants/rethinking-grc/ [accessed 2 March 2016]

Risk and Insurance Management Society, Inc. (2011) *An Overview of Widely Used Risk Management Standards and Guidelines*, Risk and Insurance Management Society, Inc., New York

Steinberg, R M (2011) *Governance, Risk Management, and Compliance – It Can't Happen to Us: Avoiding corporate disasters while driving success*, John Wiley & Sons Inc., New Jersey

Toogood, R J (2013) What are the barriers to implementing an integrated approach to governance, risk management and compliance (GRC) and what can be done to address them, in terms of best practice guidance? Unpublished MSc research dissertation, University of Portsmouth, UK

Operational Risk Management

04

EDWARD SANKEY, WITH DR ARIANE CHAPELLE

Why does Operational Risk Management matter?

Resilience is the watchword: achieving corporate goals the aim. Firms need to ensure that they have adequate resources to be resilient against the combined effects of all the risks they are exposed to over the course of a year and in the longer term. Operational Risk Management (ORM) was developed for this purpose. The developments have resulted in improved value of risk management to the board and executives in decision making in the business, and in better assurance of reaching corporate goals.

Although banks started introducing ORM in the mid-2000s, the banking crisis accelerated the need for implementation. The huge credit and market losses made by many banks had their origin in operational risk events. It also demonstrated the importance of understanding much better the potential for major risk events, in addition to the day-to-day ones.

In financial services, regulators place great significance on the quality of ORM, systems and controls, and governance in firms, in fulfilment of the aims to protect customers, and prevent firms in distress from causing financial market instability.

Achieving corporate goals is the business aim: whilst clearly executives want their firms to satisfy regulations, their own aims for risk management are to be confident they will meet the objectives they have set out to the board and shareholders, as well as minimizing the chances of serious losses or failed new ventures. This is illustrated in Figure 4.1.

FIGURE 4.1 Achieving objectives by controlling risks in balance with resources

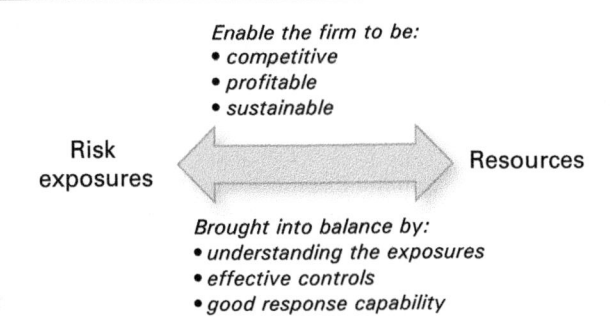

```
                    Enable the firm to be:
                    • competitive
                    • profitable
                    • sustainable
        Risk      ⇐========⇒   Resources
     exposures
                    Brought into balance by:
                    • understanding the exposures
                    • effective controls
                    • good response capability
```

Thus regulation provides a minimum standard, and firms have to make the policy decision about how much in excess of this standard they need to go for their own management purposes.

Whilst ORM has been coined in the financial services sector, its scope can and should be applied in all sectors. Particular developments brought by ORM are:

- aggregation of risk exposures and emphasis on probability assessments;
- a source of information for use in planning and decision making;
- the importance of formulating and articulating board risk strategy and risk appetite/tolerance;
- use of risk analysis to assess financial requirements.

In connection with the last item above, ORM assesses the total losses from each risk and all risks over a given period of time such as a year or longer, as well as from an individual instance.

What is Operational Risk Management?

Systematic and integrated risk management

From a genesis in the need to ensure firms had the financial resources and risk controls to be resilient, ORM aims to provide a platform for the assessment of risks on a consistent basis, and to reflect the inherent uncertainty about the degree and frequency of impact of any given risk. It is systematic and consistent across the whole organization, and integrates the management of risks with each other and with corporate strategy.

Measuring risks on a common metric is the crucial step to achieving this. Key developments have been:

- the identification and assessment of risks on a common metric;
- the assessment of the combined exposure to these risks individually as well as over a period of time, and of the possibility of extreme events taking place;
- introduction as a systematic discipline into well-established firms, often very large companies, at a time of significant technological, economic, and competitive change such as the banking crisis;
- the development of frameworks – policies and procedures – to manage the risks effectively;
- the achievement of compliance with major regulation, which in financial services has made Operational Risk Management mandatory for banks and insurance companies and others.

As well as the ongoing risks of the organization, ORM embodies the risks of new ventures, major projects and ultimately corporate strategies.

Prioritization in risk management through common metrics

Given that an organization is constrained in its resources for managing risks, the ORM approach of measuring risk on one or two common metrics provides corporate management with the information to see the most pressing needs for control improvements.

The risk management regime needs to balance the costs of risk controls with the level of losses expected to arise across the organization as a whole. ORM enables investment in additional controls to be directed to those risks where the reduction in expected losses will be greatest, as well as in excess of the new control costs. The minimum point must be sought in the sum of expected losses and expected costs of control, illustrated in Figure 4.2.

This is especially important when assessing the potential of some risks to create extreme losses in exceptional instances. ORM sets out to ensure management attention is directed to these potential high-severity events, and not just to those risks with more frequent occurrence, albeit with more modest losses in their scale. The use of common metrics for risk, together with comprehensive identification and assessment of risks, provides high-quality risk information to be used in decision making at all levels.

FIGURE 4.2 Seeking the lowest combined cost

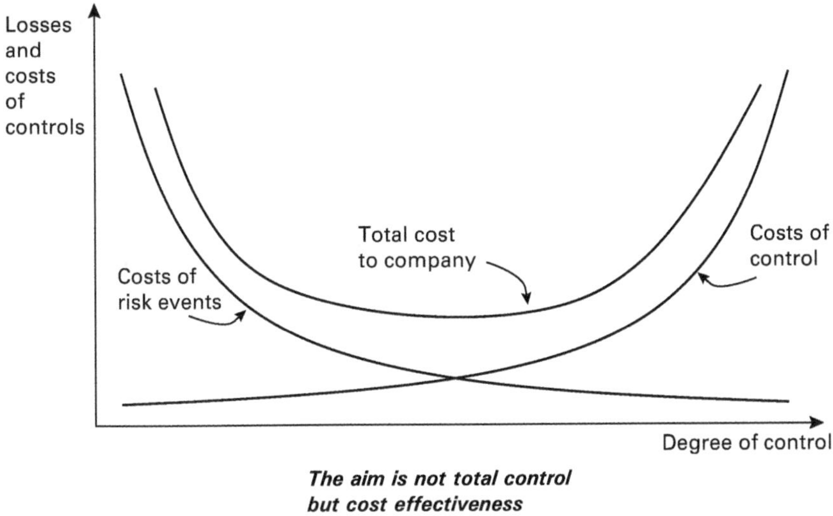
Losses and costs of controls
Total cost to company
Costs of control
Costs of risk events
Degree of control
The aim is not total control but cost effectiveness

Special risk situations

It is important to look for risk situations with the potential to generate high losses. These include:

- the potential for small-scale risks to accumulate large losses, which might have an underlying systematic cause (eg mis-sold products due to poor training);
- interrelated risks, such as systemic fraudulent loan applications creating excessive credit losses;
- risks whose losses would only become apparent years after the risk event has occurred.

An example of the first and last is the many instances of PPI mis-selling that led much later to immense losses in restitution, compensation, damages and legal costs, running across UK banks at the time of writing at £27 billion.

Risk exposure modelling and risk aggregation

Central to ORM is the use of risk assessment, risk modelling and risk exposure aggregation methods. The application of these techniques is growing in step with greater confidence that the data sets of recorded loss events are of good enough quality. However, even with moderate weaknesses in the data, important information is brought out about the levels of losses expected in a year from all risks and the scale of losses in a 'bad' year, especially when combined with the loss experience of other firms.

Techniques for risk aggregation, using simulation methods or mathematical statistics, are gaining ground as data quality improves, with striking impact at director and board level.

Dealing with political and regulatory developments

The potential for changes in the way business is conducted arising from political or regulatory change has to be recognized and brought into the systematic framework of ORM. Whilst it might not be the specific responsibility of the operational risk core team, the OR leader must ensure that it is handled adequately somewhere, and is subject to the same assessment, monitoring and reporting system as the other risks.

What is risk in this context?

Defining operational risk

The international Basel Committee of Banking Supervision, in setting out the need for ORM, defined operational risk, in brief, as the risk of losses caused by failures by people, processes, and systems, or by external events. This has been a useful definition to start the introduction of ORM in the systematic way intended. Regulation leaves open the possibility that a firm may use another definition of operational risk (including strategic risk or reputational risk) for its own purposes (Pillar I compared to Pillar II in the Basel terminology for banks – see Chapelle *et al.*, 2004 for definitions of the Basel Pillars).

A very useful definition which fits the board and directors' purposes for risk management is that based on the Turnbull Report on Internal Control, incorporated into the 'Guidance on Risk Management, Internal Control and Related Financial and Business Reporting' (FRC, 2014), namely that a risk is what prevents the achievement of objectives.

Loss and impact measurement

Many of the operational risks – using the term in the broader definition used for business management purposes – bring impacts to the organizations beyond the immediate direct costs of repair, replacement or reworking (and therefore perhaps extra overtime costs). Some of these are shown in Figure 4.3.

FIGURE 4.3 Illustrations of impacts and costs of risk events

	Direct costs	**Indirect costs**	**Long-term impact**
Examples:	Repair	Investigation	Loss of client
	Replacement	Management time	Poor reputation deterring many new clients
	Overtime and temps	Cost of new prevention or control	
	Alternative facility		Deferred major initiative
	Compensation	Diversion of time and attention from client and corporate development	

Most will certainly impact the current and planned balance sheets, and the expected financial resources of the organization through the year. In addition, some will affect the organization's ability to achieve its objectives. The diversion of management time from new initiatives is an example. In all cases ORM sets out to assess risks and measure impacts of events in monetary terms. Considerable effort is made in defining how impact and loss is measured in the defining policies of the risk management framework.

Some risks entail damage to relationships with important stakeholders and even breach of law or regulation. Clearly these aspects of the risks are very important, and are modelled in terms of loss of future income (impact on future financial condition and firm's objectives) including consideration of potential fines, etc. An additional metric, albeit often qualitative, is used specifically to reflect the loss of confidence of a stakeholder. For example a regulator's increased concern about a firm may lead to the trouble of greater scrutiny, intervention and restriction of activities. The scope for criminal or tort proceedings needs to be reflected.

Link with other risks in financial firms

The other principal areas of risk in the financial services firms are credit, market/investment, and underwriting. Operational risk is commonly called a *non-financial* risk, as a reference to its causes rather than its consequences, ie not directly caused by purely financial activities. In other sectors, 'Operational Risk Management' is synonymous with 'risk management'.

In the regulated financial industry, however, operational risk is treated as a single risk class with regard to capital planning and risk tolerance decisions, and needs to be considered along with credit, market, actuarial, and liquidity risk. The collection of these different risk classes is diversification *inter* risk, illustrated in Figure 4.4. It supplements the diversification *intra* risk, which is the diversification within each risk class and will be covered in a later section of this chapter.

FIGURE 4.4 Exposure aggregation across risks

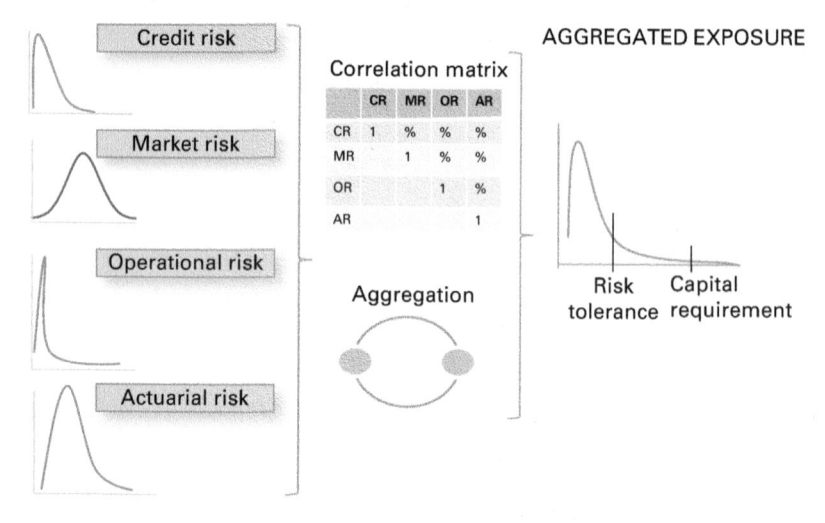

How is operational risk managed?

As well as the crucial matter of managing risks as a portfolio based on common metrics, another key element is the linkage of the management of operational risks from the working-level units (including functional and administrative units such as Finance and Accounts, Marketing, etc.) in a joined-up process to the top risks of the organizations. Conversely, the cohesive body of Operational Risk Management enables the directors to include risk in the strategy of the organization. Banks and insurers, under regulation, have to link their corporate financial planning to the combined risk exposure and this has application in other sectors.

Directors have choices about what sorts of risk they want the firm to take on in the pursuit of success ('no firm can survive without taking some risk'). Big oil companies accept very large project risks (in an informed, planned and controlled way) in their major exploration and development ventures, but run very low-risk balance sheets. Many banks have outsourced IT operations rather than hold all the technical risk themselves.

Setting out a risk strategy is a valuable directive to divisions and operating units, carrying not only messages about tolerance (or not) of various types of risk, but also quantitative measures of the amount of exposure the board is prepared to accept in various businesses, activities and types of risk.

This key strategic feature of ORM has produced noticeable changes in many banks' structures and business areas.

As illustrated in Figure 4.5, ORM provides the balancing of bottom-up perspectives of risk exposure with top-down direction and constraint about the scale of exposure in businesses and risk type. Risk assessment is largely done in operating units, supported by loss data, expert information, and special exercises on major exposures. This can be aggregated to provide corporate totals, and the directors can determine whether the resulting picture meets their plans, and direct divisions accordingly.

FIGURE 4.5 Developing the risk strategy and tolerance from bottom up and top down

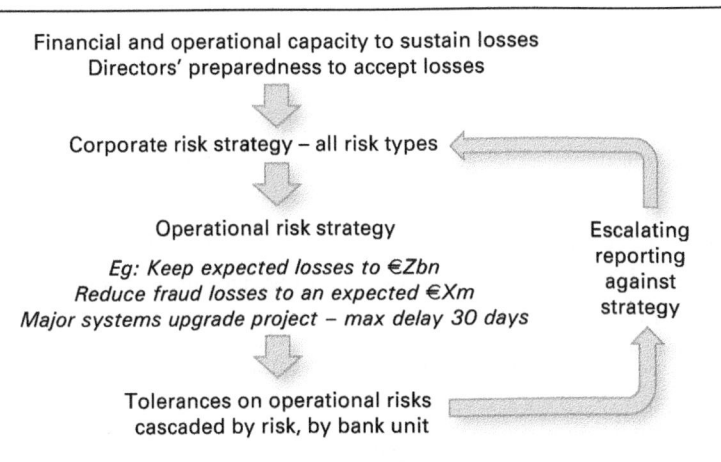

Financial and operational capacity to sustain losses
Directors' preparedness to accept losses

↓

Corporate risk strategy – all risk types

↓

Operational risk strategy

Eg: Keep expected losses to €Zbn
Reduce fraud losses to an expected €Xm
Major systems upgrade project – max delay 30 days

↓

Tolerances on operational risks cascaded by risk, by bank unit

Escalating reporting against strategy

As set out later, best practice for risk assessment in ORM involves statistical modelling based on loss data, conditioned by expert opinion about how future stochastic behaviours of the risk may in some way be different from the past.

For many firms, the loss data quality is not yet sufficiently good for purely quantitative work. In many firms a structured process has been developed for gathering together the best information, based on expertise, experience and also the loss data whilst acknowledging its weaknesses. This activity is often called a Risk and Control Self-Assessment (RCSA). Here the focus is on risk exposure, both gross and net, in comparison with the similarly named Control Risk Self-Assessment (CRSA) where the emphasis is on the effectiveness of controls. In practice, control effectiveness is subsumed into RCSA.

Accountability

Each risk is formally allocated to a manager to be accountable for its effective control, sometimes called the Risk Owner. Day to day, the job of monitoring a risk may be given to a designated 'risk manager' in the unit. It is essential though that responsibility for the control of a risk is clearly attributed to a senior named individual.

Effective management of a risk requires familiarity and proximity to the risk, or at least to its events. These are line locations. Moreover, very few central operational risk managers have the authority or resources to change a unit's way of working. The Risk Owner should be a local unit manager.

Communication and training

Consequently the implementation of a comprehensive, integrated and universal risk management framework has to involve a large number of people in the organization, all briefed and trained to understand how the framework will operate, and their roles and responsibilities in it.

ORM places great store in training and communication of all sorts. Good practice includes features like:

- Ensuring new employees understand how risk arises in all work places, and their role in managing it.
- Thorough training for nominated local operational risk managers in their roles and responsibilities, including relevant techniques in, for example, assessing losses and conducting qualitative risk assessments.
- Providing all levels of management with briefings and training, as appropriate to each level, in ORM and how it impinges on them.
- Ensuring that when there are personnel changes for jobs that include ORM responsibilities, the new incumbent is given all the technical training required within a short period of time.
- Periodically refreshing everyone in the importance of ORM and how the organization does it, and the benefits that come out. For most people, involvement in ORM only happens once in a while, and people lose touch with it.

Risk modelling – the Loss Distribution Approach

Modelling activities require a lot of observation data points. Models are a simplified, theoretical representation of the reality, built on repeated observations to derive stable patterns and common laws governing the data observed.

When regulators decided to require banks to hold capital for operational risk, data on incidents were barely collected. To increase the number of data points at their disposal to fit statistical distributions, modellers use the Loss Distribution Approach (LDA). Risks are decomposed into two of their components: how often they occur (frequency) and how much they cost (severity). This multiplies the number of observation points available for modelling. The application of LDA to operational risk has been published by modellers at the French bank Credit Lyonnais (Frachot et al., 2001) and it has become common practice, despite some technical reservations (Coleman and Young, 2009; Hassani and Guegan, 2013). The LDA allows the fitting of two types of distributions:

- Frequency: a discrete distribution, counting the number of operational risk events per period of time, typically one year. Frequency is most commonly modelled by a Poisson distribution. Poisson is the simplest frequency distribution, with a single parameter, λ, that is both the mean and the variance. Most banks using sophisticated methods approved by the regulator use this simple distribution (BCBS, 2009).
- Severity: a continuous distribution, asymmetric and heavy tailed, to account for the dual nature of operational risk: ie a large number of small losses and a few, very large incidents. The most common distribution used is the lognormal (BCBS, 2009), also favoured for the simplicity it brings. The lognormal distribution has the same properties as the well-known normal distribution (Gaussian) but it is the natural logarithm of the losses (assumed to be normally distributed) instead of the losses themselves.

Frequency and severity distributions are then compounded ('convoluted') into an aggregated loss distribution, illustrated in Figure 4.6. The following convolution methods exist to aggregate frequency and severity distributions:

- Monte Carlo simulations, an empirical method where the final distribution is made of a million or more points, all points being the results of random computer draws of severity and frequency. It is the simplest approach and is most commonly used in practice, although it requires the largest computational resources.
- Fourier transforms or Panjer recursions; equations-based solutions requiring more coding but less computer time.

For a detailed review of all available statistical techniques in operational risk modelling, refer to Peters et al. (2015).

60 Multidimensional Risk Management

FIGURE 4.6 Frequency and severity aggregation – illustration

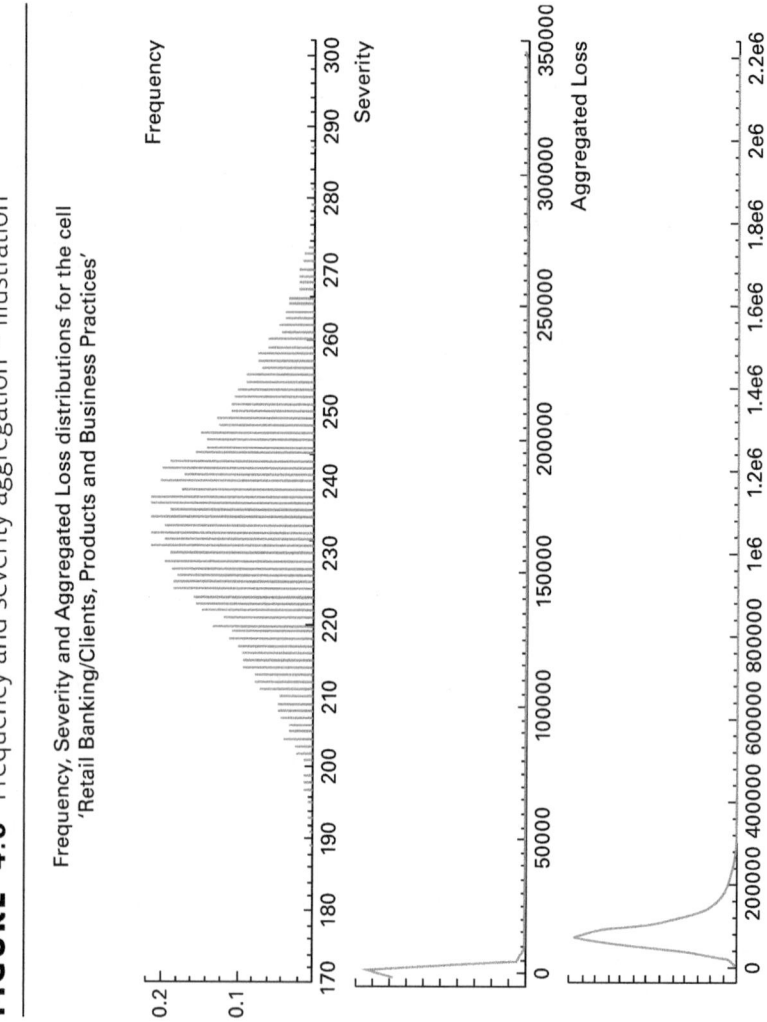

Frequency, Severity and Aggregated Loss distributions for the cell 'Retail Banking/Clients, Products and Business Practices'

SOURCE: Chapelle, et al. (2004)

The LDA process is operated for each cluster of similarly behaved losses that will then be aggregated into a total distribution where, under banking regulation, the 99.9th percentile will correspond to the stand-alone capital for operational risk.

Risk and Control Self-Assessment

In the absence of adequate loss data, RCSAs are used to assess likelihood and frequency. Good practice involves not only assessing averages of both, but also estimating an extreme event and its likelihood.

A good RCSA process frequently leads to fresh insight and understanding of a risk in the context of the whole firm, including for line staff and managers. In this regard, process mapping and process risk assessment are powerful approaches. To best design cost-effective controls, root cause analysis should be used, typically with Fault Tree techniques. However, RCSAs require preparation and follow up – the workshop itself is only a part. The best way to aggregate such assessments together with the unlikely severe event is Monte Carlo.

Assessing extreme events

Operational risk disasters, whether due to systems failures or disruptions, cyber-attacks, physical damage, systematic mis-selling, or compliance breaches, have the potential to wipe out years of revenues, significantly damage reputation and durably damage the firm's earning capabilities. One reason for this for example is the potential for an operational risk event to have a knock-on effect to other risks – in banking and insurance even going into credit, market and underwriting exposures.

Scenario analysis is the assessment and management of exposure to high-severity, low-frequency events. It focuses on the extremes and is not limited to financial impact. There should be a high level of repeatability of the process of generating scenario data, through consistent preparation and application of the qualitative and quantitative results. To reduce as much as possible subjectivity and biases in the process, assumptions must be based on empirical evidence, analysts must explain the rationale behind the level at which a scenario is analysed, and assumptions and process for generating scenario analysis should be well documented. Peachey (2011) provides a large number of cases of major losses which can assist in planning extreme scenarios.

Scenario analysis considers the likelihood of such disasters and, more importantly, assesses resilience if they occur. For modelling, scenario analysis provides an important input to the tail of the distribution, and a yardstick for capital adequacy. For management purposes, it informs directors about the large exposures to the firm, possible vulnerabilities, and thus the necessary level of preventive controls and mitigating measures.

Increasingly techniques such as Decision Trees (Event Trees) are being used to understand the impact of large events. Equally importantly but less widely adopted are Fault Trees and Causal Network modelling, which provide important insight into root causes, enabling prevention and control to be more cost-effective.

Stress testing and scenario analysis are sometimes synonymous in operational risk. Stress testing however, also refers to two different exercises:

- Macro stress testing: evaluation of the sufficiency of capital level in cases of large macroeconomic shocks, such as sharp variation of interest rates or severe economic downturn.
- Micro stress testing or sensitivity analysis: variation of one or more parameters of the operational risk model, to assess the stability of the results.

Combining day-to-day risk management with high-impact eventualities

Operational risk is largely dual, contrasting a mass of minor losses with rare, extreme failures. Every loss data consortium analysis has demonstrated over the years the asymmetry in operational losses. Reports from ORX (a membership organization that maintains a database of members' loss events) show that for the period 2008–2012, the smallest losses reported (€20,000 to €50,000) have represented 52.4 per cent of the frequency but only 2.4 per cent of the severity, whilst the largest incidents reported (above €10 million) represented 0.5 per cent of the occurrences but 73.5 per cent of the severity. In other words, three-quarters of the yearly operational losses are caused by 1 in 200 incidents, while more than half of the smallest losses do not make even a fortieth of the annual losses (ORX Association, 2014).

In modelling, the dichotomy between small and frequent 'ordinary' losses and large, rare events is captured by the combination of a body and tail of the loss distribution as illustrated in Figure 4.7.

Pure statistics models often use different distributions to model the body and the tail, while hybrid models typically use a combination of LDA approaches for the body and scenario analysis for the tail. An illustration of different distribution fitting combined with scenario assessment, based on real bank loss data, can be found in Chapelle *et al.* (2004).

Figure 4.7 illustrates schematically the structure of a real and complete LDA model (referred to as Advanced Measurement Approach (AMA) by the regulator) and the components of the operational risk framework informing the body and tail of the distribution.

FIGURE 4.7 Combining management of ordinary risks with high-impact eventualities: body and tail

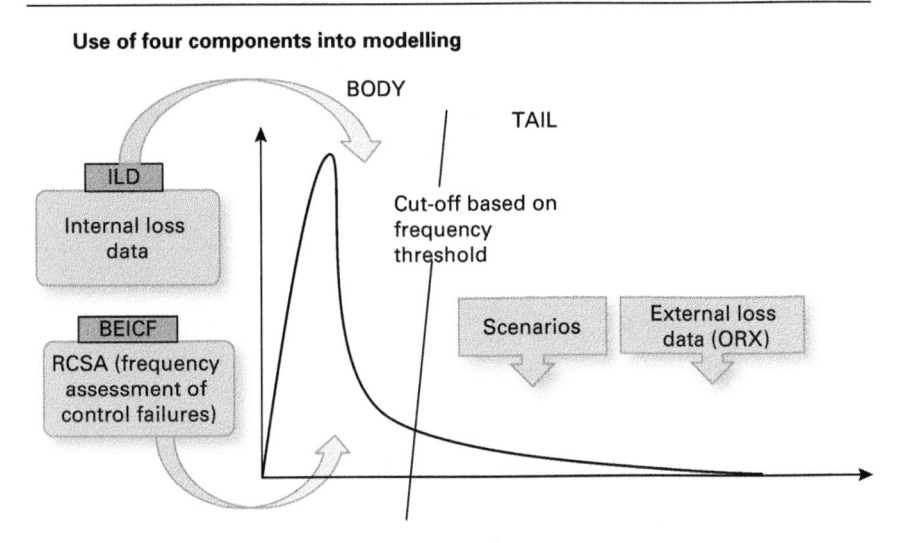

SOURCE: Chapelle, A (2015b) University College London

Aggregation within risk groups

Statistical methods are available to aggregate risk distributions. The very wide range of operational risks – from IT system failures to, say, internal frauds, and between operating units of very different nature – means that the stochastic characteristics can vary considerably (Cope and Carrivick, 2013). If the data quality and quantity is adequate, risks can be grouped together where their nature is similar. More on the potential groupings and the trade-off with data can be found in Cope (2010).

Within the banking industry, the leading and most commonly used approach for aggregating risks of similar type uses copula techniques. These techniques are the regulators' requirement for banks' implementation of AMA, the highest standard of minimum risk exposure modelling for the purposes of establishing the minimum capital required by the regulator (BCBS, 2011).

Copulas are a generalization of correlations and can be used to model advanced dependency structures, including tail dependence and dependence between extreme values. Intuitively, a copula is a multidimensional function that allows for coupling marginal distributions functions of two or more random variables with their dependence scheme. A simplified representation of copulas is illustrated in Figure 4.8. The intra risk group aggregation process of an existing AMA institution is illustrated in Figure 4.9. For extensive discussions on copulas and their application to operational risk, see Peters et al. (2015).

FIGURE 4.8 Intuitive representation of marginal distribution, joint distribution and copula

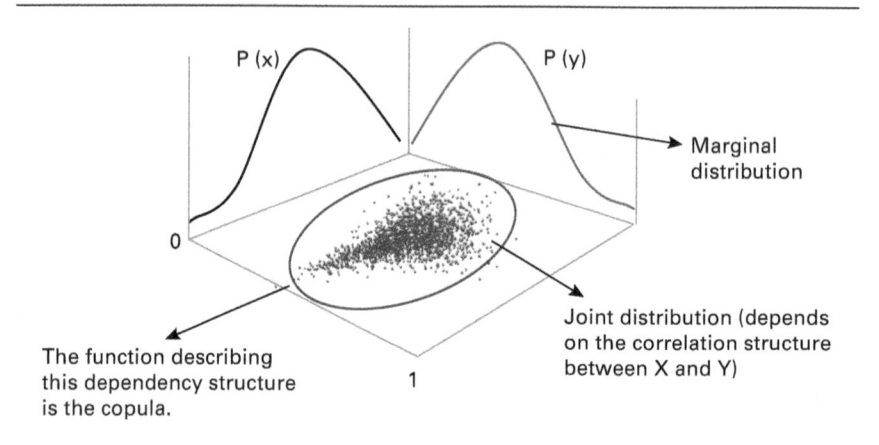

FIGURE 4.9 Intra-operational risk aggregation process – example of an AMA institution

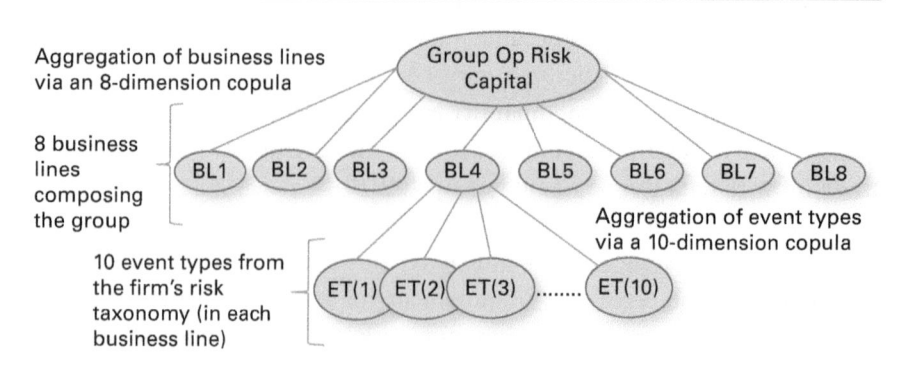

SOURCE: Chapelle, A (2015b) University College London

Operational Risk Management: risk appetite, tolerance and indicators

Risk appetite/tolerance is cascaded down through the different decision levels of an organization. In the business, decisions taken by senior management, like downsizing or increasing a business activity, increasing or decreasing risk taking, should reflect the risk appetite of the firm. At department level, risk appetite is expressed in risk scales, in the types and thresholds of key risk indicators, and in the monitoring of incidents against tolerance and loss budget:

- Risk scales: eg red, amber, green. The colours of the Risk and Control Self-Assessment (RCSA) matrix (or heatmap) to express risk tolerance for each combination of impact and likelihood. Amber and red typically reflect a risk above risk tolerance.
- Key risk indicators (KRIs): the metrics of operational risk drivers. They monitor an activity and give assurance that it stays within the boundaries of risk tolerance. The type of indicators selected and the thresholds between green, amber and red alerts are linked to the level of risk tolerance of an organization. The more critical the activity to the firm, the lower the risk tolerance, and the more numerous and strict will be the KRIs and thresholds. For more on KRIs see Chapelle (2013a, 2013b, 2015a).
- Incident data: monitoring the incidents compared to their tolerated levels helps evaluate performance and controls, as well as whether a firm operates within risk appetite.

Unlike financial risk, operational risk reporting using qualitative indicators faces the challenge of aggregating such data. Even when expressed in numbers, risk ratings are no more quantitative or additive than colours or adjectives.

There are basically three options when aggregating qualitative data:

1 Conversion and addition:
- Metrics can be converted to a common, linear and continuous metric, usually monetary units (£, $, €); some large firms convert non-financial impacts results of their RCSA (reputation, regulatory, etc.) into financial data, to be able to sum and group risks.
- Simple addition of the individual risks or exposures into a total bears the implicit assumption of zero correlation between the individual parts. Care should be taken as to whether this

simplifying assumption is reasonable in each case. Interrelationships between operational risks are still underexplored, mainly due to the lack of adequate data.

2 Worst case:
- Most conservative, where the worst score of a set, such as a group of key risk indicators, is reported as the indicator value. This is an option when risk tolerance is low and data are closely correlated to risk levels, ie the KRIs are strong predictors of the risk, and risk assessments produced are quite reliable.
- It has the advantage of being prudent, but the drawback of potentially generating too many alerts to the point that management starts to disregard the indicator.

3 Categorization:
- Report the risk scores per percentage of categories: per cent of red, amber and green, or per cent of low, medium and high risks. Rather than collapsing complex information into a single datum point, this approach is more informative to management whilst still being economical in presentation.

Many firms choose to report an aggregate score, alongside the red alerts and issues that are escalated as such.

Risk reporting to risk committee, directors and management

ORM places great importance on monitoring and management reporting of operational risk exposures. Regular reports advise management at all levels of significant changes in important exposures. Given the wide range of risks, reports are most effective when prepared by the operational risk manager to highlight areas of concern, such as a risk exposure becoming unacceptably large, or a control improvement running late.

The selection of risk indicators, and leading indicators in particular, is crucial. Considerable work is done to identify indicators, and the necessary data sources, to enable proactive action to be taken to improve controls, rather than only responding to risk events that have taken place.

In combination with thresholds based on risk tolerance from the risk strategy, indicators provide a structured and consistent approach to deciding which adverse trends need action by management to limit exposure. This is illustrated in Figure 4.10.

FIGURE 4.10 Use of KRI with management alert level and tolerance level

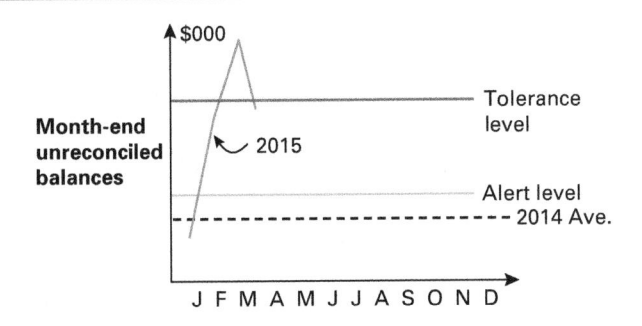

[Figure: Graph showing Month-end unreconciled balances ($000) over months J F M A M J J A S O N D, with a 2015 line peaking and dropping, a Tolerance level line, and an Alert level / 2014 Ave. dashed line]

Good practice reporting to directors focuses on selectivity of reporting. At increasing levels of reporting the degree of selectivity should increase. Providing too much information runs the risk of key matters being overlooked, and a report that does not get key information across has failed. The featured information may change from report to report, as different matters of importance arise. The focus should be on issues where the risk manager believes action needs to be taken. The use of summary risk 'dashboards' is favoured, in which the contents may well change from report to report, as different priorities arise.

How does Operational Risk Management fit?

ORM has developed as a discipline within risk management to meet the need for integrating the scale and nature of an organization's risk exposure into governance and management at all levels, into corporate strategy, and into financial planning. This is in addition to the aim of improving for each risk the preventions and mitigations.

With the operational risks managed as a systematic whole, ORM is placed as a key part of the governance of an organization in a way in which, as disaggregated risks, it was not before. The focus on the potential for severe losses – stress testing and scenario analysis – enables organizations to plan to have financial and well as operational resilience. Operational risks cover the full range of risk types, so ORM teams work with all the approaches in the various risk fields. In this sense Operational Risk Management is a multi-disciplinary activity. ORM is far and away most widely adopted in the financial services sector. Firms in this sector, such as banks, insurance companies and asset management firms tend to have relatively little equity and long-term debt compared to the risk exposures they carry.

Major areas of operational risk for such firms are:

- IT operations – reliability and security. Financial services firms, especially the banks, have many systems which are not only real time, but are the essence of their services to customers and to linking with markets and inter-bank payments systems.
- Poorly designed products and services, and mis-selling towards customers. Recently this has begun to be called conduct risk.
- Transaction processing – losses caused by incorrect recording, checking, processing and completing market transactions.
- Internal and external fraud – these firms have high volumes of money and financial instruments under process at any one time. The firms are very aware of the scope for fraud to take place and have extensive controls. Nevertheless there are instances of rogue traders for example.

What's next?

For further reading about good practice in the management of operational risks see Blunden and Thirlwell (2010), Institute of Operational Risk (no date) and BCBS (2014). ORM continues to develop. Implementation to achieve the distinctive features of ORM – improved high-level governance, consistent and complete risk modelling, integration of risk exposures, and linkage to strategy and financial resilience – continues with more sophistication possible as data becomes of better quality (consistent and accurate) and its value, especially to senior management, becomes more evident.

With developing methodology and evolving implementation of the risk strategy, risk tolerance and KRI monitoring, the impact of these techniques on governance, resource allocation and management decision making will grow and prove very influential. We are seeing instances where better knowledge of the potential returns, risks and capital requirements of some divisions is causing groups to exit those activities. On a more day-to-day level, seeing better which are the important risks to increase control of, rather than which are the easy ones to control, is increasing cost effectiveness of the control regime.

The volume of data and information available about the threats to an organization places a premium on effectively communicating salient matters to management at all levels. Developments are taking place in:

- assisting users to readily identify key current issues;
- developing risk indicators with potential for integration across an organization, and related to performance indicators;

- improving the use of risk information in decision making;
- improving the ability to report on emerging, complex and interrelated risk situations.

Emerging risks

A number of important risk areas are developing at present, leading to considerable study in the operational risk field. These include:

- cyber risk;
- reputational risk, including conduct risk;
- new business models;
- major project risk management.

These are considered in turn below.

Cyber risk

The threats are evolving and changing – new players are using more sophisticated methods for new purposes. The effects they are trying to achieve run from major theft of personal data for resale or exposure, to causing payments to be made/client funds stolen, to subverting the proper operation of systems, to achieving improper influence on the firm or its executives (eg blackmail). The risk management response to this requires new approaches to assessment and response planning.

Reputational risk, including conduct risk

Three issues continue to make these areas difficult:

- assessing the impact – the cash costs at the time might be trivial compared to the loss of future income and fall in share price;
- handling the time between the root cause event and the discovery and costs;
- the highly uncertain nature of the potential costs. For example, will a poor staff product training programme now lead to modest numbers of restitution and compensation in the next year or two, or a large number of complaints many years out, with massive damages and fines (as in the PPI scandal)?

New business models

Speed of change in many industries is great at present. This is driven not only by technological developments such as IT/internet/microchip. Societal change is taking place, affecting how we want to conduct our personal affairs and what we look for in the work and career space. Large organizations are under threat from new businesses with new services and means of delivery of those services. Typically the challengers have very different (lower) cost structures.

In assisting directors in the decision making and risk control around initiatives to respond to these external changes, ORM needs to provide approaches that bring such initiatives into the total risk profile of the organization.

Major project risk management

There are large exposures to an organization around major projects, be they introducing new IT systems, new business ventures, acquisition or divestments. The large exposures, some of which may have long durations before they become evident, need to be identified and controlled. Firms accustomed to large physical projects (oil and gas, power, railways, etc.) have excellent project risk management disciplines. ORM needs to bring these into the consistent and integrated risk framework.

Find out more

Basel Committee on Banking Supervision (BCBS) (2009), Observed range of practice in key elements of Advanced Measurement Approaches (AMA), *Bank for International Settlements* [online] http://www.bis.org/publ/bcbs160b.pdf

Basel Committee on Banking Supervision (BCBS) (2011) Operational risk: supervisory guidelines for the advanced measurement approaches, *Bank for International Settlements* [online] http://www.bis.org/publ/bcbs196.htm

Basel Committee on Banking Supervision (BCBS) (2014) Review of the principles for the sound management of operational risk, *Bank for International Settlements* [online] http://www.bis.org/publ/bcbs292.htm

Blunden, T and Thirlwell, J (2010) *Mastering Operational Risk*, FT Prentice Hall.

Chapelle, A (2013a) Unlocking KRIs, *RM Professional* [online] http://www.rmprofessional.com/content/features/unlocking-kris

Chapelle, A (2013b) The importance of preventive KRIs, *Operational Risk & Regulation Magazine*, April

Chapelle, A (2015a) Six steps for Preventive KRIs, *Operational Risk & Regulation Magazine*, January

Chapelle, A (2015b) Operational risk measurement for financial institutions, MSc in Financial Risk Management, Course Material, University College London

Chapelle, A, Crama, Y. Hunber, G, and Peters, J-P (2004) Basel II and operational risk: implications for risk measurement and management in the financial sector, National Bank of Belgium, working Paper n°51, May

Coleman R, and Young, B (2009) *Operational Risk Assessment: The commercial imperative of a more forensic and transparent approach*, Wiley Financial Series

Cope, E (2010) Modeling operational loss severity distributions from consortium data, *Journal of Operational Risk* 5 (4), Winter 2010/11, pp 35–64

Cope, E and Carrivick, L (2013) Effects of the financial crisis on banking operational losses, *Journal of Operational Risk*, 8 (3), September, pp 3–29

Financial Reporting Council (FRC) (2014) Guidance on Risk Management, Internal Control and Related Financial and Business Reporting, *FRC* [online] https://www.frc.org.uk/Our-Work/Publications/Corporate-Governance/Guidance-on-Risk-Management,-Internal-Control-and.pdf

Frachot, A, Georges, P and Roncalli, T (2001) Loss distribution approach for operational risk, working paper, Groupe de Recherche Opérationnelle, Crédit Lyonnais

Hassani, B and Guegan, D (2013) An autocorrelated loss distribution approach: back to the time series, Documents de travail du Centre d'Economie de la Sorbonne, number 12091

Institute of Operational Risk (no date) Sound Practice Papers [online] www.IOR-Institute.org, members section

ORX Association (2014), 2014 ORX report on operational loss data

Peachey, A (2011) *Great Financial Disasters of our Time*, BWV Berliner Wissenschafts-Verlag.

Peters, G, Shevchenko, P and Cruz, M (2015) *Fundamental Aspects of Operational Risk and Insurance Analytics: A handbook of operational risk*, Wiley, Chichester

Project, programme and portfolio risk management

05

DR DALE F COOPER

Why does project, programme and portfolio risk management matter?

Project risk management has been around for a long time and there are well-established processes for doing it. Despite this, projects 'go wrong', and sometimes they fail spectacularly. They either don't deliver the value they were intended to provide, they cost more than expected, or they take longer than planned.

Risk management can't substitute for poor project management, but good risk management can go some way to identifying and managing opportunities for generating better project outcomes and avoiding major failures.

Good risk management becomes even more important, and more useful, as projects become larger or more complex and as projects are grouped into programmes and portfolios that must be managed in a coordinated manner. There are many factors that make such endeavours 'risky', as shown in Table 5.1.

Projects, programmes and portfolios

When expanding from project risk management to consider programmes and portfolios, we need first to look at some definitions (Table 5.2).

TABLE 5.1 Factors that make projects risky

Activity	Large scale, large amounts of money, many individual parts, large workforce, many interactions, competition for scarce resources, complex contractual arrangements, scope that may be not defined in detail when work starts
Technology	New or innovative technology, research and development components
Location	Difficult or remote physical location, sensitive community or environmental aspects, specific features of the region or the country where work is to be done
Stakeholders	Many stakeholders, conflicting or unclear objectives, differing perceptions, NGO interest, media interest
Approvals	Multiple regulators, detailed and sometimes conflicting regulatory requirements, increased scrutiny, stringent approval processes, regulatory approval delays, internal approval delays

TABLE 5.2 Definitions

Project	A temporary endeavour undertaken to create a unique product, service or result (PMI, 2013a). It is a unique process consisting of a set of coordinated and controlled activities, with start and finish dates, undertaken to achieve an objective conforming to specific requirements, including the constraints of time, cost and resources (IEC, 2013)
Programme	A group of related projects, subprogrammes, and programme activities, managed in a coordinated way to obtain benefits not available from managing them individually (PMI, 2013b)
Portfolio	A component collection of programmes, projects, or operations managed as a group to achieve strategic objectives (PMI, 2013c)

The relationships between projects, programmes and portfolios are shown in Figure 5.1. The example in Figure 5.2 shows a portfolio of two public transport programmes that must be coordinated, with an integrated ticketing project that is managed at the portfolio level.

FIGURE 5.1 Projects, programmes and portfolios

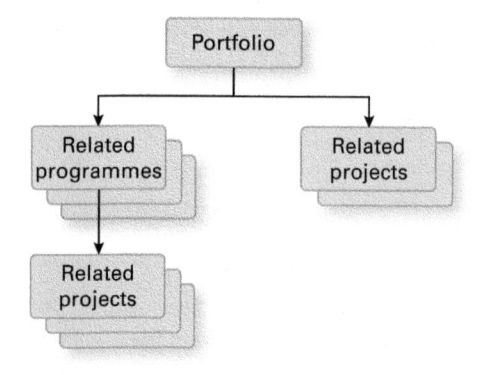

SOURCE: © Broadleaf Capital International, 2015

FIGURE 5.2 Portfolio example

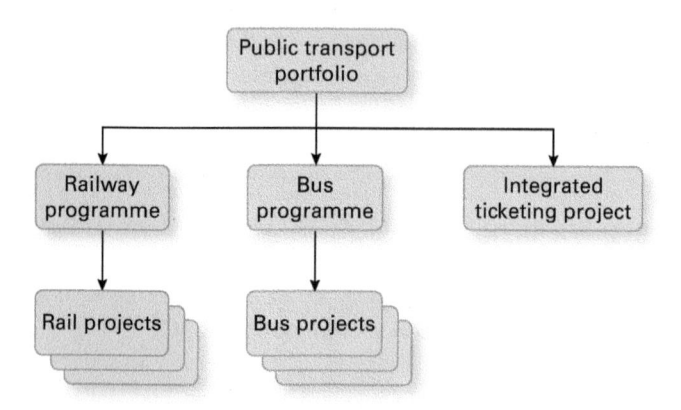

SOURCE: © Broadleaf Capital International, 2015

The essence of programmes and portfolios is the aggregation and alignment of related activities to achieve high-level or strategic objectives. Programmes and portfolios are complex and difficult to manage well, even if the component projects are relatively simple. They often involve extended timeframes encompassing the duration of several projects and a wide range of resources, including people, finance, facilities, materials and intellectual property, all of which must be coordinated.

Phases in the life of projects, programmes and portfolios

In most circumstances, projects have defined objectives or an end-state that provides those involved in the project with a clear vision and specification of their goal. The larger scales and longer timeframes for programmes and portfolios often mean that their objectives and desired end-states may be stated in more general terms, and these objectives may evolve as circumstances change.

The evolutionary nature of projects, programmes and portfolios as they move from initial ideas through to practical activities that deliver real assets, products and services is important. For example, Figure 5.3 shows the typical phases in the life cycle of a project, and similar life cycles can be developed for programmes and portfolios. In the early phases, objectives and desired outcomes may be expressed in quite general or strategic terms, there may be many ways in which those outcomes could be achieved and there is usually significant uncertainty about the detailed way forward. As the project moves towards delivery, the scope becomes better defined, objectives and targets are expressed more precisely and uncertainty decreases as risks are addressed and resolved. (The pre-delivery phases are often referred to as front-end loading, or FEL.)

FIGURE 5.3 Typical project life cycle

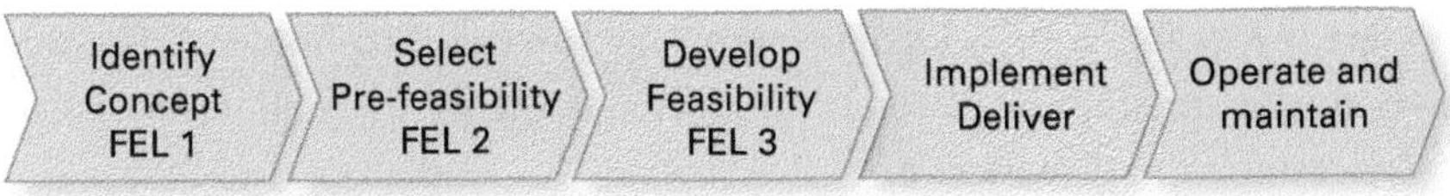

Identify Concept FEL 1 → Select Pre-feasibility FEL 2 → Develop Feasibility FEL 3 → Implement Deliver → Operate and maintain

SOURCE: © Broadleaf Capital International, 2015

The changing nature of uncertainty is a key focus for project, programme and portfolio (P3) risk management, as are the evolving definitions of the objectives and the desired outcomes.

What is project, programme and portfolio risk management?

Purpose of P3 risk management

The purpose of risk management is to provide confidence that an organization can achieve its objectives and to identify and take advantage of opportunities for obtaining better outcomes. This is true for the projects, programmes and portfolios an organization chooses to pursue.

Risk management enhances business and project outcomes. It does this by providing insight, knowledge and confidence for better decision making.

It guides actions and allocation of resources to increase certainty, support more effective management in the face of uncertainty, reduce exposure to detrimental outcomes, and promote prudent risk taking where this would lead to benefits for the organization.

What is risk in this context?

Following ISO 31000 and IEC 62198, we define risk as 'the effect of uncertainty on objectives'.

For projects, programmes and portfolios the notion of objectives is critical. The Project Management Institute defines project risk as 'an uncertain event or condition that, if it occurs, has a positive or negative effect on one or more project objectives such as scope, schedule, cost, and quality' (PMI, 2013a).

The objectives implicit in this definition seem quite short-term and tactical in nature. However, if 'scope' and 'quality' are thought of in a broad, general sense that encompasses all that a project's stakeholders might include in what they regard as a 'good project outcome', the definition can be regarded as being wider than this. It is always important to ask: why is this project, programme or portfolio important for the stakeholders? The answer to this question leads to David Hillson's interpretive definition of risk as 'uncertainty that matters'.

The PMI's definitions of programme and portfolio risk take a more general view (see Table 5.3).

TABLE 5.3 Programme and portfolio risk

Programme risk	A programme risk is an event or series of events or conditions that, if they occur, may affect the success of the programme... These risks often arise from the programme components and their interactions with each other, from technical complexity, schedule and/or cost constraints, and with the broader environment in which the programme is managed (PMI, 2013b)
Portfolio risk	A portfolio risk is an uncertain event or condition that, if it occurs, has a positive or negative effect on one or more project objectives. A risk may have one or more causes and, if it occurs, the corresponding effects may have a positive or negative impact on one or more portfolio success criteria (PMI, 2013c)

There are several features of these definitions that are important in shaping how P3 risk management is conducted.

The definitions all refer to positive or negative effects. This accords with the purpose of risk management being concerned with improving outcomes, both by recognizing and exploiting opportunities as well as by avoiding or reducing detrimental outcomes.

The definitions are concerned not just with events but also conditions. While specific acute events may be important, so too are chronic conditions that may evolve or accumulate through time. For example, a programme manager might focus on events that restrict the availability of resources right now, as well as gradual changes in economic conditions that might lead to changes in both the availability and the price of resources in the future. Climate change is another condition that may have limited immediate effect but may be critical for the long-term strategic outcomes of a large portfolio.

Because the purpose of projects, programmes and portfolios is to support organizational objectives, the objectives that are addressed in risk management are commonly very similar, and sometimes identical, to those of the organization. This means that P3 risk management is very similar in both its general process and its focus to Enterprise Risk Management (ERM) for the organization.

How is risk managed in projects, programmes and portfolios?

Relevant standards and guidelines

There is an international standard and several guides for P3 risk management. IEC 62198 describes how ISO 31000 can be applied to projects. Cooper *et al.* (2014) expand substantially on this approach, with many case examples.

The Project Management Institute (PMI, 2013a, 2013b, 2013c) and the Association for Project Management (APM, 2010) also provide useful guidance.

The risk management process

The basic risk management process for projects is the same as that for ERM, illustrated in Figure 5.4. However, its focus changes as it is applied at different points in the project life cycle shown in Figure 5.3. For example, early in the life of a project, attention is on strategic matters, whether the project could ever be worthwhile, and the identification of any fatal flaws. In the pre-feasibility phase, risk-based selection of design and delivery options becomes important. Later, when the scope of the project becomes more clearly defined in the feasibility phase, so the risk management activities address finer details of the design and the delivery strategy.

FIGURE 5.4 The risk management process

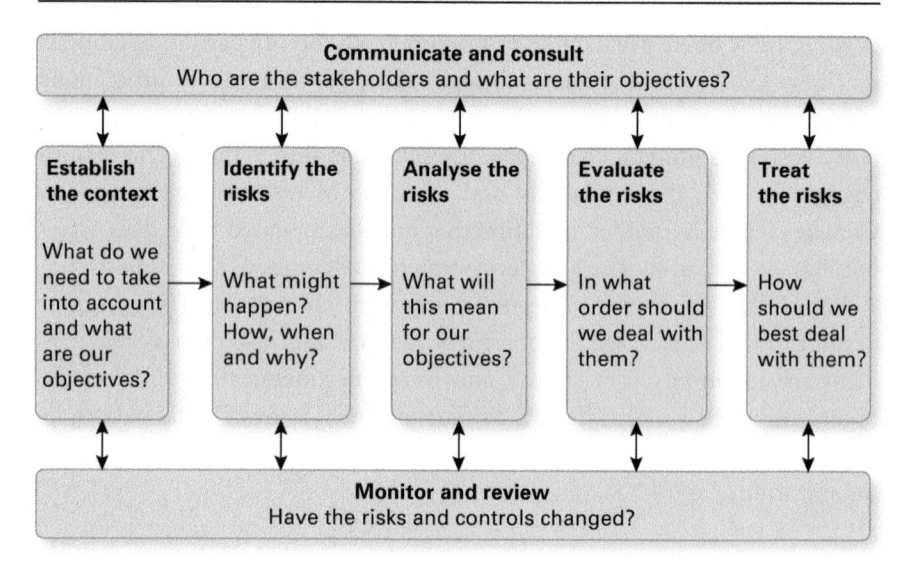

```
┌─────────────────────────────────────────────────────────────────────┐
│                      Communicate and consult                        │
│         Who are the stakeholders and what are their objectives?     │
└─────────────────────────────────────────────────────────────────────┘
  ┌───────────┐  ┌───────────┐  ┌───────────┐  ┌───────────┐  ┌───────────┐
  │ Establish │  │ Identify  │  │ Analyse   │  │ Evaluate  │  │ Treat     │
  │ the       │  │ the risks │  │ the risks │  │ the risks │  │ the risks │
  │ context   │  │           │  │           │  │           │  │           │
  │           │  │ What      │  │ What will │  │ In what   │  │ How       │
  │ What do we│→ │ might     │→ │ this mean │→ │ order     │→ │ should we │
  │ need to   │  │ happen?   │  │ for our   │  │ should we │  │ best deal │
  │ take into │  │ How, when │  │objectives?│  │ deal with │  │ with them?│
  │ account   │  │ and why?  │  │           │  │ them?     │  │           │
  │ and what  │  │           │  │           │  │           │  │           │
  │ are our   │  │           │  │           │  │           │  │           │
  │objectives?│  │           │  │           │  │           │  │           │
  └───────────┘  └───────────┘  └───────────┘  └───────────┘  └───────────┘
┌─────────────────────────────────────────────────────────────────────┐
│                        Monitor and review                           │
│              Have the risks and controls changed?                   │
└─────────────────────────────────────────────────────────────────────┘
```

SOURCE: © Broadleaf Capital International, 2015

For programmes and portfolios, which have a broader scope than an individual project and include many interconnected components and projects, the scope of the risk management process extends too. The way the components fit with the organization's evolving objectives, their interactions with one another and their aggregate effects, particularly their combined requirements for resources, become critical. Because programmes and portfolios are usually important parts of the organization's strategy, board members and the most senior executives are often active participants in risk management activities.

The following discussion concentrates on those areas of P3 risk management that differ in interesting ways from ERM or where the focus might need to be adjusted to achieve effective and efficient outcomes.

Communicate and consult

Communication and consultation is an important step in project risk management, just as it is in ERM. For programmes and portfolios, the range of stakeholders who need to be taken into account increases. The spheres of influence and the interests of individual stakeholders change over time in a programme and portfolio environment, and this may affect the approach that is taken to communicating and consulting with them.

For project managers, interactions with stakeholders having programme-wide or portfolio-wide roles may be quite different in this broader context. For example, these stakeholders might have roles relating to human resources and staffing, information technology, market research, investor relations, allocation of pooled equipment, maintenance or any of the myriad other functions that are often organized and managed far more efficiently at a programme or portfolio level.

For risk management, consultation with this wider set of stakeholders should lead to a broader view of the context, identification of a wider set of risks, particularly risks related to interactions between projects and programmes within a portfolio, more nuanced treatment activities that take into account the requirements of other parts of the programme and portfolio, and different mechanisms for monitoring, review and assurance of controls.

Stakeholder communication plans are often formulated and coordinated at a programme or portfolio level rather than within individual projects.

Establish the context

The context for P3 risk management must take external and internal factors into account, just as for ERM. Additional factors for projects, programmes and portfolios include the range of components and activities involved, the overall scale of the workforce and the management effort required, interactions between the components and constraints on aggregated resources at a programme and portfolio level, as well as the stakeholder matters noted above.

Criteria for thinking about success or failure will generally be broader for a project within a programme or portfolio than for a stand-alone project, and will be expressed in higher-level terms. As noted above, criteria are far more likely to reflect organizational objectives than be linked to simple measures associated with scope, time, cost or quality.

As discussed later, risk identification, the next step in the risk management process, is best if it is structured clearly. Key elements, developed in the context step, provide this structure. For a project, they are often based on the project's work breakdown structure (WBS) or its phases. Within a programme or portfolio, the key elements for a project must be extended beyond the WBS to encompass interactions with other projects and programmes across the portfolio.

For programme and portfolio risk management, the key elements should include the main individual projects. Smaller projects might appear as single elements; larger projects might be represented by several elements, perhaps linked to high-level components of their WBS. There are also likely to be elements that reflect programme-wide or portfolio-wide matters, such as critical resources, dependencies and other interactions.

Identify the risks

Methods for identifying risks for individual projects are well established: brainstorming based on the key element structure developed in the context step, guideword and prompt systems, questionnaires, examination of previous projects and so on. They are all similar to the processes used in ERM.

Similar approaches can be used for programmes and portfolios, but there is usually a far heavier reliance on the detail of the risk management work that has been implemented in individual projects, supplemented by fresh risk identification associated with interactions between projects, shared resources, outputs of one project providing enablers for others and external influences.

Risks that are important or rated highly in individual projects, such as a difficult location for Project A, complex technology development for Project B or important stakeholder relationships for Project C, may be managed best at the project level, but programme managers and portfolio managers need to be aware of them and the status of the actions to address them. Some may need additional resources from the programme or the portfolio.

Risks that may not be rated highly in any one project but that appear in several places, such as lack of skilled personnel, poor maintenance processes, dependence on a common supplier who is under pressure, or restrictions imposed by outdated information systems, may have important aggregate effects. They may be managed better at programme or portfolio level rather than piecemeal within individual projects.

Risks that can only be seen properly at the programme or portfolio level, such as strategic matters associated with the wider economy or the political environment, prospective changes in regulations, or externally derived constraints on resources, are best managed within the programme or portfolio.

Analyse the risks

Risk analysis for P3 is similar to that for ERM, with only small adjustments for the specific project context, particularly in relation to the objectives and the way the consequences of risks are rated. The five components included in qualitative risk analysis are described in Table 5.4.

TABLE 5.4 Risk analysis components and purpose

Control effectiveness	Measures the adequacy of the design of the controls and the effectiveness of their implementation, in relation to the best that could be achieved in a project like this
Consequences	Measures the effects of a risk on the project, programme and portfolio objectives, taking into account the controls and their effectiveness
Likelihood	Measures the chance of the consequences arising at the indicated level, again taking into account the controls and their effectiveness
Level of risk	Combines the consequence and likelihood measures into a single measure of risk
Potential exposure	Measures the maximum consequences of a risk for the objectives if all the controls were to fail

The way in which controls are perceived and analysed for projects, programmes and portfolios needs some discussion, as this differs significantly from common practice in ERM. For an ERM process that follows ISO 31000, risks are analysed as they are now, with the current controls and their current level of effectiveness. This poses a problem for projects because they will not have controls in place in their early phases when a project team and associated infrastructure has yet to be established. Controls are addressed in one of two ways in these circumstances.

The first approach is to assume the existence of controls that the organization always puts in place for a project like this one, under existing policies, processes and procedures. For example, when analysing risks at the concept or identify phase for a construction project it would be very unlikely (and unnecessary) for the project team to have formulated test and commissioning plans, and a primary risk allocation and control measure, the contract, would not be in place. Nevertheless, it would be quite reasonable to assume that a test and commissioning plan would be developed later in the feasibility phase, and that the contractor would be required to prepare an appropriate quality management plan, as long as that's what the organization always does. This approach provides an analysis of risks as would be expected in later phases of the project.

The second approach is to consider the adequacy of the controls in relation to those that might be expected for a project at this phase of its life. There might be few controls, but that would be expected and so the control effectiveness rating, which is really a measure of management effectiveness, would be quite good. In this case, many risks might be rated highly, which provides an indication for the project manager about what needs to be done to fill in the gaps in controls as the project progresses.

The value and use of quantitative risk analysis for projects, programmes and portfolios is discussed later.

Evaluate the risks

The outcomes from risk analysis provide a guide for where project managers should focus their attention. The principles are the same as for ERM:

- For risks with high consequences and high likelihood, examine options for changing the level of risk.
- For risks with high level of risk and low control effectiveness, examine options for increasing the effectiveness of the controls.
- For risks with low level of risk but high potential exposure, develop assurance plans to ensure controls remain in place and effective. This is especially important where the existence of controls that the organization always puts in place has been assumed.

Treat the risks

Treating P3 risks follows a similar process to that for ERM: identify options, evaluate their benefits and costs, select worthwhile options, develop action plans, include action plans in project plans and budgets, and monitor the implementation of action plans as for any other activity in the project. Treatment options are noted in Table 5.5.

Monitor and review

There are several aspects to monitoring and review in projects, programmes and portfolios.

TABLE 5.5 Treatment options

Do something different	Avoid the circumstances in which the risk might arise, remove a hazard or make the project more susceptible to recognizing and exploiting an opportunity
Change the likelihood	Reduce the chance of something going wrong or increase the probability of a benefit arising
Change the consequences	Reduce the extent or duration of negative impacts or enhance the positive impacts
Share the risk	For example, set contract terms or purchase insurance
Accept the risk	Make a conscious decision to manage outcomes as they arise

Regular management meetings provide the most appropriate forum for monitoring, and risk management should be a routine agenda item. Items that should be addressed include high risks, the status of associated treatment plans, any control failures, particularly for risks with high potential exposures, and lessons learned from project activities, both successes and failures.

Periodic assurance reviews should be scheduled to examine the effectiveness of the controls associated with risks having high potential exposures. The effectiveness of the project risk management process should itself be reviewed regularly, and the context might change within the duration of an extended programme.

At a programme and portfolio level, sound communication processes are needed to ensure the outcomes from monitoring and review activities are communicated appropriately to other projects and other parts of the portfolio. In the medium to long term, this might have to accommodate changes in the make-up, objectives and relative influence of multiple stakeholders.

Frameworks and governance

When implementing P3 risk management in practice, the framework within which the risk management process takes place and its interaction with governance and decision making must be specified. Good management practice for projects uses tollgates for reviews and approvals at the end of each project phase (Figure 5.5).

FIGURE 5.5 Governance through the project life cycle

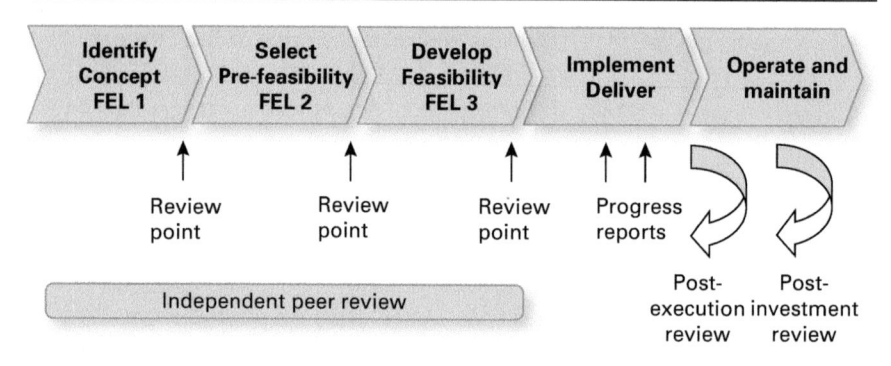

| Identify Concept FEL 1 | Select Pre-feasibility FEL 2 | Develop Feasibility FEL 3 | Implement Deliver | Operate and maintain |

↑ Review point — ↑ Review point — ↑ Review point — ↑↑ Progress reports — Post-execution review — Post-investment review

Independent peer review

SOURCE: © Broadleaf Capital International, 2015

Risk management is an important contributor to the information provided to decision makers at each tollgate, with the focus changing as the project proceeds (see Table 5.6). In a programme and portfolio context, the relationship of one project to other existing and planned work needs to be taken into account.

TABLE 5.6 Risk management focus

Phase	Purpose	Risk management focus
Concept or Identify	Appraisal of opportunities. Could the project ever be worthwhile?	Strategic threats and opportunities. Are there any fatal flaws?
Pre-feasibility or Select	Select the preferred option for the project. What is the best way of proceeding?	Risk-based selection of options. Which option provides the best balance of risk and reward?
Feasibility or Develop	Finalize the preferred option, scope, design and delivery strategy. What exactly is to be implemented, and how?	Risks related to the design and delivery approach.

Figure 5.6 illustrates the governance structure within which each tollgate review and approval takes place. In this framework, the project is viewed as an investment opportunity: the organization invests resources of many kinds – including capital, management attention and time – in order to achieve desired beneficial outcomes. The key decisions to be made are whether or not, and with what conditions, further resource expenditure is to be authorized for the

FIGURE 5.6 Investment governance

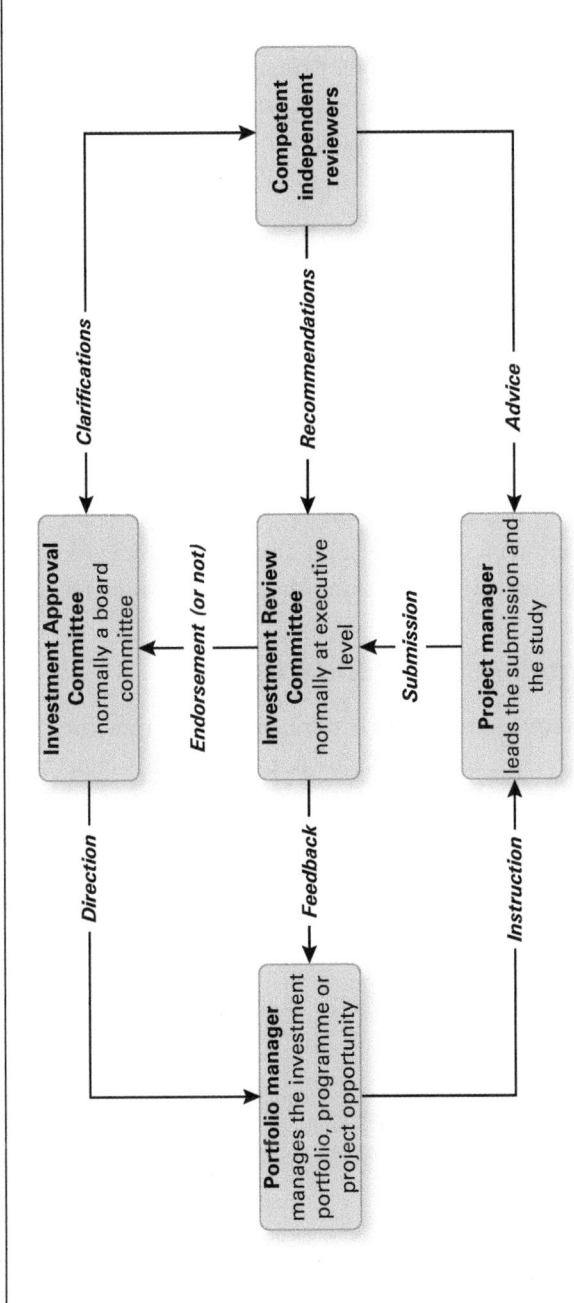

SOURCE: © Broadleaf Capital International, 2015

next project phase. The Investment Approval Committee is usually a committee of the board, or of the equivalent decision-making body in a public sector organization. It acts on the recommendation of an Investment Review Committee, which examines, usually in great detail, information submitted by the project manager. The portfolio manager oversees the work undertaken by the project manager, and competent independent reviewers provide independent assurance of the completeness and validity of the data, analyses, interpretations and recommendations submitted by the project manager.

Risk management contributes to the governance process in several ways. It helps the project manager allocate resources by highlighting areas of major uncertainty that should be addressed in the investment submission. It also helps the reviewers focus on major uncertainties or weaknesses in the submission. The risk assessments prepared by the project manager as part of the submission help the Investment Review Committee and the Investment Approval Committee to balance uncertainty and risk against the benefits to be derived from the project. At the portfolio level, questions of the organization's capacity to manage several concurrent projects effectively will arise, over and above the direct risks associated with each of the individual projects and the resources they require.

Risk management in tendering

The governance matters above were discussed from the perspective of a project, programme or portfolio owner. Contractors undertake similar processes when they examine a request for tender, decide whether or not to bid, and what price and conditions they should include in their response. The risk assessments and decision processes undertaken by a contractor in the tender response step in Figure 5.7 may look remarkably similar to the

FIGURE 5.7 Risk management in tendering

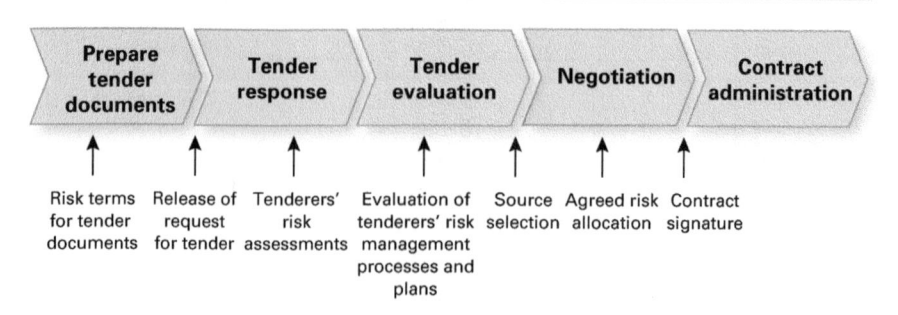

Prepare tender documents → Tender response → Tender evaluation → Negotiation → Contract administration

- Risk terms for tender documents
- Release of request for tender
- Tenderers' risk assessments
- Evaluation of tenderers' risk management processes and plans
- Source selection
- Agreed risk allocation
- Contract signature

SOURCE: © Broadleaf Capital International, 2015

approval process in Figure 5.6, particularly for large projects. Contractors' approval processes are usually at least as stringent as those for owners: contractors rarely have balance sheets that are strong enough to accept large risks that might threaten their shareholders' capital.

Quantitative analysis of uncertainty

A major focus of the risk management process seen in Figure 5.4 is on individual risks, but this does not help if an overall view of the 'riskiness' of a project, programme or portfolio is needed. Such a holistic perspective requires a quantitative analysis of the uncertainty involved. Some of the more important applications for projects, programmes and portfolios are noted in Table 5.7. Of these applications, schedule uncertainty is an important input to analyses of capital cost uncertainty and many aspects of value uncertainty.

TABLE 5.7 Applications of quantitative risk analysis

Schedule uncertainty	Delivery timetable, schedule control, dependencies of one project on the outputs of others, time commitments to stakeholders such as banks, regulators and users of the asset, product or service the project creates
Capital cost uncertainty	Capital requirement, financial drawdown, capital cost contingency, contingency management and control
Value uncertainty	Uncertainty in ramp-up to full capacity, capacity attained (volume of product or service), price and revenue stream, operating cost
Contractual liability	Exposure associated with specific outcome or loss scenarios

Quantitative risk analysis is most easily described with an example of estimating capital cost. The process begins with a simple model of costs, usually a spreadsheet based on a standard estimate at a high WBS level. This is then structured to identify the main drivers of uncertainty in quantities, unit rates, productivities and the schedule, and any discrete sources are identified too (Figure 5.8). Uncertainties in the drivers and the discrete risks are expressed as distributions, and these are combined, usually with Monte Carlo simulation, to calculate a distribution of the capital cost.

FIGURE 5.8 Sources of variability in cost estimates

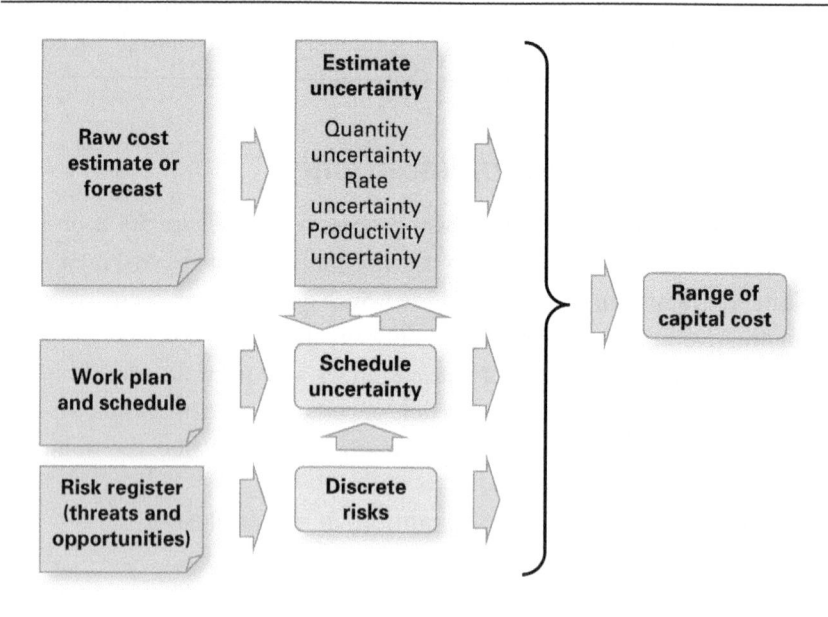

SOURCE: © Broadleaf Capital International, 2015

Distributions of cost like Figure 5.9 can be used to determine the chance of achieving any specified spending limit, to set a budget according to the organization's appetite for risk, or as a basis for negotiating a target cost in an alliance contract.

FIGURE 5.9 Chance of achieving a capital cost budget

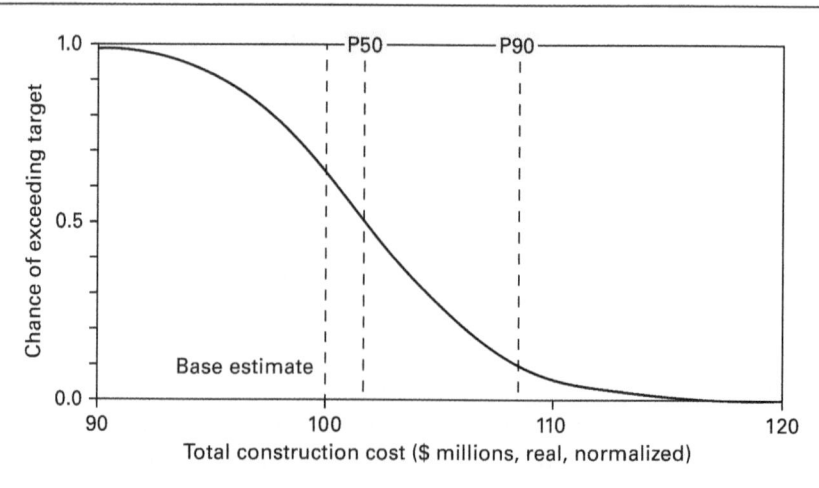

SOURCE: © Broadleaf Capital International, 2015

Analyses like these may be required for many purposes. Within a project, contract negotiation and project control may be important. At a programme and portfolio level, uncertainty analyses are required internally for coordination and the allocation of capital and other constrained resources. They also support external communications and negotiations with finance providers, regulators, security exchanges and other stakeholders.

How does project, programme and portfolio risk management fit?

Like most aspects of project management, P3 risk management ideally should be integrated with standard management processes and functions. Full integration may be difficult, but clear two-way communication is essential if the organization is to achieve the greatest benefits.

Portfolios and programmes (and often projects, depending on their size) are directed to achieving the organization's strategic goals. This means that close liaison with the executive, the board and the organization's strategic planning function is usually critical, and close liaison with the corporate ERM function is recommended. Table 5.8 summarizes some of the links with the business that may be needed.

TABLE 5.8 Risk management integration

Focus	Links to the business	Links from the business
Business strategy	Progress, achievements and forecast outcomes; escalation of risks to the executive and the board	Strategic and business objectives; changes to objectives; changes in the high-level context
Major risks	Integration with the corporate ERM function	Risks that may affect the project, programme or portfolio
Uncertainties in specialist areas	Requests for specific specialist risk assessments (eg community, stakeholder, environment, market, operations, health and safety)	Outcomes from specialist risk assessments, including risk treatments and assurance plans

(Continued)

TABLE 5.8 (*Continued*)

Focus	Links to the business	Links from the business
Risks and controls generic to specific functions	Requests for functional responses to treat risks and assure controls	Confirmation of treatment actions; confirmation of control effectiveness
Uncertainties in capital requirements	Forecasts of capital requirements, their timing and the currencies involved	Capital constraints; capital allocations; financing strategy; treasury strategy; lenders' caveats; exposure limits
Uncertainties in resource requirements (eg people and skills, physical resources)	Forecasts of required resources and associated timing; associated infrastructure and related requirements	Forecasts of available resources; resource constraints

Particular project features may require forms of risk management with a narrower and more specific focus, some of which are discussed in other chapters of this book. For example: management of risks associated with stakeholders, the environment, community health and safety; operation of the asset or service created by the project; security of physical or information assets and so on.

What's next?

PPPs and alliances

The projects within a programme or portfolio may involve a variety of contract forms and contractual relationships.

Public-private partnerships (PPPs) usually involve the project owner, one or more contractors and one or more providers of finance. The risk management process for a PPP is substantially the same as for any other project or programme, although there may be constraints on the specific allocation of responsibilities for risks, and quantitative analysis of project value may be complicated by the contractual and financial structures in place.

Alliances between an owner and a contractor often involve a sharing of the risks and benefits from a project as well as agreements to forego the right to resort to the courts to resolve disputes. Quantitative analysis of uncertainty is commonly used as a basis for determining the agreed time and cost targets that underpin risk and benefit sharing formulae. The open-book nature of many alliances makes many aspects of project management, including risk management, far more transparent during the delivery phase. Nevertheless, clear contractual allocation of responsibility for risks is necessary to avoid disputes and ensure both parties share a common interest in sound risk management of the work.

Mega-projects and complexity

There has been considerable focus recently on mega-projects and the supposed weaknesses in project management and risk management, with concern being fed by some very public failures, cost overruns and schedule overruns. It is unfortunate that some of the criticisms show a poor understanding of good risk management practice. A 'solution' that is often proposed is to do everything better and in more detail, and to make all management practices more rigorous and stringent, but this does not really address the underlying issues.

A mass of detail is not needed for sound risk management. In the early stages of very long-lived projects it is often futile to seek to define a project completely, not least because the context in which it is to deliver its value will have changed before it is implemented. Useful risk assessment can be undertaken at the concept and select phases of projects, when detail is scarce and uncertainty is high. Fatal flaws can be identified and a sound strategic approach can be developed without an exhaustive detailed analysis. There are proven workshop processes that can at least reduce if not eliminate the worst aspects of the over-confidence and anchoring biases that are often blamed for cost and schedule overruns, and quantitative uncertainty can be explored in a meaningful way using models and scenario analysis.

Nevertheless, implementing risk management in a very large and complex project is a challenge, especially where the time from concept to completion might exceed 10 years, as is common with some major infrastructure projects. Formal risk management policies, frameworks and plans that recognize the fluid nature of the work must be developed, and a risk management function must be established and resourced adequately, preferably early in the project life cycle. One of the most significant barriers to success is the reluctance of senior management to commit fully to risk management and allocate the necessary resources in these early stages.

Project complexity introduces challenges over and above those affecting routine project risk management (Grey, 2014; Williams, 2014). These can emerge from the interactions of multiple stakeholders seeking to influence a project or programme so that implementation details or even the end objectives might change as work is underway. Programmes seeking to address complex social requirements, such as major infrastructure and public service delivery, often cannot be specified in detail in their early phases. Their objectives can be expected to evolve as circumstances change, not because of lax management but because of the fluid nature of the real needs that they seek to address.

In complex projects there are many interactions, not all of them formal, and mechanistic forecasts may be unable to accommodate unavoidable uncertainty. Very often, day-to-day management will require decisions to be made quickly, with insufficient time for exhaustive analysis of the changes arising from these decisions. The consequences of these changes, and the influence of external factors, may not always be predictable. The project manager must be capable of recognizing when this results in beneficial or detrimental effects and react accordingly.

A conventional approach to risk management is still essential. However, for complex projects, it may also be necessary to bolster monitoring and response processes that can operate on a shorter time cycle than conventional reporting mechanisms, or to introduce communication channels specifically designed to provide early warning of emerging trends while there is time to influence them. This might require funding for what would otherwise be regarded as spare capacity in the management team, to allow for informal communication or for systems to gather informal real-time input from the workface.

While some mega-projects are complex, not all complex projects are necessarily large. A large number of component parts, many stakeholders, significant uncertainty and a need to act swiftly can result in even modestly sized projects exhibiting complex behaviour.

While established risk management methods can work well with mega-projects, their success in dealing with complexity is not clear. Different tools are likely to be needed to help project and programme managers, and their risk managers, make sense of the environment in which they are operating if it is truly complex. Some of these tools are themselves evolving, and so are the risk management processes they support. An increased emphasis is likely to be required on real-time monitoring and review while maintaining traditional approaches based on the medium- to long-term forecasting and anticipation of risks.

Find out more

APM (2010) *Project Risk Analysis and Management (PRAM) Guide*, 2nd edn, Association for Project Management, High Wycombe

Cooper, D F, Bosnich, P M, Grey, S J, Purdy, G, Raymond, G A, Walker, P R and Wood, M J (2014) *Project Risk Management Guidelines: Managing risk with ISO 31000 and IEC 62198*, John Wiley and Sons, Chichester

Grey, S J (2014) What does risk look like in a complex project, and how should we address it? *Connect*, newsletter of the International Centre for Complex Project Management, December [online] https://iccpm.com/content/december-2014

IEC (2013) IEC 62198:2013, *Managing risk in projects: Application guidelines*, Edition 2, International Electrotechnical Commission, Geneva

ISO (2009) ISO 31000:2009, *Risk Management: Principles and guidance*, International Organization for Standardization, Geneva

PMI (2009) *Practice Standard for Project Risk Management*, Project Management Institute, Newtown Square, PA

PMI (2013a) *A Guide to the Project Management Body of Knowledge (PMBOK Guide)* 5th edn, Project Management Institute, Newtown Square, PA

PMI (2013b) *The Standard for Program Management*, 3rd edn, Project Management Institute, Newtown Square, PA

PMI (2013c) *The Standard for Portfolio Management*, 3rd edn, Project Management Institute, Newtown Square, PA

Williams, T (2014) What is complex project management? *Connect*, newsletter of the International Centre for Complex Project Management, September [online] https://iccpm.com/content/september-2014

Political risk management

06

ROBERT MCKELLAR

Why does political risk management matter?

Political risk is relevant to international companies not least because politics, as carried out by governments and transnational organizations, sets the rules for business. Companies are bound by laws and regulations wherever they operate.

Political risk also matters because, especially in emerging markets where national consensus and institutionalization can still be fragile, politics can be a very intense arena, and companies exposed to political volatility and intense socio-political stakeholder interests can face very severe risks. The stakes in business are high, but for most managers business is still just a job. For a committed political actor or ideologue, fighting for one's values and rights can entail severe risk, and there is often little consideration for the potential 'collateral damage' on companies or other bystanders.

Finally, although a company might not be an explicit political actor, it might well be seen as such by socio-political interests which perceive a company as taking sides in a rivalry, or as acting irresponsibly towards the societal values where the company operates. In some cases, just being in a particular industry or from a specific part of the world is enough to incur socio-political dislike, or in some cases even wrath.

When a company from a long-standing liberal democracy operates at home or in similar terrain, the political environment is well known. Political institutionalization, broad national consensus on core socio-political values, and a relatively robust rule of law mean that politics is seldom the source of major surprise, severe damage or strategic disruption. Staying in safe terrain might seem like a sound choice given the challenges that many emerging and frontier markets present.

The pressure to go beyond conventional geographic boundaries comes partly from globalization, particularly in terms of communications and logistics, but also of business and liberal market values. Globalization makes new terrain more accessible, even if not necessarily more stable. Another aspect of the compulsion to seek new horizons is that 'emerging' markets, taking off from a low initial economic base but applying recent technologies to 'leap-frog', generally have higher demand growth, lower input costs and stronger long-term market demographics than the home terrain of most international firms. Increasing access to new frontiers, plus their commercial allure, forms a compelling logic in the business mindset: if Firm A does not seek new terrain while others do, then Firm A's competitive position is likely to erode.

Therefore companies are drawn to new frontiers, away from known and stable socio-political terrain, into geographies and jurisdictions where weak governance, instability and conflict can be severe challenges. To summarize, there is actually a strong commercial logic to go where political risk is a more serious issue.

This brings us to the importance of political risk management. If firms need to move into intense and volatile political terrain to remain globally competitive, then political risk management must go from being a peripheral function to a core competency. This is especially so for more adventurous companies which seek early mover advantages in frontier markets.

Political risk management is not a specific business function and perhaps should not be, given the diversity of skills that comprise it, but as emerging and frontier markets become a larger share of the overall business pie, this competency will need to become more explicit and well honed. It is still an emerging management field, but it has come a long way from its academic beginnings to practical and strategic application.

What is political risk management?

Political risk management means helping the firm or business operation to achieve a harmonious fit with its socio-political environment, and to legitimately protect its people, assets, contractual rights and day-to-day business continuity from politically motivated threats.

On the one hand it is about fitting in, learning the culture and rules, complying, showing respect and taking local sensitivities and values into account in how business is done and how the firm presents itself. This minimizes friction with relevant legitimate stakeholders who could present risks if they were frustrated or angry with the company, and in the case of officialdom, corporate diplomacy and knowing whom one is working with can go a long way towards facilitating necessary approvals (in many more traditional societies a personal touch is required, but this in no way implies a need for favours or bribes, which are addressed later).

On the other hand, political risk management is about recognizing that an international company often carries political symbolism (eg Western, capitalist, secular, profit-seeking, American, British, 'colonial'…) that could fit within the target set of terrorists or insurgents, and also represents a 'cash cow' predatory opportunity to be exploited by illegitimate and politically connected criminal interests. The company has a legitimate right to look after itself, not through mercenary armies or paying off officials for protection, but through situational awareness and discrete, legitimate and responsible security and crisis response capabilities. Above all, it is about knowing the risks, and putting intelligence to good use to in preparing to avoid, prevent, deter and mitigate, not to mention simply not going to a location which, if good intelligence so informs us, is beyond the company's risk appetite.

On a strategic and global level, political risk management manifests in global portfolio management, wherein planners seek a risk-reward balance in the spread of international operations and supply chains. Knowing the inherent political risk in a proposed new venture, planners can take an informed decision about whether or not that operation would help the global risk-reward equation, or skew the portfolio towards a high-stakes gamble. Such decisions also depend on a concept of international risk appetite, which is seldom an explicit statement, more often a gut sense of what represents unacceptable challenges (perhaps risk appetite in this context should be explicit, but the trade-off between risk and reward is often a dynamic decision and adjusted with each new potential opportunity).

Who manages political risk, and how, is addressed later in this chapter. Next we turn to a conceptualization of political risk, looking mainly at the instance where it can be most acute: an international company's direct presence in a complex emerging market country (also known as frontiers – a developing country facing challenges from weak governance and socio-political friction, or any country that has been through traumatic or violent change and has yet to fully recover).

What is risk in this context?

Political risk is potential harm or loss through exposure to actors, conditions and trends in the socio-political operating environment. The behaviour of explicitly political actors, such as governments, activist groups, and insurgent or terrorist groups, is often a source of political risk. But so too can be civil society when it coalesces around particular issues and seeks political attention to its cause. And the potential friction or violence which can arise in the interplay of these forces is another key aspect of political risk. The risk is not just to immediate profits. Political risk can affect personnel, reputation, legal standing, business continuity and management control over an investment or business entity, all of which ultimately affect a firm's ability to achieve a particular strategic objective.

Political risk is a broad domain and addressing all aspects at a brief introductory level is not feasible. The focus here will put aside geopolitical risk, the issues that arise from international relations, and will also sidestep regulatory and political-economic issues in developed countries, where politics is relatively straightforward and seldom presents severe risks to companies. Instead, the focus will be on a foreign company's direct presence in an emerging market country. This might seem self-limiting, but by focusing on the most intense arena of political risk it is possible for readers to extrapolate lessons and concepts to other aspects of the phenomenon.

Political risk can affect international companies in a variety of ways, and what follows only provides some significant reference points.

First, an overseas presence might be premised on one set of regulatory rules and a particular fiscal regime, and if the government changes these without much warning (perhaps because the government itself changes), a company can face delays as it readjusts its own compliance, and potentially faces financial underperformance if the new rules carry a heavier financial burden.

Government behaviour can cause losses even aside from adverse regulatory changes. In a context of weaker governance or institutional rules, a government or relevant ministry might favour more politically connected (or corrupt) competitors and expedite their approvals while holding the foreign company back through delays or even extra tax or environmental audits. It might change or bend regulations to extend the control of state company partners, weakening the management control of the foreign partner. This is especially relevant when the operation concerns natural resources or national infrastructure: a government might seek foreign expertise in developing these sensitive national assets, but once the bulk of expertise has been handed over, exerting national control can take precedence over notions of contractual fair play. In more dire cases this can lead to outright expropriation.

Dealing with officialdom in many developing countries also means corruption pressure. To get what should be a routine approval or even access to a public utility, a company might be pressured to pay bribes, often cloaked as expedition fees or indeed as personal favours. Foreign companies are often approached by agents who suggest that additional fees can solve a problem, and in most cases they are intermediaries of corrupt officials. Not paying can cause serious delays. For example, an international food retailer nearly closed its recent Nigeria operations because corruption seemed to hold up nearly every approval and even access to basic public services. Paying bribes, however, carries serious liabilities, as indicated by 80 prison sentences handed out to international managers across OECD countries in 2014, mostly for cases which occurred in emerging market countries.

Bureaucratic weakness is another common issue for foreign companies. Red tape, redundant or shifting application processes, and a lack of bureaucratic capacity or professionalism can lead to bottlenecks and approval delays. A European company working in Algeria in 2013 desperately needed an environmental approval and also more work permits for relevant foreign experts, yet months of reapplications and bureaucratic meetings went by before they could start the project, leaving a large team and assets unutilized (this also increased the risk of perceived contractual underperformance in the eyes of the contracting ministry).

With respect to civil society, a company might inadvertently insult a host community, or threaten long-standing socio-economic interests with its presence and operation. This can incur severe distrust, which can manifest as organized opposition, catching the attention of regulators, and drawing in activist groups and sympathetic media to turn the issue into a reputational challenge. At worst, distrust can lead to protests, and if these are met with a heavy-handed police response, then the company's image can be badly damaged. An oil company working in east Africa faced several occasions in which local operations were blocked by host communities, who felt that the relevant tribal elders had not been consulted, and in some cases over land access rights (a challenging question in traditional societies because much land ownership is customary and unrecorded). Similarly, international retailers in developing countries often come up against resistance organized by coalitions of street vendors, who see their livelihoods as threatened by the nearby presence of a modern supermarket.

Similar issues can arise when dealing with unions. Unions are often desperate to get their members into lucrative employment with a foreign firm, but can be sensitive to perceived slights or even highly opportunistic in their approach to the relationship. A mining company with a huge operation in Mauritania had smooth union relations for years, but in 2012 a dispute over bonus pay and prayer time during Ramadan started a spiral of distrust. The company has faced several strikes and violent protests which have seriously hurt performance. One such protest met with police violence, and the company's reputation in the country and indeed with its own investors has yet to recover.

A foreign company in a developing country can also be exposed to political violence. This might be targeted at the company, for example by politically connected criminal groups seeking a new racketeering opportunity or potentially extortion through a kidnap, or terrorist groups who see the firm as an ideological target. Or it could take the form of inadvertent exposure to riots, violent protests, terrorist attacks or skirmishes in a civil war. Political violence is most obviously a danger to people, but it can cause property damage, and severe delays as the company faces disruptions to public services and travel as the state imposes a security crackdown.

While terrorist attacks make the headlines, perhaps the most insidious form of political violence is kidnapping, which is severely demoralizing and also poses a number of moral dilemmas with which most companies have no experience. This brings into question the links between politics and criminality, and in many developing countries there is some overlap between these domains. Political insurgent groups often apply criminal extortion to obtain funding, while organized criminal groups often maintain useful political connections via family or clan overlap, bribery or blackmail of security officials, or indeed by way of a direct 'sub-contracting' relationship as outsourced 'deniable' political party enforcers. When there is such overlap, dealing with extortion and kidnap can be especially challenging and reliance on local law enforcement is not an option.

The most spectacular and tragic manifestations of political risk, such as the attack on the In Amenas gas plant in Algeria in 2013, or going back to an old classic, the Iranian Revolution, which took many big investors by surprise, are relatively rare. In most cases in complex environments, political risk manifests incrementally on a number of fronts, and is more like slow entanglement as opposed to a dramatic 'blow out'. But the end result can be just as bad. BP's experience in Russia is a good example: the company was hit by a variety of commercial disputes which drew in predatory political interests and by most standards politically-connected criminal interests, resulting in official harassment and even threats. AES in Georgia was a particularly hard lesson in entanglement. This upbeat US firm took on the modernization and operation of the power grid, and in the process met full face with an intersection of traditional/clan, mafia, and corrupt political interests for whom paying standard rates for electricity was anathema. AES sold at a significant loss of five years of heartache and severe personnel risk (and to add to AES' frustrations, there is evidence that the Russian firm they sold to was partly involved in orchestrating AES' hassles).

Such cases, while not always this dramatic, are in fact common, and even if a company makes its planned profit, the ride is often far from smooth. External or inherent risk in the environment, for example an insurgency or endemic corruption, cause distractions, and the company is more inclined to make mistakes. Mistakes lead to vulnerability and distrust. Threats or pressures go from general, to specific to the company. Meanwhile the firm is likely also dealing with a convoluted bureaucracy, and this is further distraction. There might not be one big risk, but the combination of issues in the environment and direct pressures can wear down managers, and after such an experience some people simply say 'no thank you' when offered another overseas position. This makes it harder to recruit experienced people for new frontier opportunities.

Political risk is relevant in any country and at the global level, but certainly its most acute forms manifest when a company is directly exposed to a volatile socio-political environment in a complex emerging, or 'frontier' market, which often presents a strong business opportunity for more adventurous companies or those seeking a boost after facing market saturation and competitive pressures in their home terrain.

Despite these issues, the fact that many international businesses have successfully played in challenging markets for decades indicates that this is a manageable phenomenon.

How is political risk managed?

As political risk management is an emerging field, or perhaps it is better to say an un-codified field, there are in fact few formal standards and guidelines for handling it. ISO 31000 is rather generic in this context but still applicable. ISO 26000 is a lesser-known standard (International Organization for Standardization, 2010), and is aimed at guiding companies on social responsibility, a critical component of positive stakeholder engagement. In fact when it comes to political risk management planning, the best practice players, though they might not call it political risk management, apply a combination of general standards and good practice from intelligence, security, and stakeholder engagement/sustainable development. Companies have even learned from international non-governmental organizations (NGOs), who routinely work in very challenging circumstances and who rely heavily on local stakeholder acceptance and relationships to secure themselves and to seek positive change.

A company looking for guidance in self-comportment and risk management in complex emerging markets will find a range of voluntary standards, most pertaining to social responsibility, which in the political risk context translates to stakeholder engagement and the minimization of socio-political friction which could lead to risk. The UN Global Compact and UN Principles on Responsible Investment (PRI) are two codes that companies can officially align with in order to help ensure that their business practices are developmentally aligned, although many firms prefer to use them as guides and develop their own aligned principles.

Extractives companies can sign up to the Extractive Industries Transparency Initiative (EITI), aimed at ensuring that extractive operations lead to development benefits and not just a profit split between the company and a corrupt or militaristic state. Governments can also sign up, and this increases their chances of transnational assistance to develop their extractives sectors, and minimizes a company's risk by way of potential association with an abusive regime (if a company is regarded as helping to fund despotism, it is likely to encounter severe ethical criticism which ultimately affects its markets' and shareholders' perception of the firm).

The Voluntary Principles on Security and Human Rights (VPSHR) is another standard that guides companies in the use of security so that host communities do not suffer security abuses at the hands of company security personnel, be they private or seconded by the government. Additionally, for companies working in countries or areas where there is ongoing conflict or intense socio-political rivalry, the domain known as conflict sensitivity has afforded much valuable guidance on how a business can comport itself in high-tension areas to avoid making rivalries worse or indeed being perceived as a conflict actor (as Shell has, for example, in the eyes of insurgent groups in the Niger Delta, or as Talisman did in Sudan in 2000). International Alert and other NGOs have extensive publications on conflict sensitivity and they are very useful guidelines for companies working in the most arduous environments.

The above might imply that good practice in political risk management comes from outside the company or needs to be imported. In fact, companies with experience in more volatile terrain have developed very strong political risk management capabilities. The following key points summarize how different clients and project sponsors might seek to manage political risk in their own areas of concern:

- **Human resources:** How can we best hack through the red tape to enable access for necessary foreign experts? This often means making an argument for their necessity while still presenting a workforce plan that shows how the company will comply with national development imperatives and in particular local content stipulations over time, so how can we balance our need for expats with the state's need for local content?
- **External affairs:** How can we leverage relationships and host community interaction to gain as much socio-political acceptance and legitimacy as possible to avoid friction with legitimate interests? Which media are prone to state manipulation and which are more independent, and if the company wanted to get its own story across, with whom should we develop relationships and whom should we avoid?
- **Country management:** How are we perceived and what are the principal threats (actors) and risks (contingencies), and what does our operation have to be most concerned about in terms of personnel security, reputation, and business continuity? In terms of corporate diplomacy, who matters, and what channels, messaging and protocols are required for a strong but legitimate relationship? What is the bigger plan that could apply and help sustain the operation that we are responsible for?
- **Corporate social responsibility (CSR)/community engagement/ sustainability:** How are we perceived on the ground, how are we affecting people above and beyond what was indicated in the mandatory social-environmental impact assessment, and how should we consult with local communities? If we could offer something tangible that also aligns with our business interests, would it be micro-finance support, education, internships, contributing to scholarships, peace building, local infrastructure…? And who can help us in this? We do not want to approach directly as a commercial company, so are there legitimate local NGOs or transnational agencies with whom we could engage for social investment and CSR?

- **Strategic/business unit management:** Is this country and operation feasible in terms of the socio-political risks which it presents? Is it beyond our risk appetite? If we entered, what risk mitigation plan would we need to run alongside the commercial element to make it as feasible as possible?

- **Security:** Who are the principal threats, and how might their intentions towards us manifest? What do we need to be ready for in deterrence and crisis response? If we rely on state forces for security, what is their human rights record, and how can we best guide them on the VPSHR (or human security adherence generally)? What are the regulations governing private security, and would it feasible to have a well-trained and VPSHR-compliant private security contingent? If not, how do we best influence state-seconded forces for both attention to our needs, but also compliance with human rights standards?

- **Legal/audit/compliance:** How bad is corruption here and what pressures might manifest? Can we apply standard corporate policy, or do we need an augmented or tailored version for this location? If we train staff and managers in OECD-level compliance in this context, how extensive does it have to be and what should we focus on as key issues? What is the local cultural attitude to corruption, as well as local corruption laws, and how can we fit those into an anti-corruption programme?

The above is just a snapshot. Indeed most front-line managers in complex socio-political terrain have a role to play and actually handle political risk management every day, whether it is mitigating the expectations of a politically connected local contractor and constraining the relationship to legitimate commercial rules, or building relationships with national associates who might be able to provide some upfront warning about a change in a delicate political situation.

There was a tendency to create in-house political risk units after the Iranian Revolution in 1978–79, when many multinationals who had big investments in Iran were taken by surprise and left behind substantial assets. The 1980s brought in the fad of process reengineering and the lean company, and non-operational units tended to be cut, including these new political risk units. The hype following the collapse of the USSR seemed to affirm that such units were no longer necessary and that commercial values seemed universal, and political risk as a management domain was shelved. As usual, taking a long-term view, perceived global stability was fragile, and the world seemed to enter a new period of instability, our current apparent 'clash of cultures' as opposed to the communist-liberal capitalist rivalry. Political risk management as risk mitigation and an opportunity enabler has regained ground, and this time might be here to stay.

Extractives companies, long accustomed to working in some of the most volatile operating environments, along with infrastructure and construction, have tended to be on the leading edge of good practice in political risk management. Following the In Amenas attack in 2013, several large oil firms decided it was once more time to set up political risk management teams, and some made sure that the new unit was positioned above departmental politics and made it an attachment to global strategic planning, albeit with a capacity to advise on specific overseas operations.

Whether or not a specific unit or department is required, or a company can just apply policy and guidelines in conjunction with common sense based on experience, is probably a question of corporate culture and the degree of exposure in frontier environments. There is a strong argument for a multi-functional political risk task force in specific sensitive operations in high-risk locations, and it should be steered and overseen at corporate level, but this need not equate to a permanent department. However, going back to the argument about the near inevitability of increasing international business exposure to emerging markets, whichever model the firm chooses, political risk management needs to be a more explicit skill and area of learning. International firms cannot rely on the 'customer, competitor, company' model anymore to sustain their growth. They need to look beyond the commercial domain and understand and optimize their fit with the socio-political environment, and their ability to protect themselves against harmful trends or illegitimate interests within this environment.

The political risk management planning process

Figure 6.1 provides a snapshot of a political risk management planning process applicable to a specific operation or country presence in a complex emerging market. It has been compiled through project experience and is not 'one size fits all', rather indicative of the thought process which companies should take into account when entering potentially volatile terrain.

The process explicitly takes into account the company's aims and exposure, since conditions and stakeholders only present risk in relation to specific assets (and the wider objective of an operation can be regarded as the ultimate asset, sustained by secondary assets directly affected by risk factors). The plans which result from intelligence and analysis should not

FIGURE 6.1 Political risk management planning process

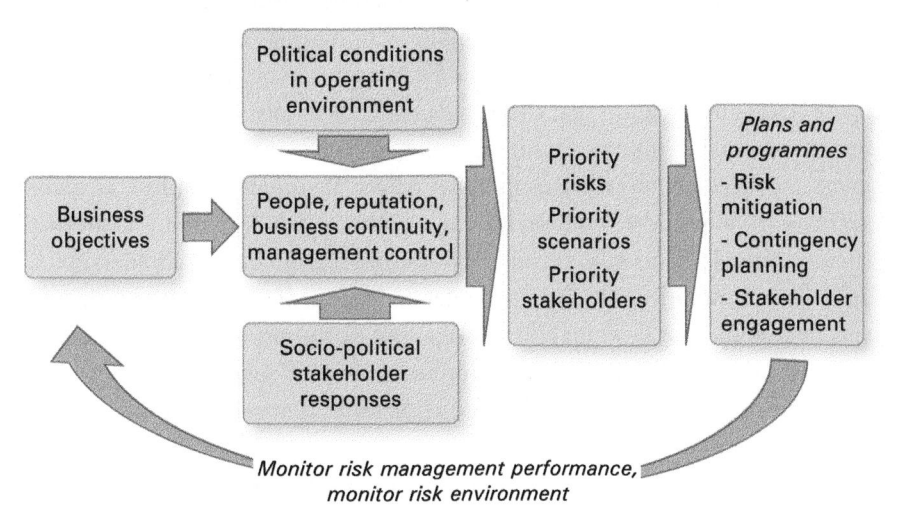

```
                    ┌─────────────────┐
                    │ Political       │
                    │ conditions in   │
                    │ operating       │
                    │ environment     │
                    └────────┬────────┘
                             ▼
┌──────────┐       ┌─────────────────┐      ┌─────────────┐      ┌──────────────┐
│          │       │ People,         │      │ Priority    │      │ Plans and    │
│ Business │  ──▶  │ reputation,     │  ──▶ │ risks       │  ──▶ │ programmes   │
│objectives│       │ business        │      │ Priority    │      │ - Risk       │
│          │       │ continuity,     │      │ scenarios   │      │   mitigation │
│          │       │ management      │      │ Priority    │      │ - Contingency│
│          │       │ control         │      │ stakeholders│      │   planning   │
└──────────┘       └─────────────────┘      └─────────────┘      │ - Stakeholder│
                             ▲                                    │   engagement │
                    ┌─────────────────┐                           └──────────────┘
                    │ Socio-political │
                    │ stakeholder     │
                    │ responses       │
                    └─────────────────┘
              Monitor risk management performance,
                    monitor risk environment
```

be regarded as a series of independent initiatives, rather integrated for coherence and mutual support. Finally, the scenario aspect is important. In more unstable environments, the entire environment could shift depending on some long-term variables such as an election or the outcome of a major political rivalry. The result of the process is a holistic strategy to sustain the operation. Monitoring both the performance of risk management and the risk environment is key to maintaining a close fit between them for optimal long-term endurance.

How does political risk management fit?

Political risk is both operational and strategic, and it can also be a market risk where government and central bank decisions impinge on business-relevant interest rates and currency valuation. It is operational in the context of affecting a specific time-sensitive business operation, even a very localized task such as getting government permission to repair a broken pipeline. It is strategic in that global changes can affect the value and robustness of a global portfolio of overseas operations and supply chains. Political risk does not align well to the 'operational-strategic' scale. It can affect a person's individual safety on any given day, or the risk-reward balance of the entire company. It is best defined as issues arising from the socio-political variable, not pegged to a preconceived niche. In other words, it cuts across different established areas of risk and challenges preconceptions.

There is a relationship between political risk management and the more well-known notion of sustainability. Sustainability as a concept in terms of companies trying to keep a 'green' image with markets and shareholders, is not all 'green wash', or misleading public relations hype. Within the concept is the strong implication that the company needs to ally with its host society and development imperatives, and that a company can indeed help development and become a partner to its host society. If seriously applied, sustainability can help address one half of the political risk equation – achieving socio-political fit and minimizing friction from legitimate stakeholders, such as host communities, NGOs, and independent media. A political risk perspective would put sustainability in one half of the risk management equation, and stakeholder engagement and acceptance alongside the other half: self-protection based on a hard-nosed realization that not everyone is going to like us no matter what we do.

Turning to Enterprise Risk Management (ERM), political risk can certainly be accounted for in ERM planning and there would be a gap if it were not. But unlike many risks that go into ERM registries, political risk is perhaps less about things going wrong than what a company can do to become an accepted and astute socio-economic entity, and manage the very severe threats represented by potential innately hostile and predatory interests. These skills enable business to proceed, rather than just work against potential downsides. Because of the unique distinction from day-to-day business risks, for the foreseeable future political risk is likely to remain the purview of experienced international managers, VPs of international organizations, and specific functional heads with a remit for security and socio-political fit, rather than chief risk officers concerned with the wider corporate picture.

What's next?

Political risk management as an area of expertise and interest among international managers has seen an upsurge in recent years, partly because most international companies have realized that the world is not getting less complicated or safer in spite of globalization. The hope and promise sensed at the end of the Cold War have not been justified. Democratization and institutionalization have increased in pace around the world, but new 'hot spots' keep popping up, and the current threats from sectarian strife and Islamist extremism in the Middle East have ramifications far beyond the region. As the world becomes more interconnected, so too do issues in one region reverberate globally. It is doubtful if, as happened in the 1980s, political risk will end up on the shelf again anytime soon, and indeed it is likely to take its place among core business competencies, at least for internationally ambitious companies.

From its beginnings in political science in the 1960s and '70s, the concept of political risk has undergone some fundamental transformations, and is now only just becoming a real area of management expertise. By necessity and experience political risk is becoming a part of the daily thinking and focus of international managers. As practical lessons from political risk management become more widely shared and codified, it might still engender a political risk management function or even specific professional standards. While a common perspective might be useful, given the diversity of businesses' risk appetites and company cultures, the value of standards is an open question. It could be sufficient that international managers are well aware of the challenge and the options to address it.

Find out more

Bartlett, S and Rogan, D, eds (2015) *The EITI Standard*, Extractive Industries Transparency Initiative Secretariat, Oslo, Norway

Bray, J (2007) *Facing Up to Corruption: A practical business guide*, Control Risks Group Ltd. and Simmons & Simmons LLP, London, UK

Bremmer, I (2010) *The Fat Tail: The power of political knowledge in an uncertain world*, Oxford University Press Inc., New York, USA

Henisz, W J (2014) *Corporate Diplomacy: Building reputation and relationships with external stakeholders*, Greenleaf Publishing Ltd., Sheffield, UK

International Organization for Standardization (2010) *ISO 26000: Social responsibility*, International Organization for Standardization, Geneva, Switzerland

Kobrin, S J (1979) Political risk: a review and reconsideration, *Journal of International Business Studies*, **10** (11), pp. 67–80

McKellar, R (2010) *A Short Guide to Political Risk*, Gower Publishing Ltd., Surrey, UK

Moran, T H, ed. (1998) *Managing International Political Risk*, Blackwell Publishers Ltd., Malden, USA

The Secretariat for the Voluntary Principles for Security and Human Rights (2013) The Voluntary Principles for Security and Human Rights [online] http://www.voluntaryprinciples.org/wp-content/uploads/2013/03/voluntary_principles_english.pdf [accessed 9 September 2015]

UN Global Compact (2015) *Guide to Corporate Sustainability*, UN Global Compact Headquarters, New York, USA

UN Principles for Responsible Investment (2013) *Understanding the Impact of Your Investments*, UN Global Compact Headquarters and UN Environment Programme Finance Initiative, New York, USA

Voluntary Principles on Security and Human Rights (VPSHR) [online] http://www.voluntaryprinciples.org/

Reputational risk

07

ARIF ZAMAN

Why does reputational risk matter?

To understand the importance of reputational risk, we first need to consider the two concepts of reputation and risk, and how they are related. Recent years have seen an increased attention by a range of stakeholders including regulators, investors, customers and employees on both reputation and risk. In tandem with this there has been a fresh focus on reputational risk which clearly relates to both reputation and risk but has a specific set of drivers and dimensions.

Mentions of reputational risk on the Internet, the establishment of Reputation Research Centres following the lead of Henley Business School, conferences, publications and references by opinion leaders, and the interest of large and niche management consultants have all contributed to this rise in interest (see 'Find out more' section for details).

In the last decade there have also been advances in thinking and awareness in key areas that influence and impact reputational risk, such as behavioural finance, governance, trust, social psychology, consumer behaviour, the psychological contract with employees, diversity, and community development in established and emerging markets.

The risk challenges addressed by reputational risk are unique for several reasons. Reputational risk relates to tangible and intangible dimensions in terms of both its origins and effects. Moreover, much of the current material on reputation still tends to concentrate primarily on 'reputation management'. Too often this is completely synonymous with two areas that have negative connotations and are more about value destruction than value creation – 'crisis management' and 'loss prevention'. Reputational upside means that reputation risk can also be seen in terms of opportunities to be seized and value to be created. Innovative companies view risk through the lens of opportunity rather than just internal control and compliance, ie they see risk as both upside and downside, as an opportunity platform as well as a safety net. Implicit in this is moving from a reactive to a more proactive approach. In fact the biggest reputational risk that a company may face is to deny that it has one.

Current approaches to reputation are neither 'strategic' nor 'integrated'. Often there is a superficial and weak understanding of either reputation or risk (and often both). There are two reasons for this, one obvious, the other less so: the use of both terms by so many people across functions and disciplines, and the way in which the meaning of language changes over time.

The consequences of 9/11, the disruption to conventional weather patterns from climate change across all continents (highlighting the political/safety aspects of risk) and a wave of high-profile scandals including in finance, sport, amongst car manufacturers and oil companies and – in the UK at least but also beyond – by politicians, charities, media and the police have all served to highlight the fragility of reputation when trust is lost and show how events can give lead to new twists on familiar words. Since 2014 in particular a long list of well-known companies have seen their reputations tarnished by unexpected incidents – product recalls, data breaches, offensive language on apparel and in customer communication, fraud investigations, money laundering charges, inappropriate remarks or behaviour by company executives and supply chain disruptions. Major headlines about massive data breaches, large-scale product recalls, mysterious plane crashes, and aggressive government investigations have raised concerns about corporate reputation and brand damage. In the "Panama Papers", the biggest leak in history, 370 journalists from 70 different countries worked in an unprecedented scale of cooperation of investigative journalism in conditions of tight secrecy for six months, highlighting the new norm of collaboration amongst usually fiercely competitive organizations in the pursuit of greater transparency and accountability.

Reputational risk is also too often used in far too narrow a context to refer to corporate social responsibility, and while community perceptions of corporate impact are important, reputational risk needs to be understood as an outcome of relationships with key stakeholders including customers, investors and employees. Reputation risk is diminished when corporate culture and strategy are closely aligned, but it is heightened when they are divergent (Dowling, 2006).

The decline of loyalty in organizations may be the irreversible consequence of globalization, the growth of market-based economies, and the dynamics of creative destruction and innovation. However, what happens when trust is lost and reputational risk is crystallized? For reputational risk, trust is the degree of confidence you have that another party can be relied on to fulfil commitments, be fair, be transparent, and not take advantage of your vulnerability (Hurley, 2011).

The unique challenge of reputational risk is also evident in the development of what has been termed as 'place branding' in applying to cities. This was well illustrated by Delhi's disastrous Commonwealth Games in 2010 (Comptroller and Auditor General of India, 2011) which probably put back its aspirations to host the Olympics by at least a couple of decades. This is in contrast to Glasgow in 2014 (Glasgow Commonwealth Games Post-Games Report, 2014), watched by 1.5 billion people worldwide, which reinvigorated the Commonwealth and not just the brands of the Commonwealth Games or of Glasgow.

All of this is made more challenging given the increasing recognition that context matters. For children that remember seeing two aircraft deliberately piloted into the World Trade Centre, or whose lives growing up were influenced by the heightened security awareness post 7/7 in London 2005, the Mumbai Taj Hotel attacks in 2007 or the Westgate Shopping Centre attacks in 2013 in Nairobi, their lived reality is different from all previous generations for which current data sets are simply significantly inadequate. To this can be added the loss of trust in so many leading corporate brands and institutions since the Global Financial Crisis of 2007–08 and the accelerating impact of technology, which was well put by PM Modi of India when he visited the HQ of Facebook in 2015 when he said 'We used to have elections every five years and now we can have them every five minutes' (Yahoo, 2015).

The consequence of this is too early to tell in definitive terms. However, two recent research reports provide some early indicators. A 2014 report from RBC in an ethnically diverse Canada highlights a dramatic shift in attitudes, behaviours and beliefs as teens age. Youth aged 18 to 21 are less happy, less optimistic, less excited about their future, and less likely to say their life has meaning and that they can achieve anything they want. The frequency of negative feelings increases among the 18 to 21-year-old cohort who are more likely to feel stressed, worried and frustrated (RBC, 2014). A 2015 report from Standard Life Investments suggests that young adults use shared knowledge to become better consumers who demand more from companies and who are making purchasing decisions in a different way. They buy less because of old-style brand values and are more likely to choose products or services from firms that have values or ethics they sympathize with. Seismic political shifts since 2014 in diverse locations including India, Canada, Guyana and Nigeria where young populations, technology and heightened stakeholder expectations all influenced electoral outcomes show what reputational risk amongst concerned citizens can achieve.

All this needs to be set against the backdrop of a changed and changing context for risk management as it applies to reputational risk. Key here is a

2012 *Harvard Business Review* report on how companies are doing in risk management (*Harvard Business Review* Global Survey, 2012). This highlighted that risk management needs to have a clear 'owner' to be effective; risk management and corporate goals must be integrated; companies must manage risk proactively; companies must look deeper and wider to determine what their most serious risks will be in the long run; and companies must break down silos and managerial bottlenecks (Tett, 2015). This has helped to focus on areas which I have described as the '3 As' of risk – risk appetite, risk attitude and risk aptitude – as well as the core areas of governance risk which are building blocks of addressing reputational risk in the 21st century (Alam, 2012).

What is reputational risk management?

Reputational risk differs from 'generic' risk management in three key respects:

1 It affects individuals, organizations, business areas, cities and countries.
2 It relates to emotions (feelings), thoughts (attitudes) and actions (behaviours).
3 History, including recent history, matters and can still shape perception.

Reputational risk needs to be understood as arising out of a tension between what affects key stakeholders (the drivers of business relationships) and what matters to key stakeholders (what they want). It is manifested through the relationship of risk with business and value drivers. If stakeholder interests are effectively navigated and managed, this can lead to companies crossing the trust threshold where reputational risk becomes reputational opportunity.

Three things determine the extent to which a company is exposed to reputational risk. The first is whether its reputation exceeds its true character. The second is how much external beliefs and expectations change, which can widen or (less likely) narrow this gap. The third is the quality of internal coordination, which also can affect the gap (Eccles *et al.*, 2007).

Effectively managing reputational risk begins with recognizing that reputation is about perception. A company's overall reputation is a function of its reputation among its various stakeholders (investors, customers, suppliers, employees, regulators, politicians, non-governmental organizations, the communities in which the firm operates) in specific categories (product quality, corporate governance, employee relations, customer service, intellectual capital, financial performance, handling of environmental and social issues). A strong positive reputation among stakeholders across multiple categories will result in a strong positive reputation for the company overall.

When the reputation of a company is more positive than its underlying reality, this gap poses a substantial risk. Eventually, the failure of a firm to live up to its reputation will be revealed, and that reputation will decline until it more closely matches the reality. To bridge reputation-reality gaps, a company must either improve its ability to meet expectations or reduce expectations by promising less. The problem is often that managers may resort to short-term manipulations.

The changing beliefs and expectations of stakeholders are another major determinant of reputational risk. When expectations are shifting and the company's character stays the same, the reputation reality gap widens and risks increase. Sometimes norms evolve over time, as did the now widespread expectation in most developed countries that companies should pollute minimally (if at all). A change in the behaviour or policies of a leading company can cause stakeholders' expectations to shift quite rapidly, which can imperil the reputations of firms that adhere to old standards.

Another major source of reputational risk is poor coordination of the decisions made by different business units and functions. If one group creates expectations that another group fails to meet, the company's reputation can suffer. Poor internal coordination also inhibits a company's ability to identify changing beliefs and expectations. In virtually all well-run organizations, individual functional groups not only have their fingers on the pulses of various stakeholders but are also actively trying to manage their expectations. Such functional groups include the following:

- Investor Relations (with varying degrees of input from the CFO and the CEO) attempts to ascertain and influence the expectations of analysts and investors;
- Marketing surveys customers;
- Advertising buys ads that shape expectations;
- HR surveys employees;
- Corporate Communications monitors the media and conveys the company's messages;
- Corporate Social Responsibility engages with NGOs;
- Corporate Affairs monitors new and pending laws and regulations.

All of these actions are important to understanding and managing reputational risks including their source and interdependence. However, more often than not, these groups do a patchy or poor job of sharing information or coordinating their plans. Coordination is often poor because the CEO has not assigned this responsibility to a specific person.

What is risk in this context?

Too often reputational risk is confused with crisis management. More accurately, reputational risk management enables successful crisis management.

Crisis management is about short-term execution, a lack of clarity as to how the issues will affect the company's reputation, a lack of control over the issue, and is driven by the media. Reputational risk management is about long-term planning, anticipating what will hurt the company's reputation the most, identifying which reputation attributes should be addressed to mitigate the issue, and the ability to manage the issue.

It is more helpful to see reputational risk as an overlap with reputation management but with its distinct aspects being more about start-of-the-pipe than end-of-the-pipe solutions, as shown in Figure 7.1.

FIGURE 7.1 Reputational risk and reputation management

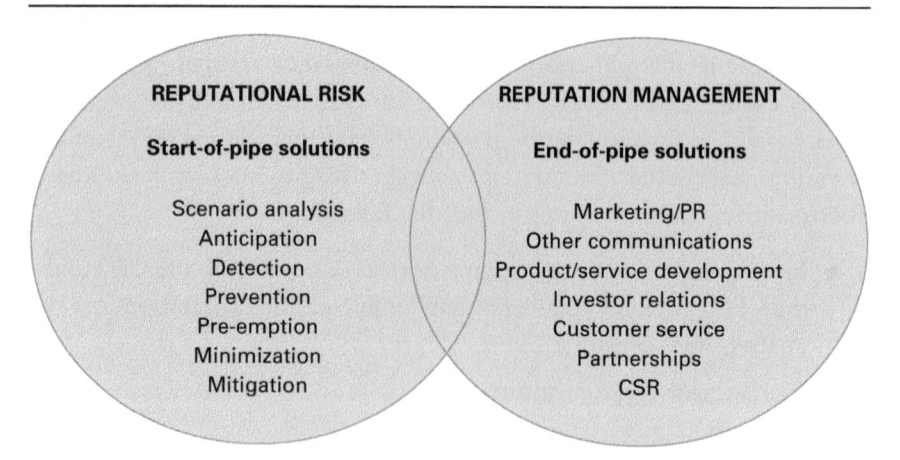

REPUTATIONAL RISK

Start-of-pipe solutions

Scenario analysis
Anticipation
Detection
Prevention
Pre-emption
Minimization
Mitigation

REPUTATION MANAGEMENT

End-of-pipe solutions

Marketing/PR
Other communications
Product/service development
Investor relations
Customer service
Partnerships
CSR

On one level, reputational risk equates to the risk of reputational failure. A reputation risk which crystallizes is a (negative) event that will impact stakeholders' perception of the company. The objective of developing a reputational risk strategy is to provide an organization with the capability to prevent the risks from crystallizing.

Reputational Risk

Reputational risk is most relevant, in a commercial context, when it potentially impairs current or prospective earnings arising from the non-delivery of the 'promise'. Even where there is no direct financial impact (eg in a public sector or not-for-profit organization), the crystallization of reputational risk increases the transaction costs of doing business, because of the time, energy and cost involved in restoring trust and confidence among stakeholders.

It can be defined as the comparison that key stakeholders make between how a company or its employees are expected to behave and how they actually behave. The key point here is that it can be positive as well as negative, and that practical measures and action strategies aim at performance management as well as perception management. Its sources lie in trust and key stakeholder relationships. Reputational risk needs to be understood above all else in relation to an organization's key stakeholders (customers/consumers, employees and shareholders).

Customers/consumers

If companies focus excessively on satisfaction, they run the risk of not understanding why customers feel drawn to return or the emotional meaning of the service experience to them. Moreover, if customer service staff rely on customers to report when they have experienced negative emotional reactions, service providers run the risk of missing subtle emotional communications that may not be expressed verbally.

There are a number of common misconceptions about customers as stakeholders:

- 'Customer satisfaction influences business performance' – this only tells part of the story. Market-perceived relative quality is correlated with profitability. The term 'market' encompasses more than just customers; it includes all potential sources of revenue – customers, competitors' customers and nonusers. 'Perceived' means quality as defined and judged by the customer, not by marketing planners or consultants. 'Relative' means quality as compared to the competition, a key differential in the firm's ability to attract and keep customers. 'Quality' in this context means exceeding customer expectations.

- 'Customer satisfaction means doing whatever it takes to keep customers happy regardless of the cost' – the ability to establish, maintain and build customer relationships depends on the perceived value of the offering. Moreover, customer budgets that are overshot in the first quarter do not provide the means to deliver customer value in the final quarter.

- 'Customer satisfaction leads to customer loyalty' – customer loyalty is best understood as a pattern of behaviour. It is the likelihood of staying with the main (ie most often used) service provider rather than switching to a realistic alternative.
- The primary drivers of loyalty in commoditized sectors are often expressed in comments like, 'I tend to use the same shop/bank/airline/computer manufacturer without really thinking about it' or, 'I can't be bothered spending time choosing between what different companies offer'. This does not build reputation. Drivers like 'I tend to stick with products/services I know and trust' minimizes the reputational risk and builds reputation.
- Secondary drivers may relate to convenience and choice where customers find it difficult to know the differences between what companies offer.

Consumers are also becoming more aware and active on a wide range of environmental, social and ethical issues. Concerns about the ethical working practices of businesses are having a significant effect on purchasing decisions around the world and the company's ethical approach must be in step with those of its valued customers. This is no substitute for a company being clear what it stands for and reputational risks can grow when gaps develop unchecked between how a company behaves in the minds of its customers and how it is expected to behave.

Employees

There is a close link between internal and external reputation. This reflects the relationship between organizational and corporate identity that has been referred to earlier. Employees' images of the reputation of the company represents an intangible asset for the company which needs to be nurtured if performance is to be maximized. This is the 'employer brand equity' in the minds of its employees, just as the awareness of, attitudes and behaviours towards a product brand such as Shell is the brand equity of Shell.

Employees' perceptions of the organization build up over a sustained period. Even so, business history's value as a tool for management development is often overlooked. It can be an extremely useful resource in a world where the labour market is becoming more flexible and many companies turn over their entire workforce in a regular cycle.

Moreover, corporate history can help us to learn from past successes and failures and avoid re-inventing the wheel. Organizational memory and corporate amnesia matter to companies and affect employee perceptions and behaviour.

Internal reputational risks increase when a focus on talent leads to a mindset which devises policies around individuals at the expense of teams and organizational systems. The 'war for talent' is to some extent a distraction from companies' real task of devising cultures and management styles that fully maximize human and intellectual capital, not just the skills and knowledge of an elite cadre.

Shareholders

Reputational risk in financial markets is driven in large part by market sentiment. There is, however, seldom any analysis of what market sentiment is, even less how it operates. Essentially market sentiment is a way of describing the central mood that drives individual share prices, sectors and the equity market as a whole. It is an emotional reaction to a piece of corporate or other stock market-related news. It can affect individual companies and sectors (for example, airlines after 9/11) and can continue for weeks or even months. Sentiment is a residual – the element in a share price that cannot be explained by reference to the fundamentals.

The best way to view market sentiment is as a pair of spectacles that enable the market to view any announcement as always bad news or always good news. Thus a company with a positive backing, a good feeling to it, a positive response, and a positive branding image within the City, can come out with the same news item as a company with a weak corporate branding. Handling it well against handling it badly can see a share price increase 10 per cent instead of falling 30 per cent. What this means is the market either views one item of news as the glass being half full or as being half empty. An example would be current market conditions where, due to economic and geopolitical uncertainty, the market views everything as a glass half empty because it has bad news about the economy and the whole of the market. This can increase reputational risk for a particular company or sector.

This is made worse where there is the slightest doubt about a company's credibility, honesty, or the opacity of its accounts (such as with Tesco and Shell in recent years), and where even minor items hidden away can trigger more negative feeling towards a company or sector. This may relate to subsidiaries, franchises, finance leases – anything that will affect the company's reputation when people look at that side. If confidence is shaken, rumours will go round the City rapidly and people will not take the risk of buying after a profits warning, even if the stock is cheap. The value of the company will then sink further and further and eventually may even disappear or be taken over. Thus market sentiment is important to manage to give each company a cushion against the fact that there will be unexpected bad news somewhere along the line.

A positive sentiment can often be viewed if the sector or company is perceived as well run – when analysts do not have doubts about it or questions about the honesty of the management. The attitude in the City is: 'So what if they've had a profits warning, I'll buy after the profits warning' and so it is the life jacket that enables the company to come up again and survive. This can increase reputational opportunity.

If everyone in the market knows the consensus estimate – the one the companies have helped develop and fully expect to beat, if only marginally – they also know that the quarterly earnings report will offer little or no valuable information unless it is negative. The focus then turns to estimating how much the company's estimate will exceed the consensus estimate. This process is accelerated by the Internet, which has led to a proliferation of gossip and news easily available to everybody. The impacts of reputational risk can be financial, political, economic or social. The best responses are to anchor these in corporate governance, not marketing/PR.

How is reputational risk managed?

There are three key areas where reputational risk can be managed.

First, it is important to make reputational risk management a top organizational priority. This involves chair and board buy-in as well as CEO and top executive support. It includes a dedicated resource – both personnel and financial – and the establishment and development of a cross-functional reputational risk team.

Second, there is a need to develop a structured system for reputational risk evaluation/reporting. An easy-to-use reporting tool should be developed (providing description, prioritization, evaluation) and this should be incorporated into existing planning and response work. Aggregate output should be used to focus risk planning/management meetings.

Third, and crucially, key reputational risks must be proactively managed. This requires understanding the changing global, regional and national context and mapping key risks, focusing on arrows and boxes or linkages and effects. Action plans should be developed around key risks and there must be top management sign-off on key risk and action plans. The risk register – which seldom mentions reputational risk explicitly – should be strengthened and reviewed and there should be a focus on net rather than gross risk. The company must actively work both in terms of its corporate reality and reputation to mitigate risks. As corporate reporting requirements increase on drivers and dynamics of reputational risk, it is also necessary to perfect the disclosure strategy.

Eccles *et al.* (2007) recommend a five-step process:

1 Assess your company's reputation among key stakeholders (such as investors and customers) in specific categories (such as financial performance and product quality).

2 Evaluate the firm's actual performance on those categories.

3 Close gaps by enhancing performance in weak categories or managing expectations by promising less.

4 Monitor changes in stakeholder expectations (for instance ask if some previously acceptable business practices have fallen out of favour with specific stakeholders).

5 Put one person in charge of managing reputational risk.

How does reputational risk management fit?

Boards should ensure that they have structures to provide them with reliable information about reputation and risks to it. Traditional 'bottom-up' risk management approaches often fail to expose important risks to reputation. Poorly designed structures can have major blind spots.

A reputational risk map is a useful, sometimes critically important, tool. However, reputational risk should not be considered in isolation but as part of enterprise-wide risk management.

Investors see reputation as an important component of value. Boards should consider reporting more explicitly on reputational matters. This requires them to answer a number of questions in deciding their approach to managing risks to their company's reputation, including:

1 How efficiently does the commonly-used specific risk-centric approach to risk analysis capture and give suitable prominence to reputational risks? Would another approach, for example centred on reputational risk, be a useful complementary tool in identifying reputational risks more comprehensively?

2 With particular reference to reputational risks but not ignoring other risks, what are the advantages and disadvantages of current hierarchical structures used within companies to identify, analyse and report on risks? Do they have potential consequences not intended by boards? And might other arrangements be better?

3 At board level, what is the appropriate level of non-executive directors' (NEDs) oversight of and involvement in dealing with reputational risks, and how might this best be structured? In particular when might a risk committee be appropriate and how might the relationships between executives, NEDs, risk managers and internal auditors best be structured?

What's next?

The pattern and profile of reputational risk will continue to grow in the short to medium term. The persistence and proliferation of examples where trust has been stretched to breaking point due to corporate misbehaviour in a range of sectors and contexts is leading to a sharper focus on reputational risk in corporate governance where it is now anchored. This is manifested in board composition, more detail on structures and stress testing, as well as on risk communication and reporting.

Emerging markets provide an area where the nature and dynamics of reputational risk will require better understanding, and local knowledge will be crucial. In this respect the presence of local staff at senior levels is one way in which reputational risk is now being mitigated, especially as changes in emerging and frontier markets can take place at a much faster and more uncertain pace.

The increasing interest by policy makers as well as businesses both new and established in alternative financing including microfinance (CSFI, 2014), crowdfunding (Miller, 2014) and Islamic Finance (Mirakhor and Askari, 2008) will provide a spotlight to reputational risk in these largely undocumented areas. To this can be added technology and cyber risk.

Find out more

Alam, K (2012) Risk index launched to track uncertainty in economy, *Express Tribune* [online] https://kazimalam.wordpress.com/2012/10/09/risk-index-launched-to-track-uncertainty-in-economy/

BSI (2014) Glasgow 2014 achieves new sustainability benchmark for Commonwealth Games, *BSI* [online] http://www.bsigroup.com/en-GB/about-bsi/media-centre/press-releases/2014/June-2014/Glasgow-2014-achieves-new-Sustainability-benchmark-for-Commonwealth-Games/#.Vi1FaNLnsY3

Comptroller and Auditor General of India (2011) Performance audit report of the XIX Commonwealth Games [online] http://www.cag.gov.in/content/report-no-6-2011-%E2%80%93-performance-audit-xixth-commonwealth-games

CSFI (2014) Microfinance banana skins 2014, CSFI survey of microfinance risk [online] http://www.citigroup.com/citi/inclusivefinance/data/2014_microfinance_banana_skins.pdf

Dowling, G (2006) Reputation risk: it is the board's ultimate responsibility, *Journal of Business Strategy* **27** (2) pp 59–68

Eccles, R G, Newquist, S C and Schatz, R (2007) Reputation and its risks, *Harvard Business Review*, February

Glasgow 2014 XX Commonwealth Games Post-Games Report [online] https://www.thecgf.com/games/2014/G2014-Official-Post-Games-Report.pdf

Harvard Business Review (2012) Risk Management: how are companies doing? *Harvard Business Review* Global Survey, April

Hiles, A, ed. (2011) *Reputation Management: Building and Protecting Your Company's Profile in a Digital World*, Bloomsbury, London

Hurley, R F (2011) *The Decision to Trust: How leaders create high-trust organizations*, Wiley, Chichester

Jackson, P, ed. (2014) *Risk Culture and Effective Risk Governance*, Risk Books, London

Kaiser, T and Merl, P (2014) *Reputational Risk Management in Financial Institutions*, Risk Books, London

Miller, Z (2014) Five common misconceptions about crowdfunding [online] http://crowdfunding.about.com/od/How-to-crowdfund/fl/5-Common-Misconceptions-about-Crowdfunding.htm

Mirakhor, A and Askari, H (2008) *New Issues in Islamic Finance and Economics: Progress and challenges*, Wiley

RBC Youth Optimism Study (2014) [online] http://www.rbc.com/community-sustainability/community/kids/optimism-survey.html

Tett, G (2015) *The Silo Effect*, Little, Brown, London

Yahoo (2015) Modi touts social media, tech development in Facebook visit [online] http://finance.yahoo.com/news/modi-touts-social-media-tech-181850141.html

Zaman, A (2003) *Made in Japan: Converging Trends in Corporate Responsibility and Corporate Governance*, Chatham House

Zaman, A (2003 and in Russian, 2008) Reputational Risk – How to Manage for Value Creation, *Financial Times*, Pearson Education

Supply chain risk management

08

LINDA CONRAD

Why does supply chain risk management matter?

The supply chain is only as strong as its weakest link

The pace of innovation and growth in business is incredible, and the slightest disruption can open the door for competitors to capture your customers, recruit your staff, and overtake your market position. Increasingly, companies are using outsourcing not only as a means of reducing costs, but also to get access to specialized knowledge and skills or to increase their production flexibility. As a consequence, the dependence on suppliers increases, as does the risk of a revenue shortfall when a supply chain breaks down. A company's operations can grind to a halt without warning due to supply chain problems arising from natural disasters, IT outages, labour disputes, regulatory issues, political unrest, transportation problems and other reasons.

Recent years have brought us natural disasters and catastrophes of unprecedented magnitude, including the earthquake and tsunami in Japan, flooding in Thailand, Hurricane Irene and Mississippi River flooding, then Superstorm Sandy in the United States. All of these physical events also caused significant supply chain disruptions which impacted local, regional and global economies, and caused significant damage to both corporate profitability and reputations. Yet, it is not only these natural catastrophes but also other accidental or man-made mishaps that can lead to value chain disruptions and financial impact. The risk landscape facing most organizations is constantly changing and becoming more challenging, so many have embraced supply chain risk management as a critical strategic discipline to strengthen their value chain and optimize enterprise efficiency.

How can organizations better manage their business risks? How can they assess their strategy and competitive dynamics, and determine where they may be asleep? Recent events suggest that organizations have become exponentially more complex and interrelated, causing significant impact to profitability and shareholder value. The strategy of a business can no longer fail to take into account critical enterprise issues such as supply chain and business resiliency. Often, this vital link between strategy and supply chain is sadly proven through the significant impact when there is a disruption.

Supply chain disruptions increasingly impact financial performance

Extensive research by Sheffi and Rice (2005) looked at thousands of company results, whereby comments in SEC reports were tied back to the stock performance of these companies. As seen in Figure 8.1, the study shows that supply chain disruptions can cause between 10 and 30 per cent reduction in share price and an impact which commonly lasts over two years. Companies can be simultaneously impacted by decreased sales and brand damage, while incurring significant extra expenses during recovery times following a business interruption. Historically, supply chain disruptions can lead to an average of 9 per cent lower sales and 11 per cent higher costs. That's a double hit. So at a time when fewer funds are coming in, the company is simultaneously faced with shelling out the cash to cover the extra expenses to try to get back up and running: higher cost of product in the open market, forced to airfreight product instead of shipping, perhaps retooling a factory or even re-engineering their product to accommodate what spare parts they can get. These factors of decreased sales and increased costs of recovery help explain why the Business Continuity Institute estimates that approximately 40 per cent of companies with extended interruptions never recover.

These alarming impacts should be of great concern to a firm's directors and officers, who are directly responsible for both results and for setting the necessary 'tone at the top' around actively addressing risks to strategy and execution. It is often said that CEOs should be heard talking about risk management as much as markets and customers, because both can have a major effect on performance. Avoiding hits to enterprise value is their responsibility,

Multidimensional Risk Management

and they may well be held accountable by shareholders, who could voice their displeasure through stock price drops and even lawsuits. Supply chain risk falls clearly here.

FIGURE 8.1 Supply chain disruptions impact financial performance

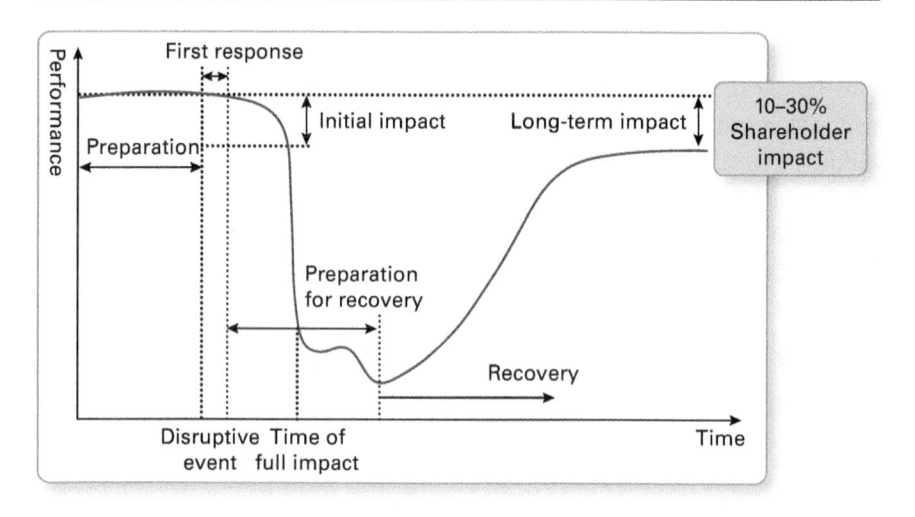

SOURCE: Sheffi and Rice (2005)

Turning risk into a competitive advantage requires risk accountability, so you do not inadvertently expose your organization to the 'blindside' of risk, potentially costing you money and preventing you from taking advantage of growth opportunities that build shareholder value. It is interesting to note that the majority of major firms list supply chain as one of their exposures in their annual reports. If this exposure is shown, might it stand to reason that it could also make sense to pursue solutions and demonstrate the steps such as risk assessments and supply chain insurance which are in place to protect the bottom line?

Benefits of risk management in supply chain, business continuity and value mapping

Supply chain risk assessments can help in the understanding of:
- critical areas of the supply chain;
- quality of supply chain risk management;
- financial impact of an interruption, including extra expenses of recovery;

- potential improvements to your risk management processes and performance;
- clearer view of risk transfer insurance and risk mitigation if the supply chain fails.

Business Continuity Management offers a structured approach which:

- enables comprehensive buy-in and efficient analysis;
- ensures that continuity planning is fit for purpose;
- makes it easier to achieve compliance with existing and future regulations and standards;
- provides an opportunity to demonstrate competence and resilience to key stakeholders;
- enables efficient planning and resource allocation;
- ensures that the right level of effort goes into safeguarding the business, ie business continuity planning;
- helps minimize uncertainty or doubt with regard to risk transfer evaluation.

Value flow mapping and modelling can help to:

- build a comprehensive framework to study effects of disruptions, and evaluate interdependencies and bottlenecks to help avoid business interruptions;
- ensure a repeatable and consistent approach;
- allow communication of risk issues in a more consistent and informed way;
- create a basis for more informed strategic decision making;
- allow more efficient resource and capital allocation;
- support better informed risk mitigation and transfer decisions.

Really knowing your business model can also increase your understanding of actual supply chain losses. One company found that supply chain losses in one country meant theft, in another country they meant natural disasters, in another it was raw material shortages, and in yet another the losses were related to infrastructure problems. An organization must be careful about simply trying to transfer one country's suppliers or solutions to other countries with a different culture and unique challenges. It's important to understand the real risks across the entire supply chain.

What is supply chain risk management?

The Supply Chain Risk Leadership Council defines supply chain risk as 'the likelihood and consequence of events at any point in the end-to-end supply chain, from sources of raw materials to end use of customers'. They propose that supply chain risk management is the coordination of activities to direct and control an enterprise's end-to-end supply chain with regard to supply chain risks, including but not limited to risk transfer of exposures which can be insured.

Supply chain risk management can often overlap with other organizational efforts, including those for business continuity and supply chain security. Supply chain security management systems seek to resist 'intentional, unauthorized act(s) designed to cause harm or damage to, or by, the supply chain' (ISO 28000:2007). Supply chain risk management goes beyond this by seeking not only to address such acts but also to promote business continuity and to mitigate any disruptions, that is, events that interrupt normal business, activities, operations, or processes (ASIS International, 2007; ASIS International and BSI, 2010). Such events may not only be intentional acts such as sabotage, but also unintentional acts such as a transportation disruption or production problem. They may be both events which may be anticipated, such as growing political unrest, or unanticipated, such as an earthquake or cyber issue.

Supply chain risk management should ideally be integrated into a broader Enterprise Risk Management (ERM) process, such as the frameworks outlined by ISO 31000:2009 or COSO. The Risk and Insurance Management Society states that ERM is a strategic business discipline that supports the achievement of an organization's objectives by addressing the full spectrum of its risks and managing the combined impact of those risks as an interrelated risk portfolio. Clearly, supply chain risk is an exposure which should be approached from an enterprise perspective, as the cost of disruptions can significantly impact the success of the organization.

Strategic risk: another link in the supply chain

A company's supply chain is the life blood running through its veins and must be seen through a wider, more strategic lens. The aim in supply chains is to lower total costs of ownership. But many companies have not properly considered the risks associated with that approach, and have failed to realize that any action taken to drive cost out can inadvertently drive risk into the business. For example, many organizations fail to identify the increased exposure associated with procurement moving to using a single source or a change in sources, often without the knowledge of the risk manager who is tasked with optimizing enterprise exposures.

Think about a company that wants to build its product in a different country. This is a potentially good move from a profitability perspective, but what risks are involved with that decision and how does it impact the overall strategy and vision for the future? Without an integrated process supported by top management, companies can fail to anticipate and connect risks on a regular basis. One NYSE-listed manufacturing company had excessive inventory concentration with a primary customer. The company chose to hedge against the likely default of that party, so they managed the financial risk. This is a good approach, but also a siloed approach. In a heated board meeting, the CEO was challenged by a board member to think beyond inventory and consider how the company would survive a loss of that supplier or customer and relationship. What would they do with the employees and the factory? Where would they sell their product? It was not a pleasant conversation. The conclusion is that risks, including supply chain risks, must be seen from an integrated perspective.

Consider other recent headlines and the next risk lesson comes into focus – supply chain problems are frequently strategic problems. The headlines and stories surrounding an airline's battery issues stated that the problems 'couldn't be higher'. Although one executive stated there was no risk to passengers, another executive correctly saw the issue as strategic when he argued that the issue was safety and confidence in the product, and that it could not occur again. For boards, executives, and risk professionals, what cannot happen again is failing to understand how the supply chain and its associated risks relate to the business model and strategy of the company. To really create, protect, and enhance shareholder value, this understanding needs to take place up front – not after a mistake occurs.

Lessons learned

One lesson to keep in mind is that sometimes the risks related to supply chain may be difficult to see at first glance. Consider the classic case of a college professor finding a flaw in maths done by a supplier of a well-known brand of computer chip. The producer's management saw the risk as minimal and not affecting normal calculations. The public saw it differently, eventually leading a major computer manufacturer (not the supplier itself) to make a recall, probably souring relations between the two businesses. The cost of this mistake was way more than the product of price times quantity, and the chip manufacturer's stock price drop reflected it. There was vendor relationship risk as well as supplier capacity risks, since the just-in-time chip manufacturer was running at near full capacity. Again, the risk was not just about a break in the production supply chain, but about how the supply chain related to reputation risk.

Consider the case of the public company that manufactures and sells its own product along the east coast of the United States. The supply chain was easy enough to manage with trucks running up and down the interstate highway. Even customer returns and warehouses were not that complicated. However, when the company chooses to manufacture in Asia what new risks exist? Perhaps more importantly, when should that company identify those risks? Years later or beforehand? This is not just an operational change – it's also a supply chain risk linked to strategy. How will this supply chain change impact the company's brand vision and financial goals? While it may not be possible to identify every new risk up front, that is the goal of a risk-intelligent organization. That is also one key way that value is added. This new supply chain resulted in slower turnaround time for new business designs and a slower response time to new consumer desires and changing consumer preferences. It also failed to factor in how consumers might view their product if not made locally, as it had always been. Additionally, this new approach resulted in the inability to return the product to be re-done, as it simply was no longer cost feasible.

Thus, customer returns needed to have a new approach. New risk metrics had to be developed to manage these new risks. Even the basic supply chain risk needed to be addressed. In the first few years, the company experienced supply chain disruptions caused by a category five hurricane, a dock strike, and a shortage of talent to manage the new and more complicated supply chain. Even worse, the supply chain disruptions occurred at the riskiest moment – right before the season of the year when this company makes a large portion of their sales. The first year into this new model, word got out that the company was having supply chain problems and it suffered stock price losses of about 12 per cent. Unfortunately, one year later, the supply chain disruption occurred again at the worst possible time and resulted in additional stock price drops near 12 per cent. Boards of corporations today are not patient with risks that could or should have been identified earlier but were not – the so called 'grey swan'.

What is risk in this context?

Understanding supply chain impacts

The number of disruptions is growing, so demonstrating resilience is essential. In the study summarized in Figure 8.2, nearly 85 per cent of those surveyed reported suffering from a supplier disruption, and more than 50 per cent reported more than one interruption. Thus, companies should plan for when, not if, their value chain will be impacted.

FIGURE 8.2 Supply chain disruptions per company per year

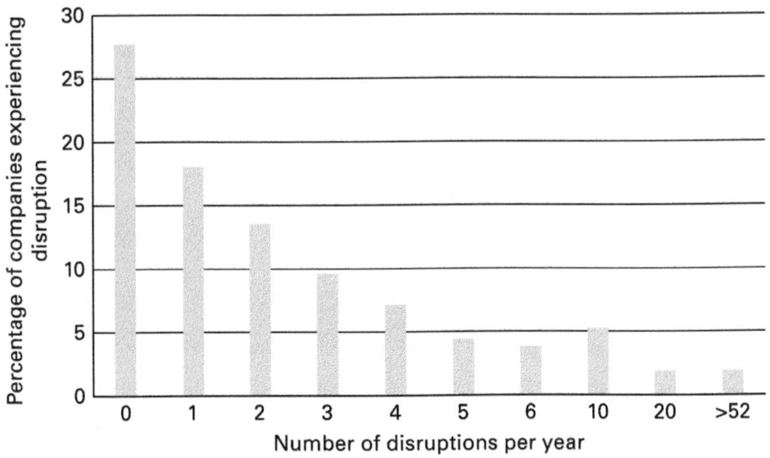
Percentage of companies experiencing disruption
30
25
20
15
10
5
0
0
1
2
3
4
5
6
10
20
>52
Number of disruptions per year

NOTE: Nearly 85% of companies suffered a supply disruption; over 50% of companies had more than one disruption; 42% of disruptions originated beyond Tier One.

SOURCE: Adapted from Zurich-sponsored BCI annual supply chain disruption study. Business Continuity Institute (2015)

As seen in Zurich's proprietary database of supply chain disruptions in Figure 8.3, some of these disruptions can last for an extended period of time. An analysis of 2,500 disruptions shows that almost 500 lasted more than a week, several hundred lasted more than six months, and some lasted over five years. Additional analysis revealed that approximately 20 per cent of these disruptions had financial consequences in excess of US $500 million. That's a big number to any organization.

Supply chain disruptions are caused by cyber challenges and a myriad of other issues

Opportunities for improvement in this area abound as the negative impacts of supply chain disruptions are growing. Interestingly, many companies only insure the assets of key suppliers against fire and other physical damages to production sites. However, Zurich Insurance Group's proprietary database of supply disruptions shown in Figure 8.4 indicates the many non-physical causes of interruptions over nearly the past 15 years. The BCI annual Supply Chain Resilience Report statistics about actual supply disruption causes

FIGURE 8.3 Matching impact and duration

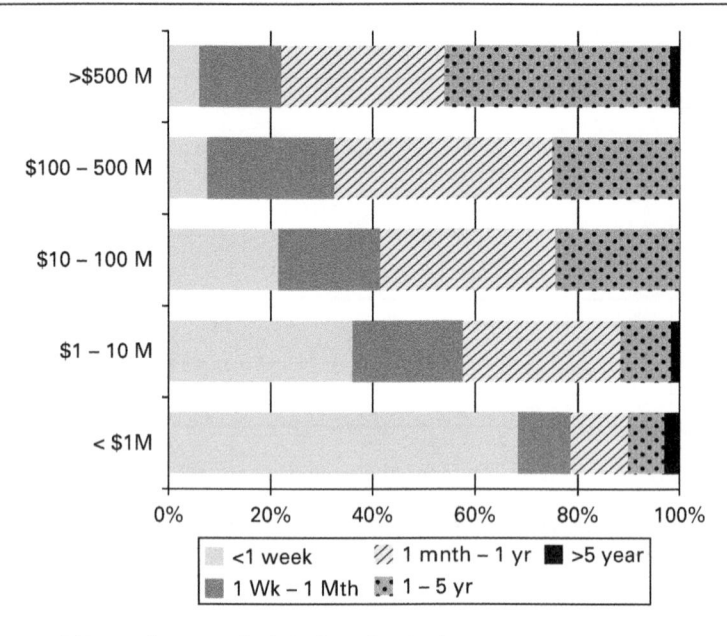

Impact	<1 week	1 Wk – 1 Mth	1 mnth – 1 yr	1 – 5 yr	>5 year

Bar chart showing distribution of disruption duration across impact categories: >$500 M, $100 – 500 M, $10 – 100 M, $1 – 10 M, < $1M

SOURCE: Zurich's proprietary supply chain disruption database

FIGURE 8.4 Cause of supply chain disruption

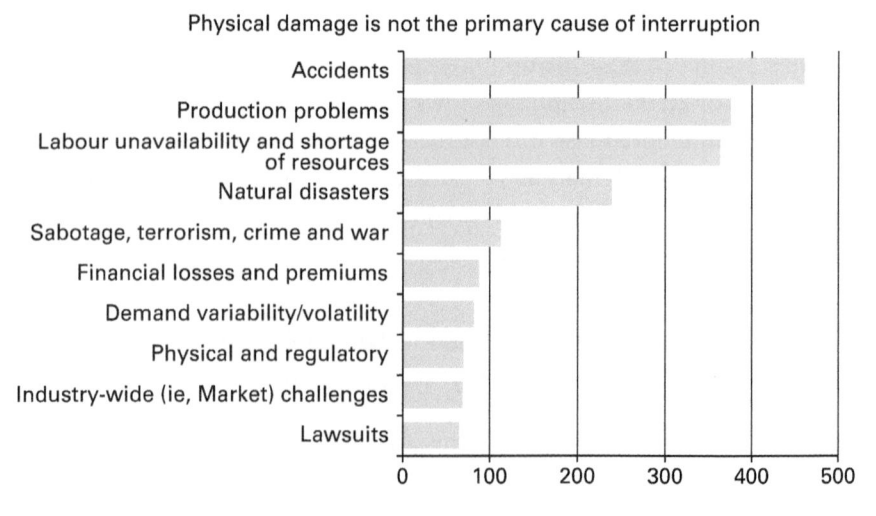

Physical damage is not the primary cause of interruption

Cause	Count
Accidents	~460
Production problems	~370
Labour unavailability and shortage of resources	~360
Natural disasters	~240
Sabotage, terrorism, crime and war	~110
Financial losses and premiums	~90
Demand variability/volatility	~80
Physical and regulatory	~70
Industry-wide (ie, Market) challenges	~70
Lawsuits	~60

SOURCE: Zurich's proprietary supply chain disruption database

show IT and communication issues as the number one challenge in 2015, comprising over 50 per cent of the interruptions. This was followed by transportation problems, labour unavailability, regulatory changes, political unrest and other reasons.

Natural catastrophe was also a key cause of interruption but, as seen following the Japanese tsunami, many of the problems were not directly tied to the physical disruption but to secondary issues like power outages, infrastructure problems, labour and ingress/egress challenges. Often, the most dramatic and widespread examples of supply chain disruptions lead to other types of disruptions. For example, the actual disruption in Thailand was a flood, but many impacted companies were scrambling to find other sources of inventory. Competitors were going to the same backup supplier[s], who in turn have 'conflicts of interest', over who they are going to give their spare capacity to. This then causes labour issues, as the suppliers have trouble trying to staff those extra shifts. This can cause a ripple effect which can spread through a supply chain.

Political upheaval was rated as the number one risk issue in the annual Global Risks Report, produced with the World Economic Forum, Zurich Insurance Company and others. Clearly, political unrest can have major implications for the unencumbered production and movement of goods in global trade. To get better insight into country risk, Zurich developed a revolutionary tool called Zurich Risk Room to visualize a company's unique risk landscape and see the interconnectedness of risk, on a country-by-country basis. This proprietary application taps into Zurich's data and numerous external sources to present global risks in an interactive way. This powerful, award-winning tool can help an organization to identify the correlation between various risks and test assumptions before making major strategic decisions. It can be a valuable resource when considering engaging a new supplier or business partner, or expanding into a new geographic territory. More information is available at **http://knowledge.zurich.com/risk-interconnectivity/zurich-risk-room/** or download a demo version of the tool that is available free of charge for both Apple and Android.

How is supply chain risk managed?

Supply chain risk management and insurance strategies

Given the variety of reasons behind supplier interruption, it may behove companies to take a more holistic approach to managing and insuring value chain risks. It is imperative that companies closely examine their supply chain exposures and the implications of deficiencies in supply chain risk management from a financial, legal, reputational and social perspective. Risk management and insurance alternative strategies should also be explored, including a protocol for evaluating an organization's readiness for dealing with and funding a supply chain disruption.

The first phase of a supply chain risk assessment and management approach (see Figure 8.5) involves the identification of the key suppliers (if this has not already been done) to narrow down to those suppliers that are most critical to protecting your profitability. The risk assessment will focus on the specific supply chains (combination of supply and supplier) you may wish to better understand (and possibly insure). This assessment provides both an in-depth understanding of the quality of management of the supply chain risk and the financial impacts of an interruption. Companies can get started toward a supply chain risk assessment by taking Zurich's supply chain questionnaire at **http://knowledge.zurich.com/supply-chain/**.

Zurich's supplier risk assessment will review nearly 25 different areas of risk, ranging from production location, transportation and security to management. The risk assessments will:

- help you to determine your key suppliers/supplies if you do not know this already;
- enable you to identify potential improvements to processes and performance;
- identify areas of residual risk, and determine the costs of extra expenses of recovery;
- quantify the estimated and probable maximum loss for each supply, to promote a deeper understanding of the potential financial impacts associated with a disruption in the delivery of particular supplies. This information will also provide the data required for underwriting, and serve as the basis and for the limit of indemnity required, should you decide to transfer some or all of your supply chain risk to an insurer.

Surprisingly, despite the guidance offered by ISO 25999, only about 8 per cent of companies reported having business continuity plans with their suppliers. Many companies are running Just in Sequence or Just in Time, but have not planned for what they would do 'just in case' a supplier does not deliver. The answer could be found in a collaborative effort between purchasing and risk financing, producing a more effective balance of risk and reward which is validated through scenario testing. Ideally, companies can establish a combined approach to managing certain exposures and insuring those risks which remain out of control of the procurement team, such as the approximately 40 per cent of disruptions that occur below Tier One direct suppliers, according to Zurich-sponsored studies by the Business Continuity Institute (BCI.org).

FIGURE 8.5 Supply chain risk assessment stages

- Determine those suppliers most critical to protecting profitability
- Develop a supply chain / value chain map
- Gather key supply / supplier details
- Evaluate risk factor information for each supplier
- Define and evaluate risk scenarios
- Develop risk grading for each supplier
- Determine risk strategies

SOURCE: Zurich

How does supply chain risk management fit?

A strong enterprise risk culture can correlate to improved profitability

Financial results studies provide evidence that a robust risk culture and enterprise process can be the basis for improved profitability and business resilience. Some organizations have implemented an integrated Enterprise Risk Management (or ERM) approach to managing risk, aggressively identifying the biggest risks so they can be proactively addressed in their strategy. A 2012 study by FERMA found that firms with 'advanced' risk management practices exhibited stronger EBITDA and revenue results over the past five years than did those with 'emerging' risk practices. This review of over 800 firms in 20 countries concluded that:

- approximately 75 per cent more firms with 'advanced' risk management practices had EBITDA growth of over 10 per cent;
- roughly 62 per cent more firms with 'advanced' risk management practices showed revenue growth of 10 per cent.

The study validates that an active risk practice and culture can directly correlate to stronger financial results, as the entire firm becomes more aware and accountable for the significant obstacles standing in the way of success. This enterprise approach helps management see the connections between the risks, in essence, linking risk management with strategy in their decision making. Perhaps nowhere is this more important than in supply chain risk management.

Eyes wide open

One executive recently stated: 'There are no black swans. All risks are identifiable.' Although saying there are no black swans may be a bit optimistic, do not tell that to one high-tech executive who in 2014 blamed 'acts of God' for profit drops of 44 per cent related to supply chain problems. Roll forward one year and that company's board is taking a more active role. Perhaps frustrated by those supply chain losses and the loss related to a recent acquisition (which was written off), the board has formed an ad hoc committee for 'directional strategy'. Organizations should take Enterprise Risk Management more seriously so they can see how strategy and supply chain risk can work in tandem or even move exponentially to create huge losses.

For example, a major manufacturer managed supply chain risks in silos and recently suffered a $1 billion write-off partly because of that silo approach. While some in management began to manage specific supply chain price increases through long-term contracts, others managed the risk through hedging. Still others in the company were managing the risks by increasing research and development and finding different manufacturing models (resulting in less use of certain high-priced inputs). An integrated approach to ERM and better communication may have saved a billion.

It might be said that: 'What is chance (or God) to the non-risk-intelligent company is not chance to the risk-intelligent company.' Companies need to figure that out. Apparently some have. There is one supply company that did not suffer major damages from the earthquake and tsunami in Japan, thanks to their ERM process and their ability to shift production and maintain extra inventory in other locations.

What's next?

Opportunities for improvement

When the supply chain function works together with risk management and corporate strategy, the synergy can create a competitive advantage and build resiliency. This can offer an expanded and cooperative role for procurement and risk management as they both seek to improve the successful execution of strategy. There are many tools available that risk managers and procurement can use to better understand the exposures their supply chain strategy can bring to the company. A firm can model its value chain to follow the profit flow to find the greatest pinch points. They can also perform a supply chain risk assessment of key suppliers to determine possible weak links. Learnings can be used to build more robust business continuity plans. There are supply chain risk management good practices available that can help a company in this area. For more information, visit the website of the Supply Chain Risk Leadership Council at **www.scrlc.com**.

Getting better in this area may also require organizations to tailor the risks to their business model. When a major retailer first got into its ERM process, the supply chain risks were about turn, turn, turn. The retailer built risk metrics around inventory movement and turn. Move a lot of goods and make more money – this was their business model. In contrast, after studying supplier and product supply chain sources, a biotechnology company saw the risk related to inventory and supply chain differently.

An integrated approach to corporate strategy and supplier risk management

FIGURE 8.6 Supply chain risk assessment

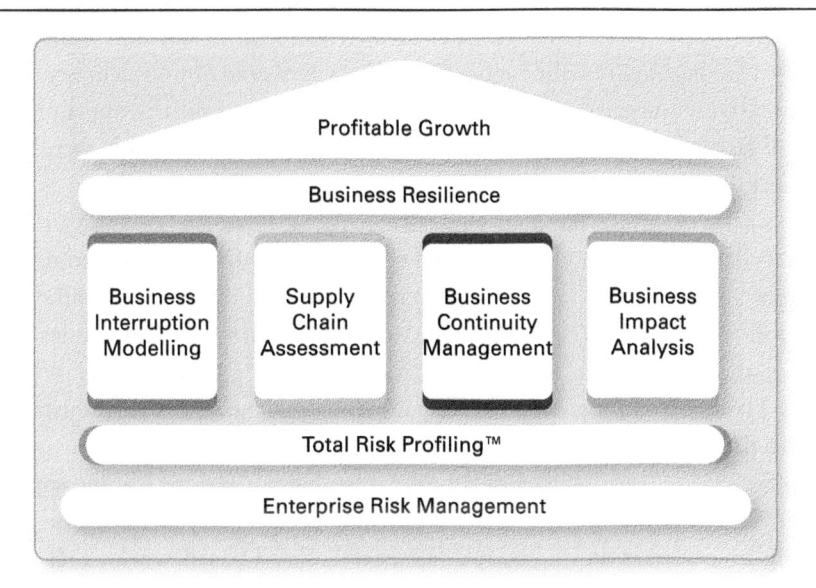

```
                    Profitable Growth
                    Business Resilience

  Business          Supply          Business         Business
  Interruption      Chain           Continuity       Impact
  Modelling         Assessment      Management       Analysis

                   Total Risk Profiling™
                 Enterprise Risk Management
```

SOURCE: Zurich

As can be seen in Figure 8.6 showing Zurich's holistic risk management framework, an integrated, enterprise approach is recommended. Zurich leverages these various risk identification and quantification tools to help build business resiliency. In addition to supplier risk assessment, Zurich can also use its Total Risk Profiling methodology to develop scenarios which could impact resiliency. Total Risk Profiling is featured in a YouTube video which can be found here: **http://www.youtube.com/watch?v=Lir9r-mzejg**.

As an example, a large firm was trying to cut costs by changing its purchasing strategy. The company was considering changing from two suppliers, which each provided 50 per cent of its raw material, to one supplier delivering 90 per cent of the necessary goods at a better price, with the second supplier providing 10 per cent of the material. Prior to making this change, the procurement manager wisely consulted with the firm's risk manager to assess the increased exposure to the firm and find alternative mitigation strategies. The risk manager obviously recognized that greater reliance on a single supplier may also bring greater business interruption exposure, including the extra expenses that could easily offset any contractual cost savings. The risk manager investigated various options such as securing an 'all risk' supply chain insurance policy to provide financial backing that can cover the value of the supplies and any additional recovery costs. The company also looked into arranging standby, make-up capacity for the critical goods, which could be built into their supplier business continuity plan. Through open collaboration, the business balanced the cost savings against the higher probability and cost of non-delivery. The cooperative enterprise approach allowed the firm to find the appropriate mix of risk and reward that aligned their sourcing strategy with their risk appetite.

It can be helpful if supplier risk management, business continuity planning, cyber security and other related control processes are included under a larger banner of a collaborative Enterprise Risk Management programme that follows ISO 31000 or COSO guidance (see Figure 8.7). Companies can review their Enterprise Risk Management by taking Zurich's free online ERM Healthcheck, available at: **https://www.zurichna.com/en/industries/financial/management** (see Figure 8.8).

In Enterprise Risk Management, one of the biggest lessons learned can be that the number one tool for better addressing enterprise exposures is simply having a conversation. In today's fast-paced, cloud-based world, that risk conversation is not occurring frequently enough, and there is often not a 'risk-aware' culture to support that dialogue. Organizations have to think – and

FIGURE 8.7 An integrated framework for Enterprise Risk Management

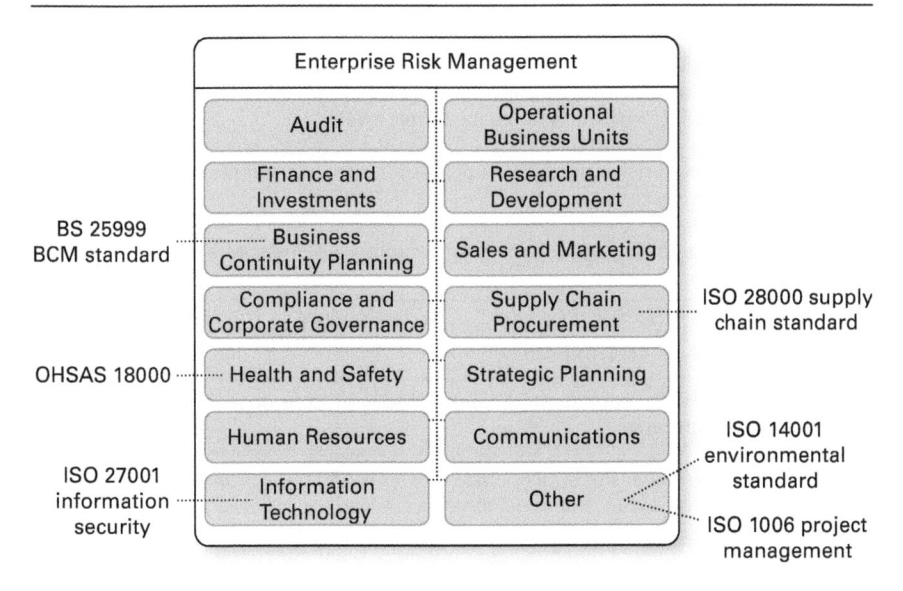

```
                    Enterprise Risk Management
          ┌─────────────────────┬─────────────────────┐
          │       Audit         │    Operational      │
          │                     │  Business Units     │
          ├─────────────────────┼─────────────────────┤
          │   Finance and       │   Research and      │
          │   Investments       │   Development       │
BS 25999  ├─────────────────────┼─────────────────────┤
BCM       │     Business        │ Sales and Marketing │
standard  │ Continuity Planning │                     │  ISO 28000 supply
          ├─────────────────────┼─────────────────────┤  chain standard
          │  Compliance and     │   Supply Chain      │
          │ Corporate Governance│   Procurement       │
OHSAS     ├─────────────────────┼─────────────────────┤
18000     │  Health and Safety  │ Strategic Planning  │
          ├─────────────────────┼─────────────────────┤  ISO 14001
          │  Human Resources    │   Communications    │  environmental
ISO 27001 ├─────────────────────┼─────────────────────┤  standard
information│    Information      │       Other         │
security  │    Technology       │                     │  ISO 1006 project
          └─────────────────────┴─────────────────────┘  management
```

SOURCE: Zurich

discuss – anew about how supply chain risk can be managed and how it impacts their business model, strategy, and vision.

One major retailer used to say that when they saw their risk in a new way or learned something new about the risk or how it impacted others, that it was an 'aha' moment. Aggressively identifying and managing supply chain risks and understanding how they are linked to other risks such as strategy can be a revelation for many companies. Senior management should verify that risk information is being shared across silos to ensure that a holistic company view of potential breaks in the chain is available as a basis for strategic decision making. They should ensure that there is a strong enterprise risk programme to help the company identify exposures earlier and operate with the proper risk/reward balance so they can attain their strategic objectives. By working in concert across business and functional areas, executives can help create a more resilient enterprise that is better able to anticipate surprises, recover from disruptions, adapt to changing conditions and leverage strategic growth opportunities.

FIGURE 8.8 Sample supply chain risk healthcheck

Do you know who your critical suppliers are, and how much their failure would impact your company's profits?	Yes/No
Have you fully mapped your critical supply chains upstream to the raw material level and downstream to the customer level?	Yes/No
Have you integrated risk management processes into your supply chain management approaches?	Yes/No
Do you have routine, timely systems for measuring the financial stability of critical suppliers?	Yes/No
Do you understand your Tier 1 production facilities and logistic hub exposures to natural catastrophes?	Yes/No
Is supply chain risk management integrated into your Enterprise Risk Management approach?	Yes/No
Do you record the details of supply chain incidents and the actions you have put in place to avoid future incidents?	Yes/No
Do your Tier 1 suppliers have business continuity plans that have been tested in terms of their viability?	Yes/No
Have you provided risk training to your supply chain management team?	Yes/No
Is risk on the agenda at performance meetings with your strategic suppliers?	Yes/No

SOURCE: Zurich

Find out more

For more information on supply chain risk management, please review the following information and visit the websites below.

Anupindi, R (2013) Cisco SCRM in action: 2011 Tohoku earthquake, Case 1-429-284 *Globalens* [online] http://webuser.bus.umich.edu/anupindi/cases/GL1429284I-Tsunami.pdf

ASIS International [online] https://www.asisonline.org/About-ASIS/Pages/default.aspx

Berkow, J (2011) A supply chain disaster survival guide, *Financial Post*, 8 Nov [online] http://business.financialpost.com/2011/11/08/dealing-with-supply-chain-disruptions/

British Standards Organization (BSI) [online] http://www.bsigroup.com/en-GB/standards/

Business Continuity Institute website: http://www.thebci.org/

Business Continuity Institute (2015) Supply Chain Resilience Report 2015, *BCI* [online] http://www.thebci.org/index.php/businesscontinuity/cat_view/24-supply-chain-continuity/33-supply-chain-continuity/140-bci-resources

Conrad, L (2013) Deciding what opportunities to fund, which risks to protect, *Zurich* [online] https://www.zurichna.com/en/knowledge/articles/2013/06/deciding-opportunities-fund-which-risks-protect

Conrad, L (2015) A Strategic Approach to Enterprise Risk Management at Zurich Insurance Group, in *Implementing Enterprise Risk Management: Case studies and best practices*, ed. J Fraser, B Simkins and K Narvaez, Wiley, Chichester

Conrad, L and Walker, P L (2013) Strategic risk: do not forget your supply chain, *Financier Worldwide* [online] http://www.zurichcanada.com/internet/can/sitecollectiondocuments/english/target%20markets/large%20corporation%20and%20multinationals/supply%20chain/strategic_risk_do_not_forget_your_supply_chain.pdf

COSO ERM Framework [online] http://www.coso.org/ERM-IntegratedFramework.htm

FERMA (2012) Risk Management Benchmarking Survey [online] http://www.ferma.eu/app/uploads/2012/10/benchmarking-survey-2012-brochure.pdf

ISO Business Continuity standards BS 25999 and ISO 22301 [online] http://www.25999.info/

ISO 31000: 2009 ERM Framework [online] http://www.iso.org/iso/home/store/catalogue_tc/catalogue_detail.htm?csnumber=43170

ISO 28000:2007 [online] http://www.iso.org/iso/catalogue_detail?csnumber=44641

Kolomeitsev, S (2011) Supply Chain Risk Management at Cisco: H1N1 Response, Case 1-428-881, *Globalens* [online] http://webuser.bus.umich.edu/anupindi/cases/GL1428881I_Cisco.pdf. Describes in detail Cisco's approach to supply chain risk management and outlines a scenario of how to address the H1N1 outbreak.

Lee, M (2009) Boeing: The Fight for Fasteners, Case 1-428-787, *Globalens* [online] http://webuser.bus.umich.edu/anupindi/cases/GL1428787I_Boeing_Fasteners_case.pdf

Sheffi, Y and Rice, J B (2005) A supply chain view of the resilient enterprise, *MIT Sloan Management Review*, 47 (1), pp 41–48 [online] http://sheffi.mit.edu/sites/default/files/ASupplyChainViewoftheResilientEnterprise.pdf

Supply Chain Risk Leadership Council best practices: www.scrlc.com

Supply Chain Risk Insights website: http://www.SupplyChainRiskInsights.com

Zurich ERM Healthcheck: https://www.zurichna.com/en/industries/financial/management

Zurich Global Risks Report 2016 [online] http://knowledge.zurich.com/risk-interconnectivity/global-risks-report-2016/

Zurich Knowledge Hub: http://knowledge.zurich.com/

Zurich Risk Room country risk analysis tool: http://knowledge.zurich.com/risk-interconnectivity/zurich-risk-room/ or download a demo version of the tool that is available free of charge for both Apple and Android

Zurich Strategic Risk resources and Risk Profiling: http://www.zurichna.com/en/kh/strategicriskres

Zurich supply chain risk questionnaire: http://knowledge.zurich.com/supply-chain/

Zurich Total Risk Profiling video on YouTube: http://www.youtube.com/watch?v=Lir9r-mzejg

Disclaimer

Zurich American Insurance Company

1400 American Lane

Schaumburg, IL 60196

www.zurichna.com

The information in this publication was compiled from sources believed to be reliable for informational purposes only. All sample policies and procedures herein should serve as a guideline, which you can use to create your own policies and procedures. We trust that you will customize these samples to reflect your own operations and believe that these samples may serve as a helpful platform for this endeavor. Any and all information contained herein is not intended to constitute advice (particularly not legal advice). Accordingly, persons requiring advice should consult independent advisors when developing programmes and policies. We do not guarantee the accuracy of this information or any results and further assume no liability in connection with this publication and sample policies and procedures, including any information, methods or safety suggestions contained herein. We undertake no obligation to publicly update or revise any of this information, whether to reflect new information, future developments, events or circumstances or otherwise. Moreover, Zurich reminds you that this cannot be assumed to contain every acceptable safety and compliance procedure or that additional procedures might not be appropriate under the circumstances. The subject matter of this publication is not tied to any specific insurance product nor will adopting these policies and procedures ensure coverage under any insurance policy.

© 2015–2016 Zurich American Insurance Company

Business Continuity Management

09

IAN CLARK

Why does business continuity matter?

A strong recovery requires strong leadership. It needs a diverse range of leaders and leadership styles that can respond to the changing needs of recovery. The right structures must be in place to support these leaders and enable effective decision making to agree the way forward, instil hope and build momentum (Davies, 2015).

However, these strong leaders are assisted in their task by having a strong process already in place before it is needed.

Traditional risk management has, in the past, promoted a widespread perception that business continuity is just about dealing with high-impact, low-probability events. This is often misrepresented as a form of disaster recovery or contingency plan for the business and often leads to a large collection of event-specific plans gathering dust on many corporate shelves.

Business activities are disrupted by a wide variety of incidents, many of which are difficult to predict or analyse. By focusing on the impact of disruption upon the organization, rather than the cause, business continuity identifies those products, services, processes and activities upon which the organization depends for its survival. It also enables the organization to determine what is required to continue to meet its obligations before any disruption is experienced. This leads to the commonly used term 'event agnostic' being a defining attribute of business continuity. Through business continuity, an organization can recognize what needs to be done to protect its resources (eg people, premises, technology and information, supply chain, interested parties and reputation) before any disruptive event occurs. Therefore, the organization is able to take a realistic view on the likely responses and associated resources needed as and when a disruption occurs. It also enables the organization to recognize the time-sensitivity of these responses, so that it can be confident of managing the after-effects of any disruption and avoid unacceptable impacts across the supply chain.

Another valuable by-product of having a Business Continuity Management programme or system in place is that the organization will be well equipped to take advantage of opportunities that might otherwise be judged to be too high risk.

It is now more generally appreciated that implementing a Business Continuity Management system can improve organizational resilience as part of 'business as usual'. This leads to the promotion of Business Continuity Management as a complementary discipline to the management of risk under an all-encompassing Enterprise Risk Management framework. The concepts contained within the development and implementation of a holistic Business Continuity Management programme can also be applied to dealing with the impact of any event, whether internal or external to the organization.

This is emphasized within the British Organizational Resilience Standard BS65000:2014 which states:

> Application of a comprehensive Business Continuity Management programme has been shown to increase an organization's resilience to disruptive events which, in turn, contributes to higher corporate performance. Resilience is widely defined as the ability of an organization to absorb, respond to and recover from any disruptions.

Implementing a Business Continuity Management programme provides a valuable framework for understanding how the organization creates and maintains value and establishes a direct relationship to dependencies that are inherent in the delivery of that value, both internal and external to the organization.

What is Business Continuity Management?

Definitions

Business Continuity Management (BCM)
Business Continuity Management is a holistic management process that identifies potential threats to an organization and the impacts to business operations those threats, if realized, might cause, and which provides a

framework for building organizational resilience with the capability of an effective response that safeguards the interests of its key stakeholders, reputation, brand and value-creating activities (ISO22301:2012).

Business Continuity Management System (BCMS)
(That) part of the overall management system that establishes, implements, operates, monitors, reviews, maintains and improves business continuity (ISO22301:2012).

Business continuity is designed and implemented by an organization to provide a means of delivery of its products or services at acceptable, predefined and agreed levels following any disruptive event. Implementation of such must bear in mind the potential for far-reaching implications for the wider community and other third parties, such as the external organizations, that it depends upon, and others that depend on it.

BCM involves:

- being clear on the organization's key products and services and the activities that deliver them;
- knowing the priorities for resuming activities and the resources they require;
- having a clear understanding of the threats to these activities, including their dependencies, and knowing the impacts of not resuming them;
- having tried and trusted arrangements in place to resume these activities following a disruptive incident; and
- making sure that these arrangements are routinely reviewed and updated so that they will be effective in all circumstances.

Business continuity can be effective in dealing with both sudden disruptive incidents (catastrophic failure) and gradual or 'slow-burn' ones (eg flu pandemics).

What is business continuity in this context?

Any incident (large, small, natural, accidental or deliberate) has the potential to cause a degree of disruption to an organization's operations and its ability to deliver products and services. Implementing business continuity before a disruptive incident occurs, rather than waiting for it to happen, will enable the organization to resume operations before unacceptable levels of commercial impact arise. Business Continuity Management is developed upon the understanding that the impact of any disruption will vary the longer the organization takes to resume business activities.

Top management commitment to implementing any form of business continuity within the organization is the essential, and most difficult starting point. It is essential that top management should:

- demonstrate leadership by being prepared to make timely decisions, allocating appropriate resources, and ensuring the motivation and engagement of other staff; and
- foster a culture and environment of awareness, participation and communication across all strata within the organization to achieve its business continuity objectives.

The risk to the organization's capability to continue providing products and services following any disruptive event is generally well documented. What is not, in an organization without any form of business continuity, is the single process whereby it can effectively manage any disruption and provide all interested parties with pre-defined time parameters and objectives by which resumption of the agreed services can be achieved.

How is business continuity managed?

Like any other management system, a Business Continuity Management System (BCMS) includes the following key components:

- a policy;
- people with defined responsibilities;
- management processes relating to:
    - policy;
    - planning;
    - implementation and operation;
    - performance assessment;
    - management review; and
    - improvement.
- a set of documentation providing auditable evidence; and
- any BCMS processes relevant to the organization.

A Business Continuity Management System emphasizes the importance of:

- understanding the organization's needs and the necessity for establishing business continuity policy and objectives;
- implementing and operating controls and measures for managing an organization's overall capability to manage disruptive incidents;
- monitoring and reviewing the performance and effectiveness of the BCMS; and
- continual improvement based on objective measurement.

Placing BCM within the framework and disciplines of a management system creates a BCMS that enables the process to be controlled, evaluated and continually improved. The International Standards Organization has two foundation standards published on the subject of Business Continuity, namely:

- ISO 22301:2012   Business Continuity Management Systems Requirements (ISO22301)

- ISO 22313:2012   Business Continuity Management Systems (ISO22313)

The former describes the auditable framework of an implemented BCMS through which an organization can be audited and accredited as having a BCMS that complies with the International Standard. The latter provides fuller advice and guidance on how to develop and implement a BCMS that conforms to the requirements, and it is the choice of the organization whether to seek accreditation.

Before any activity is considered in creating a business continuity programme for any organization, top management must provide the necessary structures to enable its implementation.

The first task addressed by top management is the publication of a business continuity policy. In this document the scope and governance requirements of the BCM programme are set out. It also provides the context in which the developed continuity-related capabilities will be implemented and identifies the principles to which the organization aspires and how its performance can be audited. As such it should be clear, concise and to the point as an extended statement will be a barrier to effective communication of top management's intentions.

Top management must be prepared to provide the necessary resources to the BCM programme that are sufficient to:

- achieve its stated policy and objectives;
- make adequate provision for people and people-related resources, including the time to fulfil BCM-related roles and responsibilities, and training and awareness to those who have to execute the roles;
- meet the changing requirements of the organization; and
- provide for ongoing operation and continual improvement of the BCM programme.

Once these are in place the business continuity programme can be initiated. Construction is governed by the well-understood Plan-Do-Check-Act (PDCA) methodology employed within all management systems. This is applied in ISO22313:2012 as detailed in Figure 9.1 below.

FIGURE 9.1 The Business Continuity Management System PDCA model

PLAN **Establish**	Establish the Business Continuity policy, objectives, controls, processes, procedures and staffing relevant to improving business continuity in order to deliver results that align with the organization's overall policies and objectives.
DO **Implement and operate**	Implement and operate the business continuity policy, controls, processes and procedures.
CHECK **Monitor and review**	Monitor and review performance against the stated business continuity objectives and policy. Report the results to top management for review. Determine and authorize actions for remediation and improvement.
ACT **Maintain and improve**	Maintain and improve the Business Continuity Management System by taking corrective actions based on the results of management review and re-appraising the scope of the Business Continuity Management System policy and objectives.

The BCM programme is a PDCA cycle that facilitates the production of a Business Continuity Management System by sequential progress through a series of stages, as illustrated in Figure 9.2. ISO 22313:2012 provides the necessary guidance through the programme stages.

FIGURE 9.2 The BCM programme

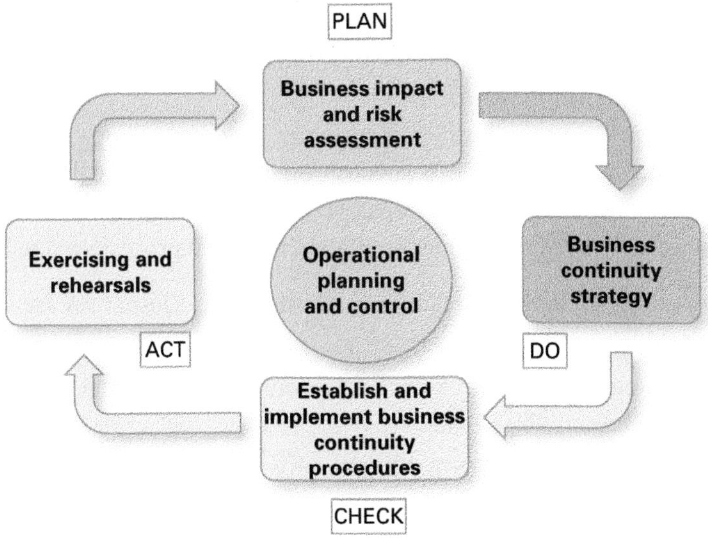
PLAN
Business impact and risk assessment
Exercising and rehearsals
Operational planning and control
Business continuity strategy
ACT
DO
Establish and implement business continuity procedures
CHECK

As the entire cycle is very intensive the exercise should be managed as a project using an appropriate project management methodology and documentation system to ensure that the complex infrastructure of the organization is adequately addressed. ISO 22313:2012 provides a concise diagram to illustrate this (see Figure 9.3).

FIGURE 9.3 The organizational ecosystem

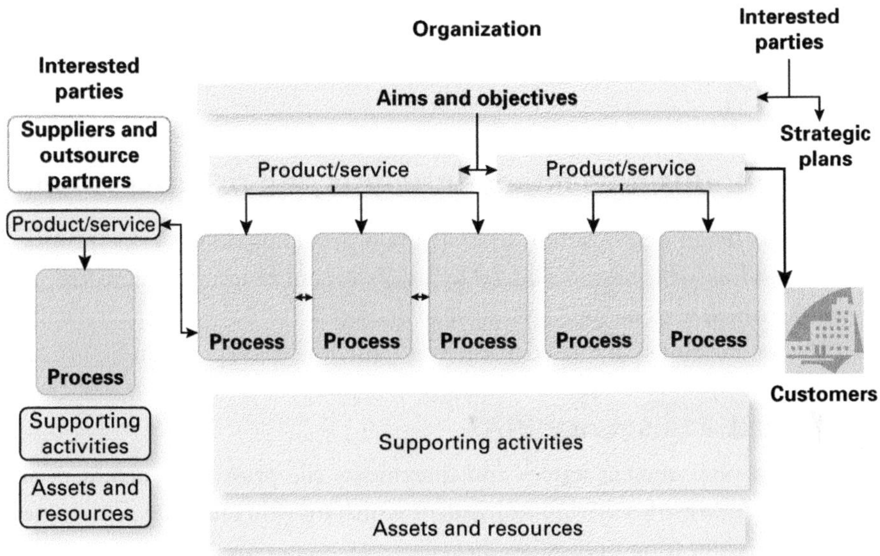
Organization
Interested parties
Interested parties
Aims and objectives
Suppliers and outsource partners
Strategic plans
Product/service
Product/service
Product/service
Process
Process
Process
Process
Process
Process
Customers
Supporting activities
Supporting activities
Assets and resources
Assets and resources

The first and most important stage within the programme is the conducting of a Business Impact Analysis (BIA) and a Risk Analysis. This is followed by the determination of appropriate measures and strategies to deal with any disruption, and construction of documentation to enable business units to respond in an appropriate manner.

Prior to initiating the business continuity programme top management commitment to the process is necessary to ensure that all of the organizational components participate effectively. Top management, in demonstrating leadership, may consider communicating the process's value by:

- ensuring the appropriate and most cost-effective responses are selected;
- providing evidence that business continuity requirements align with organizational objectives;
- emphasizing that collecting the information necessary within the programme is an essential business activity;
- identifying linkages between products and services and process, activities, and resources that support the execution of other project or change activities throughout the organization and build resilience;
- prioritizing the effective recovery of the organization's resources during any disruptive incident, focusing resources on the restoration of key product and service delivery;
- providing an overview of the organization that can be used to improve its efficiency or explore new opportunities and promote growth.

Stage 1: Business Impact Analysis and risk assessment

Generically an organization depends upon providing added value products and services. These are produced by using a number of interconnected processes which each contain a number of activities. A Business Impact Analysis (BIA) is therefore conducted at each of these layers as shown in Figure 9.4.

Product and service BIA

The top management agrees and documents the priority of products and services following a disruptive incident which may threaten the achievement of the organization's objectives because:

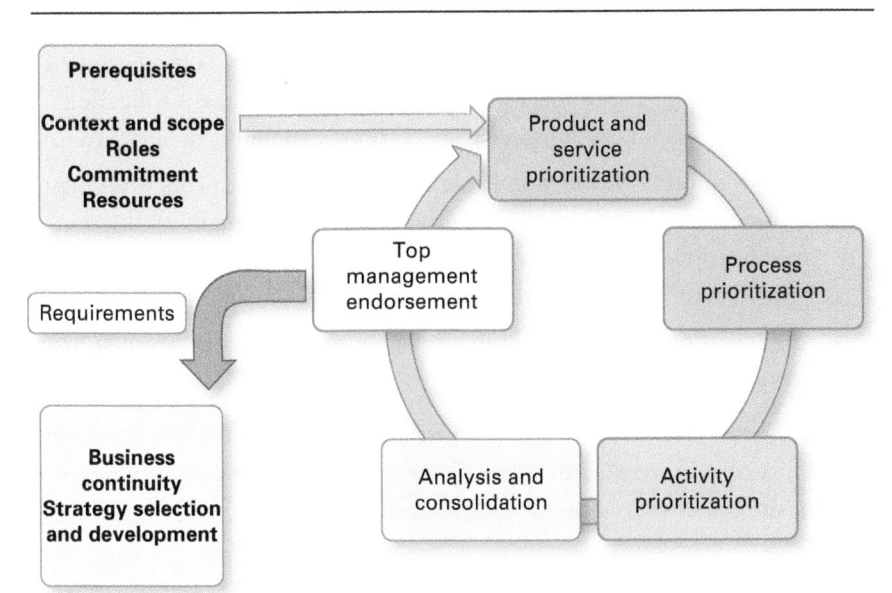

FIGURE 9.4 The Business Impact Analysis process

- they have the ultimate responsibility for ensuring the continuity of the organization and the fulfilment of its objectives; and
- they are aware of all planned future changes and other factors which may affect the organization and hence the business continuity requirements.

If the organization has too many products and services to identify individually, then those with similar priorities may be grouped together. It may be necessary for the organization to identify customers who, despite sharing the same products and services, have differing delivery timeframe expectations or value to the organization.

For each group of products and services top management should document the impacts that a disruption may cause by identifying any customer expectations and any legal recourse they may have over the organization if these expectations are not met, and the impacts they will have on the organization if such sanctions are imposed. Also taking into account the views of other interested parties in assessing impacts will provide the essential information necessary to prioritize the products and services of the organization during any disruptive event.

The outcome of the product and service prioritization process should be:

- endorsement or modification of the organization's BCM programme scope;
- identification of legal, regulatory and contractual requirements (obligations);

- a statement of the organization's strategic objectives, products and services, customers and other interested parties, and downtime requirements;
- a balanced evaluation of business impact, over time, as it relates to a failure to deliver products/services, which serves as the justification for business continuity requirements (time, capability, quality, etc.);
- confirmation of product and service delivery requirements (that may include time, quality, quantity, service levels, and capability specifications) following a disruptive incident that then sets the priorities for activities and resources;
- an indication of the maximum allowable time that each product or service can remain unavailable;
- identification of processes (that deliver the products and services); and
- a list of prioritized products and services (grouped by timeframe or customer, or individual).

An essential output from this phase is the provision of target times for resuming delivery of products and services at specified minimum levels, which is defined within ISO 22301:2012 as recovery time objective (RTO) and minimum business continuity objective (MBCO).

Process BIA

The next phase involves a process-level prioritization to determine the interrelationships between internal processes as to how they deliver the products and services. Included in process prioritization is the necessity to determine the activities that make up those processes. In addition, prioritizing processes will assist in the development of a timetable for the recovery of activities across the organization. An agreed table of impacts may be used to consider the impacts of disruption of processes. It may be appropriate to add additional internal impact categories during the exercise.

The outcomes of process prioritization should contain:

- the identification of the relationship between product and services, processes, and activities;
- the identification of dependencies on other business processes;
- an evaluation of impacts of a process failure over time;
- agreed priorities of processes;
- an interdependency analysis of the processes that deliver products and services to customers;

- an interdependency analysis of the activities that deliver processes;
- a documented list of prioritized processes that deliver products and services; and
- an initial documented list of activities that deliver processes.

Activity BIA

The next phase involves performing an activity-level prioritization to understand the resources needed to effectively operate each activity following a disruptive event and to confirm the potential associated impact. This entails obtaining information relevant to a comprehensive understanding of normal resource requirements, enabling the organization to identify the resources necessary for recovery and to help confirm impact-related conclusions developed at the process level. Such information includes:

- people/skills/roles;
- facilities;
- equipment;
- records;
- financing;
- information and communications technologies, including applications, data, telephony, and networks;
- suppliers, third parties, and outsource partners;
- dependencies on other processes and activities;
- special tools, spare parts, and consumables;
- limitations imposed on resources by logistics or regulations.

The outcomes of activity prioritization provide:

- the confirmation of impacts over time, which serves as justification for business continuity requirements (time, capability, quality, etc.);
- resource needs to perform each prioritized activity (including facilities, people, equipment, ICT assets, suppliers, and finance);
- dependencies on other activities, suppliers, outsource partners, and other interested parties;
- required currency of business operational information or data used to determine any recovery point objectives;

- analysis of impacts over time associated with activity downtime;
- analysis of interdependencies of the resources (and other dependencies) needed to deliver processes;
- a documented list of prioritized activities that deliver processes, and products and services; and
- a documented list of prioritized resources that enable activities to operate.

Included in the analysis of interdependencies is the incorporation of all aspects of the ICT services necessary to support the business continuity process. An excellent source of information in this respect is to be found in ISO27031:2011 and is eloquently represented in Figure 9.5.

FIGURE 9.5 ICT readiness for BC

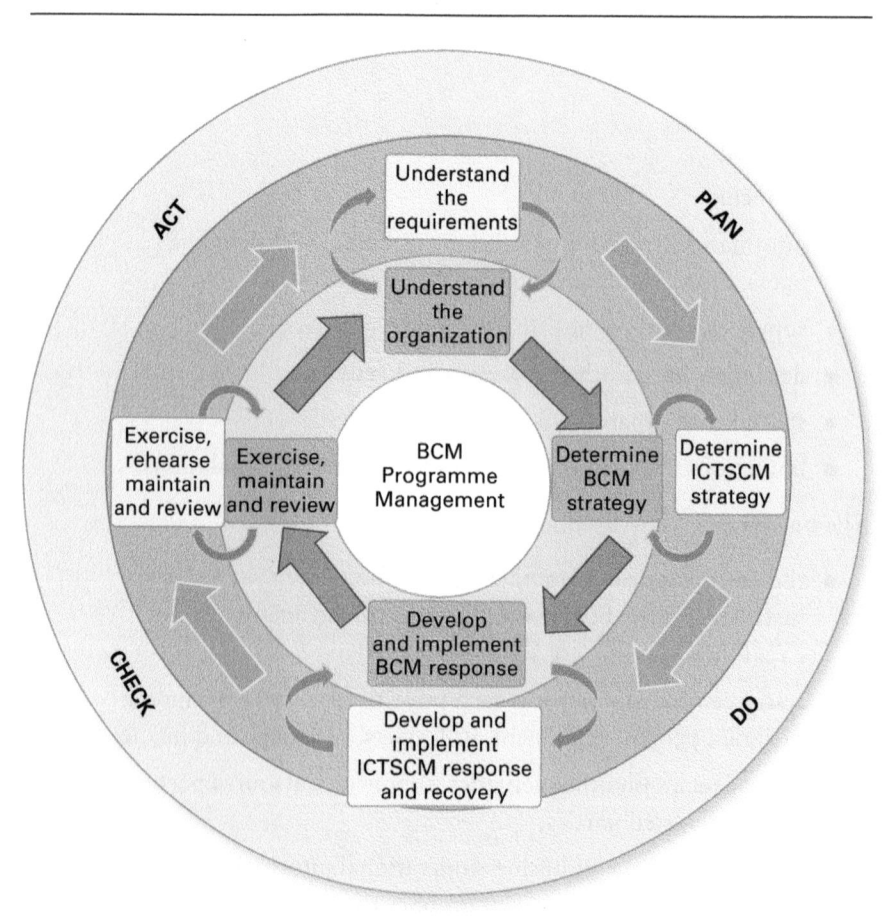

This publication emphasizes that any decision on recovery times and capability must be agreed by all parties involved. It is meaningless to have recovery time or recovery point objectives being set by the product and service or process BIAs that are unachievable by the ICT services. Discovery of such an imbalance is desirable at the analysis rather than the invocation stage and normally results in negotiations between all interested parties as to what can be achieved when a disruptive event places the entire capability under stressful circumstances. These negotiations reverberate across the entire process supply chain and successful negotiations will result in the development of a Business Continuity Management System that is appropriate and achievable.

Risk assessment

Many organizations have a well-established risk management function, maintain a corporate risk register and have risk assessment embedded as part of their normal practices and procedures. Threat assessments, therefore, may already be available for the organization's activities.

Evaluating threats as part of the BCM programme is not the same as undertaking a full corporate risk assessment, as it often takes place at a lower level of detail and incorporates aspects of Environmental, Facilities, Health and Safety and other relevant disciplines which may have an influence on the organization. Using risk assessment techniques as part of BC may inform an existing risk management programme and the normal threat mitigation techniques applied. While these may have the desired result of reducing the threat, this is not the primary purpose. The risk assessment within the business continuity programme is to provide an evaluation of existing threats inherent within the environment where the organization operates.

There are many risk management models in common usage, some of a general nature and others which have been entirely developed for a specific industry or sector. Virtually all of them involve identification of specific threats (or hazards) and use a formula based in historical information to calculate a risk value based upon threat probability and threat impact.

Whilst reasonably effective at dealing with known and predictable threats, they have serious shortcomings in evaluating the threats posed by catastrophic operational situations that are difficult to quantify, and cannot adequately reflect the relative importance of less quantifiable assets such as reputation. These models have been found inadequate in assessing the variation in impact over time. However, these assessments are essential in providing useful and usable information for developing scenarios for the exercising phase used to validate the subsequent plans.

Consolidation BIA

This final analysis (or consolidation of analyses) of the BIA process brings all of the findings together for presentation to and subsequent approval by top management. This involves reviewing the results from the prioritization activities, and drawing conclusions that lead to business continuity requirements. It also incorporates all of the recommendations for amendment of priorities, resumption timeframes, and priorities discovered during the preceding activities.

Regardless of approach used within this activity the outcome is to ensure that the data are

- Correct – accurate and reliable;
- Credible – believable and 'reasonable';
- Consistent – clear and repeatable;
- Current – up-to-date and available in a timely manner;
- Complete – comprehensive (no records missing and every field is known for each record).

Once the requirements are approved by top management all of this information is ready to be transformed into a business continuity structure that is fit for purpose. The total top-down approach to managing the BIA and risk assessment stage is illustrated in Figure 9.6.

FIGURE 9.6 BIA project management

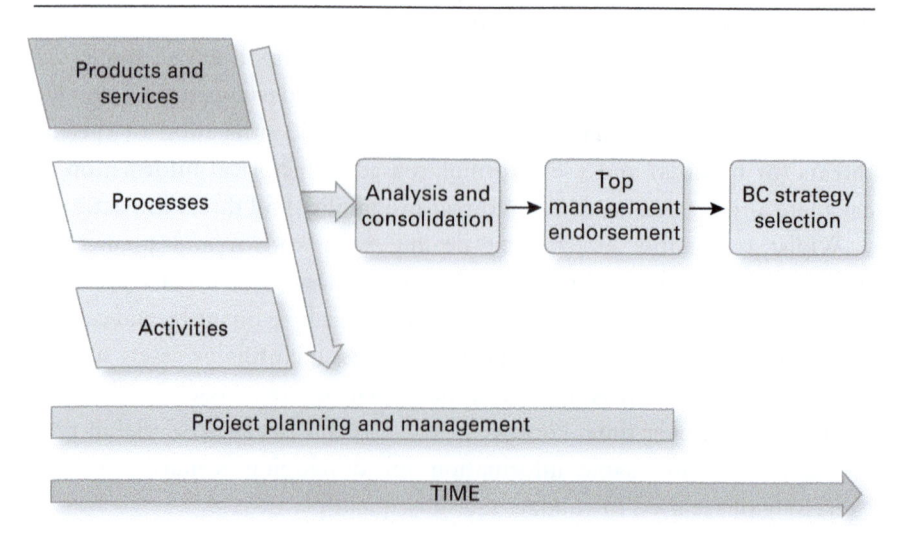

Stage 2: Design continuity strategies

The major design consideration within this stage is the production of documentation to provide the continuity and recovery strategies and tactics to agreed timescales. This documentation should also identify the means by which those objectives will be best achieved. This can be undertaken at three organizational levels:

- Strategic – products and services;
- Operational – process infrastructure; and
- Tactical – activities and resources that are essential to the processes.

At a strategic level the relative importance of various products and services has been determined in the first phase of the BIA. During a disruptive event, the strategic-level team members are accountable for the organization's stability, continuity and reputation. They are responsible for implementing and adapting the overall response strategy when the organization is threatened.

At the operational level the process infrastructure consists of the services and facilities needed to deliver a product or service. It is where the solutions that will make plans workable in practice are designed, and decisions are made that will probably incur the most expenditure. The design of operational solutions might require consultation with other experts in the field for specialist technical advice and skills. The consolidation analysis phase within the BIA verified the maximum allowable outage (MAO) and the minimum business continuity objectives (MBCO) of the organization's products and services, processes and activities. This stage finally sets the agreed period of time for the resumption of each of these, which is known as the recovery time objective (RTO).

Design considerations include a further verification process to ensure that the RTO for each product, service, process and activity is set at less than its MAO. Care should be exercised to ensure the aggregate RTO of processes, activities and dependent services does not exceed the MAO of the overall product, service or higher-level process. This will ensure that individual interruptions will not threaten the overall survival of the organization.

The recovery point objective (RPO) is the point to which information used in an activity must be restored to enable the activity to operate upon resumption (can also be referred to as 'maximum data loss' (ISO22301:2012)). In practice there is always a trade-off between cost and the speed of recovery. In most situations it is true that the shorter the time allowed for recovery and resumption of activities and processes, the greater the cost to the organization. The reverse is also true. Typically longer RTOs increase the chance that the recovery will not be achieved within the overall allowable time parameters, and that data will not be recovered. As a consequence the strategies and tactics incorporated into the plans must always look to balance continuity and recovery capability against reasonable and affordable costs.

This stage also integrates the Continuity plan with any existing Incident or Crisis Management plans. As a rule the communication, control and command structure within such plans dovetails with the strategic, operational and tactical structure of the response plans. The communications plan should address how the organization will manage communication with internal and external interested parties, including the media. The Incident or Crisis Management plan may be included within the strategic level plan or it may be referenced as a separate, essential document.

Response considerations

The design of continuity and recovery strategies requires the development of action-orientated plans covering necessary actions and minimum levels of resource availability that can be deployed in the event of the loss of:

- People – skills and knowledge;
- Premises – buildings and facilities;
- Resources – IT, information, equipment, materials, etc.; and
- Suppliers – products and services supplied by third parties.

Although these plans detail an integrated organizational approach (eg loss of a building that results in unavailability of resources, renders some of the staff unavailable for work or disrupts a local supplier of essential goods or services), they also need to have the capacity to work in isolation (eg where the only disruption is in a computer system or single production line).

Exercising

An organization's BC capability, or any other planned activity, cannot be considered reliable until it has been exercised. No matter how well designed the strategy, programme or system appears to be, conducting robust and realistic exercises will identify issues and assumptions that require attention, or provide the necessary proof of concept. The development of exercise scenarios in this stage is dependent upon the information gathered in the risk assessment phase. Using these scenarios provides assurance that all aspects of the response to an incident are appropriate to the organization by ensuring that:

- all information in plans is validated;
- all plans are exercised; and
- all relevant personnel (including deputies) are rehearsed in their respective roles.

A successful exercise programme begins simply and escalates gradually in terms of complexity and challenge. The aims of exercising include:

- evaluation of the organization's current BC capability;
- identification of areas for improvement or missing information;
- highlighting assumptions that need to be questioned;
- instilling confidence in exercise participants;
- developing team work;
- raising awareness of BC throughout the organization; and
- testing the effectiveness and timeliness of restoration procedures.

The exercise programme should use a combination of techniques to ensure that the aims are achieved across the whole organization over a planned timescale, including the following elements of the BCM programme:

- Technical – does all the required equipment work?
- Procedures – are the procedures and plans correct?
- Logistical – do the procedures work together in a logical manner?
- Timeliness – can the procedures achieve the required recovery time objective (RTO) for each activity?
- Administrative – are the procedures manageable?
- Personnel – are the right people involved and do they have the required skills, authority and experience? Does everyone understand their role?

Validation and review

Validation is the final stage of the BCM Lifecycle. It is important that the maintenance and review of the BCM programme is ongoing with the objective of improving organizational resilience. The review is essential in order to evaluate the delivered BCM programme and identify improvements to both the organization's implementation of the BCM Lifecycle and its level of organizational resilience.

There are five basic types of review:

- Audit (internal and external) – a formal impartial review process that measures an organization's BCM programme against a pre-agreed standard;
- Self-assessment – an assessment of the organization's BCM programme by itself;
- Quality Assurance (QA) – a process that ensures that the various outputs from the BCM programme meet requirements;
- Performance Appraisal – a review of the performance of individuals tasked with BC roles and responsibilities; and
- Supplier Performance – a review of a key supplier's BCM programme or a review of the performance of a supplier of recovery services.

How does Business Continuity Management fit?

Risk and Business Continuity Management are complementary disciplines and neither is an optional process in a well-managed organization. Both approaches require the adoption of structured and systematic programme management at all levels in an organization.

The Business Continuity Management cycle sets out a process that, when adopted, should lead to the design and implementation of a business continuity policy and framework that is led from the top of an organization, is sustainable, fit for purpose, and compliant with internal and external rules or guidelines. It should be culturally suited to the organization, owned by the business, regularly exercised and maintained (Graham and Kaye, 2006).

The quotation above highlights the desirable state within an organization where Business Continuity and Risk utilize their strengths as complementary disciplines. The Good Practice Guidelines (BCI2013) published by the Business Continuity Institute emphasize that risk assessment is an integral part of the Business Continuity Management process.

What's next?

Moving towards organizational resilience

Using the framework described within ISO22301:2012 and ISO 27031:2011, having Business Continuity Management System construction as a starting point to building organizational resilience is a choice of many organizations. Resilience is not fundamentally about stopping or preventing disruption happening in the first place. Reliance on prevention measures alone to provide comprehensive protection will inevitably generate misplaced confidence, because most disruptive incidents are by their nature largely unpredictable.

As previously stated, business continuity is developed with an 'event agnostic' approach, with the primary focus upon the perceived impact over time on continuity of business operations. Focusing upon impact allows the organization to develop response plans in a modular format which readily adapts to future organizational changes and provides a well-documented response and reporting system to an over-arching crisis management system.

The first obstacle facing any organization when discussing resilience is an agreement on the understanding of what resilience means to them. Disruptions may be a result of external factors such as traumatic events, or of gradual degradation of the ecosystem within which the organization operates; or any disruption created by the organization evolving or changing its operating model. Therefore an organization has to accept that to achieve a measure of resilience any management system must be able to understand the organization and the environment. There are many definitions of organizational resilience, for example:

> ANSI SPC_1: Organizational Resilience Management: a system of systematic and coordinated activities and practices through which an organization manages its operational risks and the potential threats and impacts thereon.

> ISO22313:2012: an organization with a positive business continuity culture will... increase its resilience over time by ensuring business continuity implications are considered in decisions at all levels.

> British Standard BS65000:2014 states: Organizational Resilience is the ability of an organization to anticipate, prepare for, and respond and adapt to incremental change and sudden disruptions in order to survive and prosper.

The resilience of an organization is directly related to the resilience of the other organizations on which it depends (customers, suppliers, regulators, and even competitors). An organization is also dependent on and contributes to the individual resilience of its staff and the communities they live in. Similarly, an organization's resilience is directly related to the resilience of its sector, and the sector's resilience is intertwined with the resilience of the nation.

As any form of resilience is dictated by the operational demands of the organization it needs to be embedded across the entire organization, across any inherent operational silos and hierarchical constraints. Additionally, resilience is dependent upon external and internal interoperability and dependencies. This means that to build a resilient organization we must investigate internal activities, and relationships with partners, outsourcers, suppliers, customers and other key interested parties must be incorporated within the programme.

The second obstacle is that resilience is inherently relative, and no organization, person, network or system can be absolutely resilient. Most organizations accept the fact that change is not only inevitable but the ability to rapidly change is desirable. This means that the resilience level will fluctuate as the organization adapts to change; whether caused by internal restructure, or environmental, marketplace or natural events.

From the above statements it can be seen that the organization must be strategically adaptable, operationally aware and tactically capable to respond to the impact of any change. Herein lies the one determining factor that can influence the organization's resilience throughout the business ecosystem. The one discipline that predicates impact upon business capability is Business Continuity Management.

A Business Continuity Management System can act as a central facilitator for all business impact assessments, whether resulting from Business Continuity, IT Disaster Recovery, ICT Service Continuity, Risk Management or the Executive suite. By collating all impact studies within one central repository, responses can be tailored to fit the organization with a degree of confidence that is not apparent when utilizing disparate assessment practices.

Utilizing the Business Continuity Management Lifecycle approach, and empowering the Business Impact Analysis to consider the entire business functional chain and supporting factors will provide a common, qualitative statement of impact to the business operation or function over time. Making this BIA information available to other disciplines will provide a common assessment basis. Integrating the results of the BIA and risk assessments will provide the organization with a map of how any disruptive event will impact on the entire business ecosystem and how this impact will change over time. It will also highlight priorities within the chain of actions and the essential communication requirements necessary to retain confidence and credibility of the business during the entire event. These priorities are determined by the impact to current business operations over time taken to respond, react, recover and eventually resume business operations at the previous or an amended level or location.

Ensuring that the business continuity objectives are aligned with other disciplines' capability is a fundamental keystone for organizational resilience. All disciplines understand the strengths and weaknesses of the entire business operational process chain. An example is when the business continuity cycle is connected to the ICT readiness for business continuity as described previously in ISO 27031:2011. By default, this also ensures connection to the objective-setting process within the ICT Service Continuity, IT Disaster Recovery and IT Security Management programmes. Ensuring that the BIA also addresses the layers of the supply and distribution chain must also incorporate an assessment of environmental threats and the impact upon business operations and functions. This is broadly termed 'external issues' and it can be an exhausting exercise to apply the BIA process to every supplier and distribution outlet. Selection of the time-sensitive business functions and operations will allow for selection of those areas external to the organization.

Planning appropriate response entails integrating the Corporate Governance and Crisis Management Disciplines. This introduces the personnel layer for consideration. It is the management and leadership requirements that will ensure how a resilient organization responds to a disruptive event. Failures in planning for disruption to business operations can be mitigated by having effective leadership, personnel management and willing response teams. Failure to adequately address the people aspect will often negate the perfect operational response.

Extending this interchange of information with external service providers and suppliers unites the entire business ecosystem in deriving commonly agreed requirements, objectives and timescales on which the holistic recovery, restoration and resumption strategy can be constructed and maintained. This is illustrated in Figure 9.7.

Within this concept it is vital that all response and remedial activities are rehearsed so that the personnel involved are aware of their responsibilities to execute these activities but are also empowered to communicate when the situation demands change or modification to the process. It is also vital that part of the rehearsal involves substitution of personnel to ensure that vital knowledge of such activities is transferred before a disruptive event occurs.

In conclusion, using this approach by utilizing the full capabilities of the Business Continuity Management System provides any organization with a comprehensive pathway to achieving a measure of organizational resilience that is appropriate, comprehensive and viable.

FIGURE 9.7 Organizational resilience

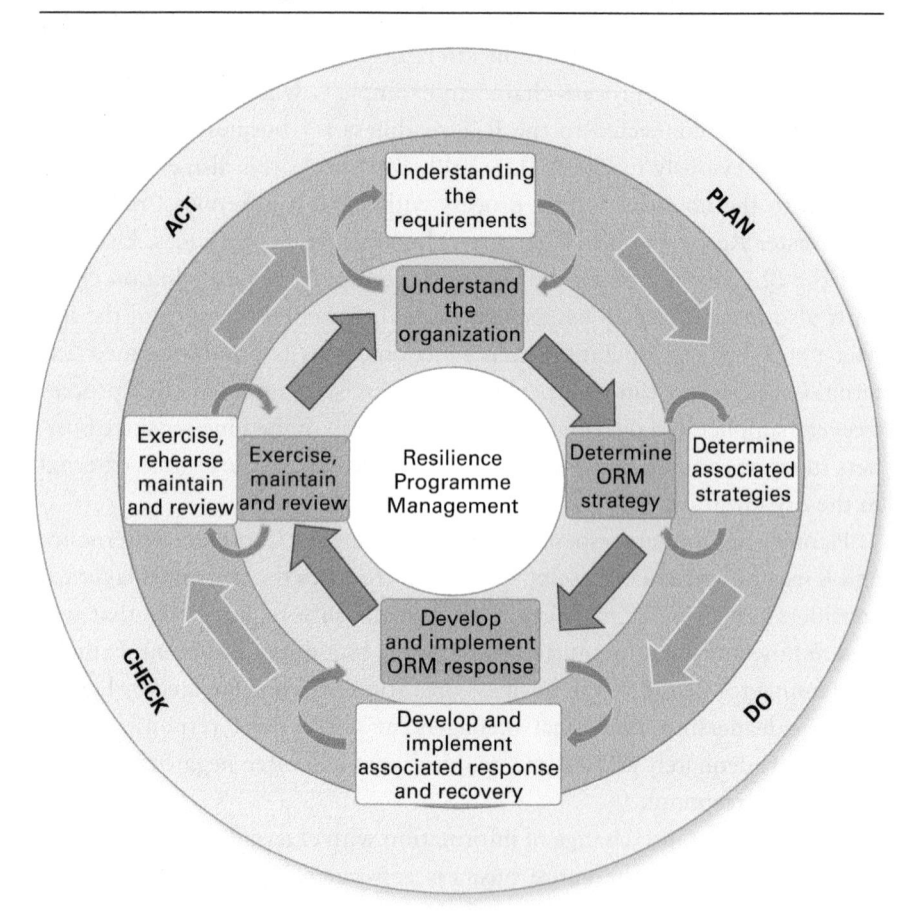

Find out more

ANSI SPC-1:2009, *Organizational Resilience: Security, preparedness and continuity management systems – requirements with guidance for use*, American National Standards Institute, New York, USA

BS 65000:2014, *Guidance on Organizational Resilience*, British Standards Institute, London, UK

The Business Continuity Institute (2013) *Good Practice Guidelines*, The Business Continuity Institute, London, UK

Davies, B (2015) Business leadership, *Resilient New Zealand* [online] http://resilientnewzealand.co.nz/business-leadership [accessed September 2015]

Graham, J and Kaye, D (2006) *A Risk Management Approach to Business Continuity Aligning Business Continuity with Corporate Governance*, Rothstein Associates, Connecticut, USA

ISO 22301:2012, *Societal Security: Business continuity management systems – specification*, International Standards Organization, Geneva, Switzerland

ISO 22313:2012, *Societal Resilience: Business continuity management systems – guidance*, International Standards Organization, Geneva, Switzerland

ISO 27031:2011, *Information Technology: Security techniques – guidelines for ICT readiness for business continuity*, International Standards Organization, Geneva, Switzerland

Managing stakeholder risk

10

DR LYNDA BOURNE AND PATRICK WEAVER

Why does stakeholder risk management matter?

People do work for the benefit of other people through projects, programmes or any other type of organizational work. Developing processes for managing risk must take into account the behaviours of the people involved or affected – stakeholders – and also consider the different elements that make each of these people unique. These elements can be categorized as culture, age, gender, personal 'reality' and inherent biases. Lack of attention to any one of these categories can accentuate risk and may lead to major issues or crises.

Theories of stakeholders have been constructed in terms of a relationship between an organization and its stakeholders. Freeman (1984) is credited with developing the seminal definition of stakeholders as:

> Any group or individual who can affect or is affected by the achievement of the organization's objectives.

Stakeholder theory has developed views of the importance of stakeholders and how stakeholder management or engagement can contribute to the success of organizational activities. Organizational wealth can be created (or destroyed) through relationships with its stakeholders.

In developing processes and practices for stakeholder management and engagement, successful risk managers understand how far key stakeholders will go to achieve, promote, or protect their stake, and adjust their behaviours accordingly. Equally important to an organization's success is understanding what it needs to do to ensure the best relationships between the organization, its activities and the contributions needed from key stakeholders for those activities to be successful. This includes recognizing the value of people's attitudes towards risk, and managing risk in an acceptable way, as a key component of building and maintaining relationships within the stakeholder community.

Who are stakeholders?

Stakeholders are defined as:

> Individuals or groups who will be impacted by, or can influence the success or failure of an organization's activities (Bourne, 2012).

Stakeholders that matter from a risk management perspective include those groups or individuals who:

- supply critical resources needed by the organization;
- place something of value at risk through their investment of funds, career or time in pursuit of the organization's business strategies or goals;
- oppose the organization or some aspect of its activities;
- are (or perceive that they are) negatively affected by a decision, action, strategy or process.

Threats can arise from situations such as:

- stakeholders' expectations not understood or not met;
- commitments to stakeholders not given or not honoured;
- decisions – purchasing, recruiting, design – made by individuals or groups that are not in the best interests of the organization or some stakeholders;
- people or other resources not managed appropriately;
- lack of risk ownership, and lack of will to plan, maintain and implement the appropriate risk responses;
- inadequate reviews of risk and stakeholders.

The stakeholder risk challenge is concerned with the complexities of dealing with people, their uniqueness and their behaviours (which generally cannot be predicted). Emergent behaviours can be extreme, driven by a combination of unidentified perceptions, miscommunication and the mismatch of risk tolerances. Stakeholder risk management is not about defining a set of processes to identify, categorize and respond to events; it is about managing the relationships between the organization, its activities and its stakeholders – the stakeholder community.

What is stakeholder risk management?

Effective risk management involves more than simply gathering data, assessing probability and impact, and applying actuarial calculations to define risk premiums or contingencies. Effectively managing stakeholder risk involves interacting with people's deepest needs for control, safety, and comfort (Rock and Cox, 2012). Stakeholders interact with risk management in three distinct ways:

1 A significant proportion of an organization's risks are directly caused by the action or inaction of stakeholders; in some circumstances this may be in excess of 90 per cent of the identified risks.
2 The perception of what is an acceptable or unacceptable risk is intrinsic to individual stakeholders and their attitudes – some people seek and enjoy risks, others are risk averse.
3 The identification, assessment and management of risks depend on the decisions and actions of stakeholders.

These factors affect perception of organizational success or failure. The perceptions are formed and held by stakeholders based on their personal experiences of the organization and its outcomes. In short, successful risk management requires effective stakeholder engagement. The stakeholder's perceptions of an organization's success or failure is intrinsically linked to effective stakeholder risk management.

What is risk in this context?

Risk is not rational

Perceptions, biases, attitudes and culture affect behaviours. It is these behaviours that create risks and influence reactions to perceived risks (opportunities and/or threats). The way people feel about risk is an amalgam of emotional reaction, learned experience and rational consideration: one person's idea of unacceptable threat may well be another person's opportunity to enjoy a thrill (think of bungee jumping).

Because the very concept of risk is tied to perceptions and emotions, attempts to manage risk as a pragmatic, rational process will lead to suboptimal outcomes. Rational processes are important to understanding the magnitude, probability and overall exposure of the organization to a risk, but they cannot specify which risks are acceptable to the stakeholders affected by the work. Neither can they indicate how others affected by the work will perceive the risk (usually threat) it exposes them to, and how they will react. In addition, the way the risk manager perceives and reacts to risk will be heavily influenced by her perceptions, biases, attitudes and culture.

Some stakeholders will attempt to avoid all risk, or pretend that certain risks do not exist. The result is a refusal to discuss or even consider the possibility of an uncertain outcome, significantly increasing risk or the consequences of the risk event occurring. There is no such thing as a risk-free activity.

Perception of risk – why does it matter?

Every person perceives risk differently. No one sees the world in exactly the same way as another person. The ability to understand another person's perceptions of risk is complicated by how an individual constructs her 'reality' and further complicated through her innate bias and other factors related to personality, culture and gender.

Each person constructs a different reality: each brain sees the world according to its own wiring, and thus selects or ignores information. Neuroscience has interpreted this process as the result of each person's brain automating much of what it perceives to ensure energy is conserved for conscious thought processes (Rock and Cox, 2012). Weick (1995) has termed the process 'sensemaking' – a filter through which everything experienced, consciously or unconsciously, is passed. Horowitz (2013) described this phenomenon of how we 'see', by describing what happened when she turned a daily 'walking around the block' with her dog into an exercise of perception. She invited people from different professions to walk with her and describe what they 'saw'. Each one of them drew her attention to different aspects of the same route she had walked many times before. Each person – psychiatrist, botanist, her 19-month-old son, an architect and eight others – 'saw' aspects of that block that she could never have imagined.

Over time every routine process tends to become an automated subconscious action or perception that frames the person's experiences of all new encounters. It also frames how we prefer to receive information and how we interpret that information. These factors affect people's perceptions of risk.

The same situation may spark a deep sense of concern in one person but be seen as normal by another, based on how the brain has retrieved information and edited observations.

The innate effect of personal characteristics on risk perception

It is not just an individual's 'reality' that affects risk behaviours; other characteristics that make each person unique will affect these behaviours and the manager's ability to interact with her.

Most people are innately optimistic, over-value their personal skills and capabilities and over-value the advice of distant experts compared to the advice from someone they know well. **Biases** that can affect people's reaction to risk (both threats and opportunities) include (Kahneman, 2011):

- Loss aversion means that most people are far more concerned about losing $100 than they are happy about gaining $100. People will try much harder to avoid a loss than to make a similar-sized gain. Given the choice of receiving a profit of $9,000 now or accepting a risk that has a 90 per cent chance of increasing the profit to $10,000 dollars, but a 10 per cent chance of receiving nothing, most people will take the $9,000.

- Hyperbolic discounting (or near-term bias) is the preference for short-term gratification over long-term benefits. Most people over-emphasize the value of short-term rewards over more substantial long-term benefits. The natural reaction is a strong bias towards not losing more money this month even if the short-term gain is far outweighed by the longer-term losses caused by an unwise *short-term focus*.

- Attentional bias: how an individual perceives and analyses a situation is affected by whatever is in her mind at that time: it is also called the *bandwagon effect*. It is the tendency to do (or believe) things because many other people also believe them: this shows in team decision making as *groupthink*.

- Optimism bias: the tendency to be over-optimistic, overestimating favourable and pleasing outcomes and playing down the less pleasing ones.

- Confirmation bias: a tendency to consider evidence that supports their position, hypothesis, beliefs or desires and to disregard or discount equally valid evidence that refutes them. For example, risk experts will be focusing more strongly on their knowledge of risk, or leadership experts on leadership theories.

Personality refers to an individual's genetically-based distinct pattern of thoughts, motives, values, attitudes and behaviours. It affects the way an individual reacts to the environment and how she prefers to receive information. **Culture** is an individual's patterns of thinking, feeling and acting learned over a lifetime, often in ways that she is not aware of. It is learned throughout childhood and continues into adult life through:

- language (particularly first language) and other symbols;
- role models and heroes such as parents, friends, celebrities;
- rituals such as recognizing 'coming of age', courtship, marriage;
- the individual's basic values.

Each cultural grouping exhibits a preferred style of communication, leadership, values and attitudes to work, and often attitude to risk.

Cultural diversity may take many forms, including:

- generational: a stakeholder community may consist of different generational groups: baby boomers, Gen X, Y;
- professional: managers, professionals (engineers, accountants, teachers), workers;
- national: consider a mix of Asian, Anglo-American and Latino cultures.

The social context we grow up in influences **gender** differences. There exists in every society a men's culture and a women's culture. In the more masculine culture found in the Anglo-American world, men are supposed to deal with facts, women with feelings (Hofstede, *et al.*, 2010). In this culture boys choose games that allow them to compete and excel, and girls choose games for the enjoyment of being together and for not being left out (Tannen, 2013). In more 'feminine' cultures, gender differences are more 'blurred'. In the Netherlands, for example, the research of Hofstede *et al.* (2010) found no significant differences in goals that children seek in playing games.

Tannen (2013) describes gender differences in conversation in the Anglo-American world as:

- 'Report talk' – the way that men communicate both formally and informally, transferring information to establish and maintain status that displays their abilities and knowledge.

- 'Rapport talk' – the way that women communicate both formally and informally to build and maintain connections, first validating the relationship to build rapport and then dealing with any business.

All these unique characteristics must be included in the mix of communication to foster effective stakeholder engagement and also in conversations with stakeholders about risk and how to manage it.

Communicating risk upwards

Understanding how best to communicate risk information and elicit cooperation and understanding from stakeholders is a major contribution to successful risk management. The other essential factor is credibility. Will I be taken seriously? Building credibility for successful management of stakeholder risk with senior stakeholders is a long-term undertaking. It requires work to develop a sense of trust and reliability.

What can the manager do to ensure that senior stakeholders are appropriately engaged and focused on doing whatever is necessary to help manage the risk in an environment of uncertainty and change?

There are three important rules for developing a strong supportive relationship with senior stakeholders – in particular with the sponsor:

1 Always communicate in business language: the sponsor may not know much about the discipline and language of risk management, and may not care. To brief the sponsor (or any other important senior stakeholder) efficiently it is necessary to provide information that is appropriate – concise, clear and in business terminology, NOT risk management terminology. Communicating in this way reduces barriers of mismatched language and creates a willingness to listen to what is being said.

2 If there are problems, offer recommendations – the sponsor (or any other senior stakeholder) does not want to be given more problems to deal with. The nature of the role of a senior manager is onerous and full of urgent issues. The best way to achieve the optimal result and also build credibility with the sponsor is to present an analysis of the problem, and some recommendations on how to solve it with information to help the sponsor make the right decision.

3 Make the sponsor, or any senior stakeholder, 'look good': this means NO SURPRISES, ever. Early warnings may also allow a senior stakeholder to act to manage or minimize the impact of the risk.

This approach will benefit all stakeholder risk management activities.

How is stakeholder risk managed?

The key challenge in stakeholder risk management is understanding who is important at any particular time and then allocating scarce resources to work with the people who matter, while maintaining a reasonable working relationship with everyone else.

This can be achieved through the application of any stakeholder management methodology. Listed here are the five steps of the *Stakeholder Circle* methodology (Bourne, 2012):

- Step 1: identification of all stakeholders.
- Step 2: prioritization to determine who is important.
- Step 3: visualization to understand the overall stakeholder community.
- Step 4: engagement through effective communications.
- Step 5: monitoring the effect of the engagement.

(The *Stakeholder Circle* software can be downloaded free of charge from: **http://www.stakeholdermapping.com/stakeholder-circle-methodology/**.)

Applying disciplined and consistent analysis of the stakeholder community – Stakeholder Analytics – is the key to efficient and effective stakeholder engagement. Analysing the stakeholder community will always involve a degree of subjectivity, but a stakeholder analytics approach can develop a set of normalized data to inform actions and decisions for developing robust relationships with the stakeholder community.

Identification

The first step in developing an effective stakeholder register is the identification of people, groups and organizations that can affect, or will be affected by the work, including those who merely perceive they will be affected (PMI, 2013). The process of stakeholder identification focuses on developing a complete list of stakeholders, their key attributes and the factors that drive the relationship.

Mutual interdependence between the organization and the stakeholder is the essential ingredient for the relationship. This is an assessment of what the stakeholder wants from the organization (expectations) and what the organization needs from the stakeholder.

- 'Stake' in the work: the stakeholder's stake may be financial, enhancement of reputation, protection or enhancement of rights or property owned by the stakeholder.

- Importance to the work: what does the project need from the stakeholder? This can be in the form of support, funding or resources.
- Requirement from the work: what does the stakeholder expect or require from the success or failure of the work?

Prioritization

The most effective way to assess the relative importance of stakeholders is to consider three factors:

- *Power* – can this stakeholder or group stop the work through withdrawal of funds or support, or is their ability to influence the work limited? Power is considered from perspective of the stakeholder's ability to impose changes and a rating applied.
- *Proximity* – is the stakeholder closely associated or relatively remote from the project? People involved in the work need more management attention than people remote from the work, such as executives.
- *Urgency* – what stake does the stakeholder have in the outcomes of the work, and what is this stakeholder prepared to do to achieve that stake?

Based on the factors of power, proximity and urgency an index can be calculated for each stakeholder. The index arranges the stakeholders in order of importance: the higher the index, the more important the stakeholder is at that time, and consequently, the higher the priority.

The process of prioritization deliberately ignores the level of support of the stakeholder and the risk profile; its purpose is to determine who is really important at the time of assessment. The next step is mapping the data so that informed decisions can be made about where to apply limited resources to achieve the most beneficial outcomes for both the stakeholders and the work being managed.

Engagement

Some stakeholders will be supportive of the work and be willing to assist, some will be unsupportive and many will simply ignore it. Three key steps record stakeholder attitudes to the work to assist in the development of effective communication strategies for building relationships:

Managing Stakeholder Risk

1. Assess the stakeholder's *current* attitude towards the work and any risks attendant on her involvement, and the risk she represents to the outcomes of the work (threats and opportunities). Attitude is a combination of the level of support for the work and the stakeholder's willingness to receive (and act on) information about the work. In Figure 10.1 this is shown in the series of 'X'.

2. Determine a realistic *target* attitude: what level of support and receptiveness to information about the work will optimize the chance of success? In Figure 10.1 this is shown as 'O'.

3. Devise a communication and risk management strategy – beyond the regular reporting cycle – to close the gap between the current and target stakeholder attitude, exploit the opportunities and mitigate the identified risks.

Attitudes can range from actively supportive of the work through to active opposition, and the stakeholder may be willing to engage in communication with the team or refuse to communicate (even if they support the work).

FIGURE 10.1 Monitoring stakeholder engagement – comparing results over time

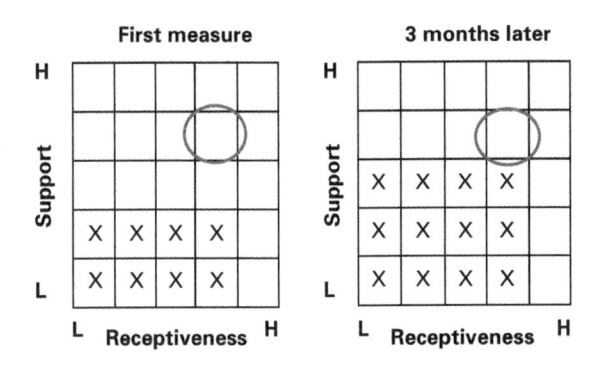

Monitoring the effect of engagement

The stakeholder in Figure 10.1 has been assessed at level (2) denoting a low level of support and at level (4) for a relatively high level of interest in information about the project. For project success, the engagement profile SHOULD BE (4) and (4). In this case, the gap between the current engagement profile and the target profile indicates that a high level of effort will be required to develop communication and stakeholder risk strategies for this stakeholder, to encourage a higher level of support for the work. The second assessment in Figure 10.1 reveals that some progress had been made, but more work is necessary to achieve the desired level of engagement. If there had been no change, it would have indicated that the stakeholder risk strategy has not been effective and that the strategy needs to be reviewed.

While the primary aim of this process is to mitigate threats and enhance opportunities through effective and directed stakeholder engagement, the process will also identify the residual risks that need managing in a more traditional way. These risk and issues should be transferred to the risk and issues registers for managing within the normal risk cycles of the organization.

The most cost-effective way to achieve a successful outcome for the work is to invest early effort to obtain the support from the stakeholder community. Most stakeholder-created risks are established by misaligned expectations and perceptions.

Identifying stakeholder risks

Every single stakeholder involved in, associated with, or affected by the work is a potential risk. It is never possible to know for certain how stakeholders will react in any particular circumstance. This generates uncertainty and, where uncertainty affects an objective of the work, a risk. The major challenge for effective stakeholder risk is deciding when an uncertainty becomes significant enough for inclusion in the risk register, or when to manage the uncertainty through normal stakeholder engagement processes.

Stakeholder engagement activities such as user consultation and community engagement are regular elements in a stakeholder engagement plan. These activities consume resources, take time and have cost consequences. Some stakeholder opposition to the change being created by the work is normal; but nothing is certain. Some of the decision points include:

- The uncertainties associated with consultation: the costs of effective engagement through consultation are far less than the costs of dealing with antagonistic stakeholders. However, if additional, unplanned consultation is necessary for an acceptable outcome it may affect the budget.

- There are always going to be stakeholders who do not respond to the engagement processes. At what point does the threat caused by important but unsupportive stakeholders become sufficiently important to become a specific risk in addition to remaining part of the ongoing stakeholder engagement initiatives?

Managing Stakeholder Risk

- A key stakeholder is replaced by a new person appointed to the role. Is this change immediately considered a risk or is it managed through an update to the communication plan and stakeholder engagement activities?
- A supportive stakeholder suddenly turns negative. There is clearly an issue to be managed but does this trigger a risk event as well?

There are no simple answers to these questions but there are a number of practices that can assist in the efficient management of the work. The starting point is using a robust stakeholder engagement methodology that has the capacity to identify and track stakeholder attitudes over an extended period. Monitoring the effectiveness of stakeholder communication and engagement processes generates usable data to feed into the assessment process: subjectivity needs to be minimized. The second key element is the recognition that people are unpredictable: for most stakeholders most of the time the best options to manage the consequences of this unpredictability are stakeholder communication and engagement.

The elements that feed into the risk management system include:

- A general contingency (cost and time) for additional stakeholder engagement activities beyond those allowed in the stakeholder engagement plan and communication management plan. These contingencies are released as needed and the drawdown monitored.
- Routine changes in the stakeholder community should be managed through updating the engagement and communication plans and strategy (in the same way schedules are routinely updated to accommodate changes in progress).
- Stakeholder risks are added into the risk register when the consequences of the specific change or condition meet the basic definition of a risk. That is, when the consequences of the uncertainty, if it occurs, will have **a significant effect on the achievement of an objective**. Determining what is significant is contextual and subjective. A good indicator of a risk warranting inclusion in the risk register is when the risk management plans involve **other actions** in addition to modifications in the stakeholder engagement and communication plans, and further actions such as the creation of specific contingencies or alterations to other plans or documents.
- Issues are realities, not probabilities, and should be managed through the issues management system. Given that virtually every issue involves one or more persons, the issues system should be an integral part of the ongoing stakeholder engagement work.

Determining when a situation has shifted from being simply 'business as usual' stakeholder engagement to a point where the risk management systems should be engaged is best done as part of a routine stakeholder review process. Ideally the stakeholder review should precede the routine risk review so that emerging risks can be transferred and processed in a timely way. However, as with any aspect of risk management, there will always be a few unexpected, emergent risks that need dealing with as soon as they are identified.

Reducing stakeholder risk

The effective management of stakeholder risk firstly requires a commitment by management and risk owners to make the effort needed to understand and manage the behaviours, expectations and risk tolerances of stakeholders supported by the development and use of effective stakeholder engagement processes.

Before developing any risk management plan or risk responses, the team must know who their stakeholders are, and how to engage them, involving important stakeholders, where possible, in decisions that affect them (Jeffrey, 2009, p 8):

> Stakeholders should be given the opportunity to comment and input to the development of decisions that affect them. In today's society, if they are not actively sought out, sooner or later they may demand to be consulted.

The value proposition for the effort involved in stakeholder engagement is derived from an understanding of the difference between crisis management (a result of inadequate or non-existing stakeholder risk management), stakeholder management and stakeholder engagement. Table 10.1 shows the main differences.

The four aspects in the table are as follows:

- *Stakeholder relationships*: Many organizations are realizing that building relationships with stakeholders is good risk management. If the relationship is strong through proactive or even interactive communication strategies, any issue that occurs can be resolved more effectively. When organizations react to crisis without a strong relationship with stakeholders it becomes difficult to resolve the crisis to the satisfaction of everyone involved.
- *Exposure to stakeholder issues*: Organizations are more exposed to issues or crises that arise through poor attention to stakeholder relationships. The stronger the relationship the less vulnerable the organization is to the impact of any issues or crises.

TABLE 10.1 Difference between crisis management, stakeholder management and stakeholder engagement

	Crisis management	Stakeholder management	Stakeholder engagement
Stakeholder relationships	Reactive	Proactive	Interactive
Exposure to stakeholder issues	Vulnerable	Anticipate	Encourage
Stakeholder involvement invited	Episodic	Regular	Inclusive
Organization/ project attitude to stakeholder involvement	Hostile	Defensive	Prepared to change

SOURCE: Adapted from Jeffrey (2009)

- *Stakeholder involvement invited*: The stronger the relationships between the organization and its stakeholders the more stakeholders are treated as partners, invited to participate in decision making and other organizational activities regularly.
- *Organization's attitude to stakeholder involvement*: When organizations move from a hostile or defensive approach to their stakeholders and recognize the need to embrace the involvement and ideas of their stakeholders, many of the sources of issues of loss of trust or reputation will reduce (or disappear).

How does stakeholder risk management fit?

The worlds of business and government are increasingly recognizing the vital importance of stakeholders in their work. Their outputs, goods and services are intended for use by stakeholders, their ability to create the goods and services is influenced by internal and external stakeholders, and the work is done by stakeholders (Freeman *et al.*, 2010).

Most advanced organizations have deployed various forms of Enterprise Resource Management (ERM) and/or Customer Relationship Management

(CRM). They have introduced programmes to support their Corporate Social Responsibility (CSR) and consultation management activities. Broader stakeholder management processes and systems and more traditional marketing, public relations (PR) and human resource management functions and processes enable effective stakeholder engagement. These developments are not simply altruistic; a consistent correlation can be demonstrated between organizational success and an organization's willingness to embrace corporate social responsibility in the broadest sense and engage effectively with its stakeholders (Bourne, 2015).

Paradoxically, the opportunity for success created by engaging with stakeholders increases the importance of understanding stakeholder risk management. This is in part because risks that remained largely hidden in the past, emerging as a sudden, unexpected crisis, can now be foreseen with a greater degree of reliability. The action of engaging with stakeholders requires the organization to open up to them and this creates vulnerabilities. The threats created by engaging with stakeholders are more than offset by the opportunities created by interaction with them, but both aspects form part of an effective stakeholder risk management system. A well-developed stakeholder risk management system should tap into the information flows in all of the other organizational systems. Where they interact with people (internal and external) they can make use of the capabilities of these systems to enhance opportunities and mitigate or avoid threats.

What's next?

With the growth of recognition of the importance of people to organizational success, it is likely that the use of stakeholder engagement and stakeholder risk management tools and processes will become as common in organizations as quality management tools and processes are today.

As the use of stakeholder management systems becomes established, meaningful data will become available that will allow stakeholder risk profiling to be used as an early warning indicator of probable success or failure for projects, product launches and other change initiatives. Some research is already taking place in this area (generally linked to the concept of 'big data').

Find out more

Bourne, L (2012) *Stakeholder Relationship Management: A maturity model for organisational implementation*, revised edn., Gower, Farnham, UK

Bourne, L (2015) *Making Projects Work: Effective stakeholder and communication management*, Young and Francis, Abingdon

Freeman, R (1984) *Strategic Management: A stakeholder approach*, Pitman Publishing, Boston, MA

Freeman, R, Harrison, J, Wicks, A, Parmar, B and deColle, S (2010) *Stakeholder Theory: The state of the Art*, Cambridge University Press, Cambridge

Hofstede, G, Hofstede, G J and Minkov, M (2010) *Cultures and Organizations, Software of the Mind: Intercultural cooperation and its importance for survival*, McGraw-Hill, New York

Horowitz, A (2013) *On Looking: About everything there is to see*, Simon & Schuster, London

Jeffrey, N (2009) Stakeholder engagement: A road map to meaningful engagement, *Cranfield University School of Management* [online] http://www.som.cranfield.ac.uk/som/dinamic-content/media/CR%20Stakeholder.pdf [accessed May 2015]

Kahneman, D (2011) *Thinking, Fast and Slow*, Penguin Books, London, UK

Kroeger, O and Thuesen, J (1988) *Type Talk: The 16 personality types that determine how we live, love, and work*, Dell Publishing, New York

PMI (2013) *A Guide to the Project Management Body of Knowledge (PMBOK Guide)* 5th edn., PMI, Newtown Square, Pennsylvania

Rock, D and Cox, C (2012) SCARF in 2012: updating the neuroscience of collaborating with others, *Neuroleadership Journal*, 4, pp 129–42

Tannen, D (2013) *You Just Don't Understand: Women and men in conversation*, Harvard Business Review, Boston, MA

Weick, K E (1995) *Sensemaking in Organizations*, Sage, Thousand Oaks, CA

Ethics in risk management

11

GIUSI MELONI

Why do ethics matter in risk management?

In her book *Willful Blindness*, Margaret Heffernan applies a fundamental legal principle (*ignorantia juris non excusat*, ignorance of the law is no excuse) to individuals, organizations and society at large in situations where relevant information was available but ignored. She writes:

> We make ourselves powerless when we choose not to know. But we give ourselves hope when we insist on looking. (…) As all wisdom does, seeing starts with simple questions: What could I know, should I know, that I don't know? Just what am I missing here? (Heffernan, 2011, p. 247)

These questions should be very familiar to risk managers whose job is to mine uncertainty and bring threats and opportunities to light, often struggling against the pervasiveness of wilful blindness.

The choice between remaining in the dark or actively seeking information, between knowing and not knowing, is a complex, mostly unconscious, mechanism, constrained by cognitive limits, emotional and relational filters, as well as personal values and cultural influences. Fear of conflict or change and the desire to demonstrate competence and control are some powerful examples of 'blinders' we experience every day. Other examples are money and/or ambition. What we commonly call 'risk attitudes' are the sum of all these and other elements.

Another significant element guiding our decisions when facing the unknown is trust. A well-known definition of trust reads: 'reliance on and confidence in the truth, worth, reliability of a person or thing' (*Collins Dictionary*) but what we normally mean by trust could be better defined as knowledge-based trust, which usually builds up over time, and is achieved when individuals have enough information and understanding to predict another person's behaviour.

Another type of trust is often at play in our life, however, particularly when time and/or knowledge is limited. Called swift trust, it is based more on social structures and actions rather than personal relationships, and its importance became evident when empirical observation, and later studies, showed that teams with a high level of swift trust consistently perform better than others.

A detailed study (Robert *et al.*, 2009) proved that the two types of trust represent two different processes and, quite naturally, are formed at different stages of a relationship. Swift trust is developed quickly, mostly on 'first impressions'. It is at work in all those situations when we don't have or cannot acquire enough knowledge and we must simply trust another person, or organization, their competence, their honesty, their reliability. Very often the less we know, the more we must trust.

In temporary endeavours such as projects and programmes – and indeed in any activity with tight time constraints – swift trust plays a crucial role for both leadership and risk management. Effective risk management requires the active involvement and commitment of various stakeholders towards the success of a project and organization. Trust, or the absence of it, becomes particularly evident when risk managers must guide their teams and other stakeholders to face uncertainty, to recognize their fears and/or their hopes and ultimately make an informed decision. Value-based leadership is particularly conducive to trust, as it builds consensus on basic values and consolidates the relationship between leader and follower at the highest level. Values connect our identity to our conduct and support our decisions: this relationship is the base of what we perceive as credibility and the heart of leading by example.

In his book *Tame, Messy and Wicked Risk Leadership,* Dr David Hancock introduces the concept of risk leadership:

> The more we stare at the jumble of equations and models, the more we lose sight of what risk is all about. Knowing how risk management works is just the beginning. Knowing how and when to use these tools is the art of risk management (Hancock, 2010, p. 35).

Risk leadership focuses on relationships with stakeholders and on helping them to understand uncertainty. Dr Hancock identifies several practical applications of risk leadership and refers in particular to 'applying concepts and frameworks which focus on risk management as value creation, whilst aware that "value" and "benefit" will have multiple meanings linked to different purposes for the organization, project and individual' (Hancock, 2010, p. 88).

If we take the meaning of 'value creation' in a broader sense, risk leadership is strongly linked to identifying and upholding shared values. Awareness that 'values' have different meanings acknowledges the possibility of ethical dilemmas.

We face ethical dilemmas when values conflict or we cannot apply an overriding and shared ethical framework. Often there is no right answer to the dilemma and both results could be argued and supported as good for the parties involved.

Examples of ethical dilemmas abound in temporary endeavours such as projects and programmes, when their innovative nature coupled with the pressure to deliver might easily influence the choice between short-term gains and the long-term good. Often after a project blunder, people ask themselves, 'should we have known?' and the question acquires a dramatic connotation when the consequences have a social and/or environmental impact.

Dr Hancock defines ethical dilemmas as 'wicked mess' (characterized by complex level of behavioural and system interaction) and writes:

> These problems require leaders whose networks extend beyond traditional confines and who can overcome silo problems within their organizations – someone who can influence groups of diverse stakeholders towards a common goal and influence others to see the value of a particular course of action, who understands the sources of power used by stakeholders but chooses not to use it themselves (Hancock, 2010, p. 71).

This is the domain where leadership, ethics and risk management meet in order to face a common challenge: to connect value-based leadership with risk management best practices.

If we consider ethics as 'primarily a communal, collective enterprise' (Ciulla, 2004, p. 28), leading by example and trust are the main tools a risk manager can use to address ethical dilemmas and uncover ethical risks alongside other threats and opportunities. Even if the dual nature of risk is now more widely recognized, in practice the amount of attention devoted to threats still exceeds that given to opportunities and it is important to note here that ethical risks are not necessarily negative. Speaking openly about ethical dilemmas will contribute to create the necessary conditions where stakeholders can express their fears but also their hopes and their values, without making them feel exposed or weak, or like an impractical dreamer.

A structured approach to ethics in risk management will provide risk managers not only with a deeper and broader understanding of the project, it will also help them to generate and sustain trust among stakeholders, assert and consolidate their leadership role and, last but not least, embrace organizational and societal benefits.

What is ethical risk management?

The word 'ethics' comes from ancient Greek 'ethos' meaning habit, custom, or character. Often used interchangeably with morals, ethics refers to the distinction between right and wrong and it transcends culture, religion, and time. On the other hand, morals are based on the distinction between right and wrong made by a specific culture and/or religion. As both terms denote knowledge of right and wrong, the distinction is often blurred but it is important to remember that the foundations of that knowledge are different.

Another important distinction is between ethics and professional conduct or professionalism. Professionalism is conduct consistent with the tenets of a specific profession, usually established in a Code of Ethics or a Code of Conduct, where the Code of Ethics governs decision making and the Code of Conduct governs behaviour.

An increasing number of organizations worldwide require their employees to adhere to a Code of Ethics and/or Conduct, as well as professional associations which require their members and certification holders to adhere to a Code of Ethics and/or Professional Conduct. While membership is optional, adherence to the Code is mandatory and internal procedures and disciplinary processes are in place.

Furthermore, leading-edge organizations have recognized the need for providing guidance to solve ethical dilemmas and have condensed the critical elements of their codes into a sequenced 'ethical decision-making model', or 'framework', that guides the decision maker through a series of steps that direct members to making the best choice possible. The practical ethical decision-making framework is closely linked to the values and codes of the organization, uses a language familiar to members of the organization, and can be illustrated with examples of situations commonly encountered in the practice of their professions. Although no code or ethical decision-making framework (EDMF) can definitively resolve most specific ethical dilemmas, a good code and EDMF can help clarify the situation, eliminate poor choices, and shine a light on better possibilities.

A good example of current practice in this area is the Project Management Institute (PMI) which has developed an EDMF to help project management practitioners and credential holders when they are faced with ethical dilemmas. A companion to the PMI Code of Ethics and Professional Conduct, the PMI EDMF places critical thinking at the heart of solving an ethical dilemma. As such, it helps to frame problems, clarify goals, examine assumptions and options, unearth hidden values, evaluate evidence, and assess conclusions.

> Since the PMI EDMF is intended to be used as a guide for critical thinking throughout the ethical decision-making process, it is represented as a sequence of questions and sub-questions to stimulate the user, beginning with the recognition and assessment of the issue, and ending with a decision and action. Critical to the successful use of the PMI EDMF is the recognition that the answers to the questions raised are the responsibility of the user. The PMI EDMF can also be effectively used at the end of a decision-making process, when a decision is about to be made, to reflectively look back to see if the important steps have been taken and if the important considerations have been made.
>
> Although the PMI EDMF is presented as a logical linear sequence of steps, it is understood that its users will likely find it useful to loop back and forth between steps. Since the PMI EDMF is not entirely prescriptive and does not include every possible step or question useful for making an ethical decision, users are encouraged to be stimulated by it to challenge themselves with additional steps and questions (PMI, 2013a).

Having thus defined ethics and its general application in the project management profession and practice, rather than a definition, we propose a working approach to ethics in risk management. Based on the ISO 31000:2009 standard which defines risk management as referring to 'the architecture (principles, framework and process) for managing risks effectively' we propose including ethics and value-based leadership among the principles guiding risk management best practices.

This approach will take ethical risk management a step beyond the current literature, which focuses mainly on tools and strategies to manage the ethical dimension of illegal actions and their impact on organizations. While these are certainly significant aspects for both business ethics and risk management, we find that limiting ethics to threats and to an Enterprise Risk Management perspective would not answer the needs of risk managers who find themselves faced with ethical dilemmas or need to guide stakeholders in identifying and assessing the ethical impact of both threats and opportunities. Furthermore, this approach will enable us, in Dr Hancock's words, 'to establish a common purpose which is arguably becoming much more of a strategic necessity in these turbulent times' (Hancock, 2010, p. 50).

What is risk in this context?

We define ethical risk as 'an uncertain event or condition that presents an ethical dilemma and, if it occurs, requires an evaluation in terms of right (ethical) or wrong (unethical).'

This definition purposely broadens the common concept of ethical risk as the unexpected negative consequences of unethical actions.

In 2006, Shawn L Berman and Kirk O Hanson presented the draft of an 'ethics assessment tool' usually referred to as the Santa Clara Alternative (the name was taken from Santa Clara University where they both worked). The tool was developed as a response to the increasing need for organizations to 'determine where ethical risks lie and either eliminate the source or mitigate the risk before it reaches headline proportions' (Federwisch, 2006).

The Santa Clara Alternative (or Tool) combined and expanded the two existing measures of the ethical dimension: the G4 Guidelines of Global Reporting Initiative (GRI) and the Ethics Quick Test of the Ethics Resource Center (ERC). While the G4 Guidelines mainly concentrate on the past, the Ethics Quick Test focuses on various areas of an organization's commitment to ethics (ie values, strategies, goals, objectives, policies and procedures). It does not, however, take into account the individual factor.

The Santa Clara Alternative, on the other hand, aims to be a preventive tool and focuses specifically on ranking risks that might relate to ethics. It includes two processes and two tools:

1 a questionnaire listing 'risk factor' and a qualitative scale to rate the answers;

2 a matrix combining the rating and the importance of each risk factor to obtain the 'Total Risk and Weighted Risk'.

The choice of words in the Santa Clara Alternative differs from common risk management terminology but we can make some easy parallels.

Risk factors are comparable to risk sources and the Santa Clara Tool takes into consideration and assesses three different sources of risk:

- the Industry;
- the Company (structure or strategy, ethics system and culture); and
- the Individual.

For each source of risk, the model provides a set of questions and sub-questions and a predefined scale (1 to 10) to assess the 'level of risk' to each risk factor (source). The level of risk is comparable to the risk probability of occurrence.

The scales used to rank the level of risk appear to be based on the assumption that the more complex and diverse the system, the higher the level of risk is, or, in other words, ethical risks are more likely to occur in complex and diverse systems. Many of the questions also seem focused on conflict of interest. Although this may appear limited, it is important to remember that conflict of interest is specifically mentioned in the Code of Conduct of several professional associations, including those of the Association for Project Management (APM) and the Project Management Institute (PMI). In particular the PMI Code of Ethics and Professional Conduct states that conflict of interest is:

> one of the most challenging (subjects) faced by our profession. One of the biggest problems practitioners report is not recognizing when we have conflicting loyalties and recognizing when we are inadvertently placing ourselves or others in a conflict-of-interest situation. We as practitioners must proactively search for potential conflicts and help each other by highlighting each other's potential conflicts of interest and insisting that they be resolved (PMI, 2006, p. 5).

The next step in the Santa Clara Tool is 'Measuring Total Risk and Weighted Risk'. These two terms might cause some confusion to risk managers for whom 'Weighted Risk' and 'Total Risk' have a different meaning. In the Santa Clara Alternative, total and weighted risk concur to determine the current Ethical Risk Profile of an organization. In the intent of Berman and Hanson the Ethical Risk Profile will help the organization to minimize negative risks by lowering ethical risks that can be controlled and creating effective countermeasures to risks that cannot be avoided. The Ethical Risk Profile needs to be re-evaluated frequently and in particular when new strategies, structures, policies, etc. are implemented.

Somewhat similar to the typical Probability-Impact Matrix or heatmap used to prioritize risks, the tool used to assess the Ethical Risk Profile is a matrix where each risk factor (source) is rated in terms of level (probability) and importance, where importance can be equated to impact. The importance of each risk factor is analysed with the same scale of 1 to 10. The sum of the level (probability) of all risk factors and the sum of the importance (impact) of all risk factors are called Total Risk. Weighted Risk, on the other hand, refers to Level Rating x Importance Ranking.

Although at the moment the Santa Clara Alternative is only available in an initial and certainly perfectible draft, its structured approach and the questionnaire are certainly worth consideration when dealing with ethical risks in projects.

While the matrix proposed by the Santa Clara Alternative to identify the Ethical Risk Profile would not be an efficient substitute for existing qualitative analysis tools, the sources of ethical risks (risk factors) documented using the Santa Clara Questionnaire could be easily integrated into risk management processes. They might be efficiently used to identify risks which are often acquiescently left in the shade and to categorize them by common root causes. These applications are discussed further below.

How is ethical risk managed?

We have seen that in the current literature the general tendency is to address ethical risk in order to gauge the ethical health of the organization's culture, to identify potential legal problems, to prevent fraud and to preserve the organization's reputation. Our approach aims to prove that ethics can and must be embedded in risk management best practices.

Our starting point is the Santa Clara Alternative Questionnaire. The following tables (Tables 11.1 to 11.3) show the most relevant questions of the questionnaire for each source of risk (Industry, Company and Individual) and the ranking scale. The slides with the complete questionnaire can be downloaded from the website of the Markkula Center for Applied Ethics at the Santa Clara University, CA: **http://www.scu.edu/ethics/practicing/focusareas/business/risk.html**.

TABLE 11.1 The Santa Clara Alternative – The industry

Question	Ranking (1–10 scale)
1. How intense is competition?	More = Higher Risk
2. How differentiated is the product?	Less = Higher Risk
3. How important are a few large customers?	More = Higher Risk
4. How closely regulated is the industry?	More = Higher Risk
5. How involved is organized crime in the industry?	More = Higher Risk

TABLE 11.2 The Santa Clara Alternative – The company

Question	Ranking (1–10 scale)
1. How hierarchical is the company?	More = Higher Risk
2. How independent are the company divisions?	More = Higher Risk
3. How much business does the company do in problematic countries?	More = Higher Risk
4. Does the company have a code of conduct?	Yes = Less Risk
5. Does the company have an effective mechanism for employees to raise questions on difficult ethical choices?	Yes = Less Risk
6. Does the company ever punish senior executives for unethical conduct?	Yes = Less Risk
7. How transparent is the company leadership about decision making?	Less = Higher Risk

TABLE 11.3 The Santa Clara Alternative – The individual

Question	Ranking (1–10 scale)
1. Does the company's ethics programme credibly emphasize that ethics is every employee's business?	Yes = Less Risk
2. Does the company's ethics programme seek to develop employee skills in identifying and reasoning about ethical issues?	Yes = Less Risk
3. Does the company seek to rein in arrogance and hubris and encourage humility and openness in its leaders?	Yes = Less Risk
4. How decisive is the company in dealing with ethical violations which arise?	More = Less Risk
5. How effective is the employee assistance programme in helping employees with personal or financial problems?	More = Less Risk

The questions presented here are those which might more easily be applied to the project environment, and they might be further adapted and/or serve as probing questions during brainstorming sessions and/or as a checklist to identify risks.

Many of the questions are of a highly sensitive nature and require a dedicated and shielded mental and physical space to be properly addressed and answered. But so do many other topics connected with risks and uncertainty: the fact of addressing ethical issues openly itself may help to break the wall of hesitancy and silence that often surrounds both risks and ethical dilemmas, thus facilitating more candid and valuable risk identification and assessment.

Furthermore, ethical risks imply that various stakeholders might have widely differing views on what could be an acceptable solution. As Dr Hancock points out, 'one of the most powerful elements of risk management is the dialogue that occurs during risk meetings' (Hancock, 2010 p. 76). It is a dialogue that must continue throughout all risk management processes, and that requires common values to be established through listening skills, trust and most of all the alignment and positive example of the Risk Manager.

In their *Harvard Business Review* blog article, John H 'Jack' Zenger and Joseph Folkman share data collected from 5,268 leaders in five different organizations, showing that 'leaders the next level down tend to be rated lower than their managers on every leadership dimension – and that includes their honesty and integrity. In other words, levels of honesty are set at the top and can only go downhill from there' (Zenger and Folkman, 2012). The lessons learned from this research point to the need for an active role towards ethics, challenging assumptions and deliberately communicating expectations regarding ethics, honesty and integrity: leaders 'should put stronger structures in place to require and enforce the level of integrity they want to protect and assume is in place. They should take a good look at their own integrity and honesty standards and consider how well those standards are communicated and made evident to their teams' (Zenger and Folkman, 2012).

Examples of ethical leadership will foster trust and thus reduce fears, minimize the feeling of vulnerability, and, in general, lower the level of stress that might be caused by facing the uncertainty. Value-based leadership will be recognized even if positive examples and opportunities are not always emphasized or even mentioned.

In risk management, this silent assumption, coupled with the negative bias (the greater sensitivity of the human brain to negative inputs), still plays a significant role and leads to a focus on threats, rather than using a balanced approach towards negative and positive risks. However, because of its value-laden nature, the process of defining an ethical dilemma often overlaps with the search for a solution: each attempt to resolve it will not only raise stakeholders' awareness but also change their understanding of the ethical issue itself and introduce a new perspective equally open towards right (ethical/opportunities) or wrong (unethical/threats) solutions.

How does ethical risk management fit?

In this chapter we have made a case for managing ethical risks at project level. An even stronger case can be made for ethics to be an integral part of Enterprise Risk Management.

Reputation – an irreplaceable asset in any organization – may be defined as a function of perceived ethicalness combined with performance, and has become, in The Economist Intelligence Unit's words, 'the risk of risks': events that can damage or increase a company's reputation are recognized as today's most significant business challenges.

Furthermore, current studies and research repeatedly show that 'ethics pays'. Although it might not be true for every industry, in the long run ethical companies generally outperform less scrupulous ones. Consumer orientation is also moving towards ethics to the point that the *Wall Street Journal* has defined ethics as 'a wise investment'. Changes in the legal and regulatory environment also show a global trend towards more transparent and ethical business operations.

Most interestingly, the trend appears to no longer be a protectionist choice but rather an attempt to achieve better business advantage through improved operations and management.

What's next?

Technologies are quickly changing our world, reshaping the way we think about knowledge, relations, organizations and individuals. At the heart of change is uncertainty and risk management, whose boundaries are now less defined than in the past.

New holistic models, integrating ethics into ERM, are emerging with the aim of managing ethics and risk and helping organizations to create and maintain a strong ethical corporate and organization culture. The fulcrum of the virtuous ethics cycle is and will remain leading by example: managers, supervisors and executives will always be the most important critical success factor in ethics management.

During a seminar in 2003, Peter Drucker was asked about Corporate Ethics and he replied:

> There is no such thing as 'Business Ethics', there is only Ethics. Confucian ethics has six types of relationships. Western ethics is simpler – don't do unto others what you wouldn't want done to yourself. The higher the monkey goes up in the tree, the more of his behind you see. There is the Mirror test – when you look in the mirror, is it something you want to see? Do you want to see a story about what you did on the front page of the *New York Times*? In this day and age, there is nothing you can do to keep it a secret.

The profile of risk managers will continue to move towards Risk Leadership and from there to Ethical Leadership.

> Leadership is a particular type of human relationship. Some hallmarks of this relationship are power and/or influence, vision, obligation, and responsibility. By understanding the ethics of this relationship, we gain a better understanding of leadership, because some of the central issues in ethics are also the central issues of leadership. They include the personal challenges of authenticity, self-interest, and self-discipline, and moral obligations related to justice, duty, competence, and the greatest good (Ciulla, 2003, p. 302).

Ethics, balance and personal alignment are among the meta-competences that risk managers will increasingly need to master, integrating quantitative and numerical-based models with a sounder behavioural approach. By meta-competence we mean the ability to read a new situation and adapt/apply appropriate competences. Therefore a meta-competence can be applied only when other competences are already set and can be used to create a logical connection between them. Usually meta-competences are considered higher-order abilities which have to do with being able to learn, adapt, anticipate and deal with uncertainty and incomplete evidence, asking the right questions, and developing the means to resolve problems. Among the most common meta-competences we find such skills as 'learning to learn' or 'thinking outside the box'.

Awareness will increasingly become another important meta-competence. Awareness can be defined as a continuous mental process which results in gaining specific knowledge. Thus 'being aware' becomes central to the concept of a 'comfort zone'. A personal comfort zone is defined by what an individual actually knows, as well as by his/her general mental boundaries, for instance risk appetite and/or beliefs and values. When an individual is in his/her comfort zone, they experience a neutral state, free from anxiety, but which might however turn into inertia or force them to stay within a limited outlook. It should not become a constrained space but a springboard for our curiosity, whose specific function is to encourage us to explore, learn and grow, expanding our knowledge, experiences and skills.

In other words, hindsight is precise but powerless; it is foresight that permanent and temporary forms of organization will need more and more, and it will be the job of risk managers to tackle wilful blindness in all its forms.

> Foresight is the 'lead' that the leader has. Once leaders lose this lead and events start to force their hand, they are leaders by name only. They are not leading but they are reacting to immediate events, and they probably will not long be leaders. There are abundant current examples of loss of leadership that stems from a failure to see what reasonably could have been foreseen and from failure to act on that knowledge while the leader had freedom to act' (Greenleaf, 1977, p. 150).

Find out more

Ciulla, J B (2004) *Ethics: The heart of leadership*, Praeger Publishers, Westport, CT

Drucker, P (2003) What are the result of measuring corporate performance, *Project Auditors LLC* [online] http://www.projectauditors.com/Papers/Whitepprs/Drucker092703.pdf

Federwisch, A (2006) Ethical risk assessment: crisis-prone or crisis-prepared, *Makkula Center of Applied Ethics* [online] http://www.scu.edu/ethics/practicing/focusareas/business/risk.html

Greenleaf, R K (1977) *Servant Leadership*, Paulist Press, Mahwah, NJ

Hancock, D (2010) *Tame, Messy and Wicked Risk Leadership*, Gower, London, UK

Heffernan, M (2011) *Willful Blindness*, Bloomsbury, New York

ISO 31000:2009, Risk management: principles and guidelines [online] http://www.iso.org/iso/home/store/catalogue_tc/catalogue_detail.htm?csnumber=43170

Project Management Institute (2006) *PMI Code of Ethics and Professional Conduct*, PMI, Newtown Square, PA

Project Management Institute (2013a) *PMI Ethical Decision-making Framework*, PMI, Newtown Square, PA

Project Management Institute (2013b) *A Guide to the Project Management Body of Knowledge (PMBOK Guide)* 5th edn, PMI, Newtown Square, PA

Project Management Institute (2014) *The Leader in the Mirror: Trust, risks and dilemmas in project leadership*, Proceedings of the PMI EMEA Global Congress 2014, PMI, Newtown Square, PA

Robert, L P , Dennis, A R and Hung, Y C (2012) Individual swift trust and knowledge-based trust in face-to-face and virtual team members, *Journal of Management Information Systems* **26** (2), pp 241–79

Zenger, J and Folkman, J (2012) The data's in: honesty really does start at the top (blog) *HBR* [online] http://blogs.hbr.org/2012/06/the-datas-in-honesty-really-do/

Acknowledgement

Some of the material in this chapter was originally written by the author for the PMI Ethics Member Advisory Group and published in the proceedings of the PMI EMEA Global Congress 2014 (see Project Management Institute, 2014). PMI has given permission for the content to be used in this way.

Cyber risk management

12

BEN RENDLE

Why does cyber risk management matter?

It is estimated that by 2020, 30 billion wireless devices will be connected, supporting a global digital services market worth as much as the entire UK economy. In 1984, the Internet consisted of 1,000 computers hardwired together, but its rapid growth, along with mobile connectivity and computing capabilities is creating a continually renewing global digital landscape – roughly 90 per cent of the data in the world was created in the last two years. The change is happening so quickly that we cannot see more than a few years into the future. We can anticipate, however, that most of us will soon be connected to the Internet everywhere we go, all of the time.

This growth has in turn developed new cyber opportunities and cyber risks which frequently outstrip the ability of businesses, organizations and individuals to anticipate and effectively adapt. In practice, this means that the online activities of these three groups can blur (see Figure 12.1 as a high-level example).

For individuals, the cyber opportunities are vast and they can open up new ways of communicating through online social media, entertaining through online gaming, learning from online courses and even careers through upskilling to desirable IT jobs. This in turn leads to subsequent advantages for not-for-profit organizations to benefit society and businesses with more highly skilled and competitive workforces. However, individuals may also suffer the adverse impacts of cyber risks and fall victim to cyber bullying, online grooming, personal scams and online thefts and malware attacks. If left unchecked and unmitigated, these can impact on an individual's performance and productivity in their organizations and businesses.

Cyber Risk Management

FIGURE 12.1 Example of blurring online activities between individuals, organizations and businesses

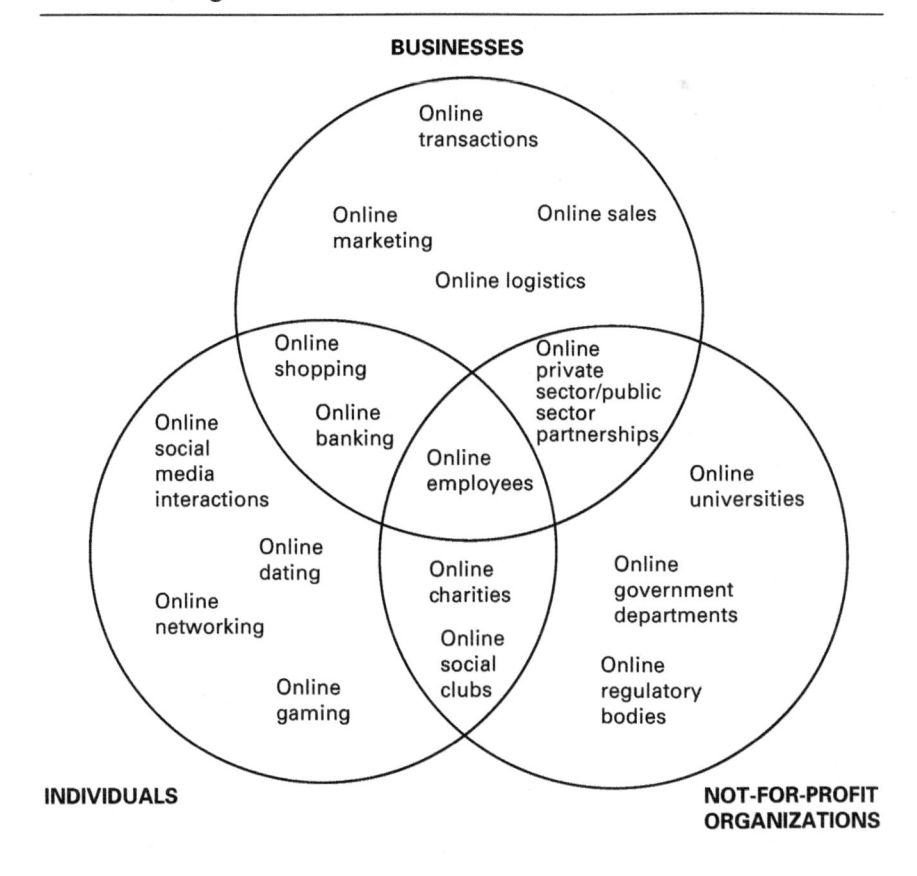

BUSINESSES

- Online transactions
- Online marketing
- Online sales
- Online logistics
- Online shopping
- Online private sector/public sector partnerships
- Online social media interactions
- Online banking
- Online employees
- Online universities
- Online dating
- Online charities
- Online government departments
- Online networking
- Online social clubs
- Online regulatory bodies
- Online gaming

INDIVIDUALS   **NOT-FOR-PROFIT ORGANIZATIONS**

For not-for-profit organizations such as charities, universities, public sector departments and government, cyber opportunities can include new ways to research more efficiently, communicate information and awareness to a wider audience, collect donations and tax revenue more easily and become more cost effective in the way they operate. On the flip side, the cyber risks for organizations can include vulnerabilities to online customer data and intellectual property theft, and subsequent legal and regulatory impacts. This in turn may result in not-for-profit organizations having to react and invest in costly IT security measures, often without the scale or depth of resources available to businesses.

For businesses, the ability to exploit cyber opportunities through online and digital initiatives can significantly increase their productivity, profitability, branding and competitiveness. This may turn into a virtuous circle – highly skilled IT professionals may want to work for them, and prestigious universities may want to conduct research for them. Alternatively, cyber risks for businesses can have huge impacts, especially for businesses that operate solely or largely online. The number of online security breaches has increased, and the scale and cost of these breaches nearly doubled in the year 2014–2015. Nearly 9 out of 10 large organizations surveyed have now suffered some form of security breach, such as distributed denial of service (DDOS) attacks which can bring down their websites – suggesting that these incidents are now a near certainty. It is interesting to note that these cyber risks are as relevant to small businesses as they are to large ones, and, without the resources and resilience of large businesses, they may suffer disproportionately.

Managing cyber opportunities and risks to businesses, organizations and individuals matters because they are increasingly reliant (in some cases, completely reliant) on online or automated services and infrastructure. Moreover, it is common for other individuals, not-for-profit organizations and businesses to expect that cyber opportunities and risks are being managed effectively. Individuals will want reassurance that a website is genuine and up to date. Boards of directors will want to see the measures being put in place to address a not-for-profit organization's online activities. Insurance companies will want to see the cyber risk management processes in place for businesses before they offer more competitive cover. However, in all these cases, it is not just a case of providing a one-off investment in firewalls and anti-virus software. As technology advances apace, so do the opportunities and risks. A control measure that may have been effective a year ago may now prove to be a vulnerability. There is a growing demand that individuals, not-for-profit organizations and businesses need to regularly review their management of cyber risks and treat them seriously.

Mismanagement of cyber opportunities and risks may result in:

- loss of adaptability to the evolving digital landscape resulting in increased operating inefficiencies and overheads, leading to a subsequent loss of knowledge, productivity, competitiveness and prosperity;
- suboptimal and limited control of the availability, confidentiality and integrity of online assets (data, finances, intellectual property);
- a restricted ability to protect, influence and enhance an online image, brand and reputation;
- a growing inability to demonstrate compliance with online and digital legal and regulatory requirements to regulators, investors, employees, customers, partners and lenders.

Traditionally, managing cyber risks and opportunities may have been seen as purely a technology problem and the preserve of IT specialists. There is now an increasing expectation that businesses, organizations and individuals are able to deal with their cyber opportunities and risks as part of an Enterprise Risk Management framework.

What is cyber risk management?

One of the challenges of cyber opportunity and risk management has been to define itself. The *Oxford English Dictionary* defines 'cyber' as 'relating to or characteristic of the culture of computers, information technology, and virtual reality'. Cyber risk management shares many common elements with other similar and related disciplines (eg IT security management, information management, data and privacy management) but it should also fit into an Enterprise Risk Management framework within an organization to be truly effective.

There are many special challenges for cyber risk management when compared to other risk management areas. These are included in Table 12.1.

TABLE 12.1 Unique types of cyber risks

Cyber Risk Challenge	Description
The speed at which online and digital objectives change	New and groundbreaking technologies are emerging all the time across the world, and they are having profound impacts on the way that businesses operate. With this in mind, it is becoming impractical and uncompetitive for many businesses to be locked into five- or ten-year strategies.
	Many now define strategic objectives as where they want to be in three years' time or less. This means that risk practitioners cannot assume static and stable online objectives and must be prepared to adapt accordingly at a faster pace than most other risk areas.

(Continued)

TABLE 12.1 (Continued)

Cyber Risk Challenge	Description
The enhanced way to communicate with both internal and external stakeholders	The ability for a business to connect in an immediate and personal way to employees, customers, third-party suppliers and others through e-mails, websites and social media creates vast opportunities and risks at the same time. Communicating the right message in the right way can win significant new business and boost the business reputation and brand to a global customer audience. Communicating the wrong message in the wrong way can lead to serious reputational damage, legal and financial consequences, demotivated staff and loss of business. It is also worth bearing in mind for organizations that once a misguided message is sent out online, they may lose control of the message and it may not be possible to take it back or delete it. In conjunction with Human Resource departments, risk practitioners can manage these cyber opportunities and risks through developing a clear and comprehensive social media policy and providing effective training for employees. They should also handle online customer feedback and complaints carefully and actively monitor their own online presence and perception by others.
The trade-offs between opportunities and risks for employee-led or organization-led technologies	Many employees now use their own IT devices for work purposes (eg working from home) or use work IT systems for social or personal reasons (eg downloading articles of interest or purchasing goods online). Whilst this provides opportunities for businesses to be flexible, incorporate new and different types of technology and improve employee morale, this also can introduce cyber risks for organizational security.

(Continued)

TABLE 12.1 *(Continued)*

Cyber Risk Challenge	Description
	Research has found that over 90 per cent of respondents said that their organizations allowed the use of personal mobile devices for business use, but only 37 per cent exercised any controls in relation to the configuration and security of these devices (Dimensional Research, 2014). Risk managers will need to be creative to find a balance between what the user wants and what the organization needs.
Difficulties estimating the probabilities and impacts of cyber opportunities and risks	Online activities and threats to businesses and not-for-profit organizations often have a high degree of uncertainty over how and when they might take place. There is usually limited relevant data or case studies to compare due to the under-reporting of incidents and unawareness in wider industry. Subsequently, this would make more conventional forms of quantitative risk analysis (eg cost risk analysis) ineffectual, as this limited cyber data may not lend itself to meaningful quantitative modelling. Estimating the probability of 'Black Swan' cyber risks is very difficult for businesses as their impact can be very high and yet they are nearly impossible to predict or rationalize in terms of probability (Taleb, 2007). The cyber risks may not be identified or they may be downplayed (eg senior managers being overconfident in their IT security culture and making untested assumptions that a highly damaging extortion attack would never happen to their business).

(Continued)

TABLE 12.1 *(Continued)*

Cyber Risk Challenge	Description
Managing the organizational culture and attitudes around cyber opportunities and risks	With little or no facts available about how cyber opportunities and risks may affect their business, the way employees subsequently estimate and perceive them is often based on personal views and convictions.
	This can lead to a varied and polarized culture within organizations on how they operate online, with some stakeholders being indifferent to or taking high-levels of risk online which could damage an organization's reputation, whilst others may be risk adverse online, which could reduce productivity and competitiveness.

What is risk in this context?

Before discussing cyber risks, it also is worth noting the different types of cyber opportunities available for businesses, individuals and not-for-profit organizations. Risk is linked to reward – and with cyber opportunities, the rewards can be huge and can often justify the trade-off against cyber risks.

Individuals, businesses and not-for-profit organizations may encounter many types of 'cyber risks', which the Institute of Risk Management defines as 'any risk of financial loss, disruption or damage to the reputation of an organization from some sort of failure of its information technology systems.' The root causes behind these risks can be technology-led, process-led or human-based, and can be deliberate, unintentional or accidental. Businesses and organizations must subsequently identify, assess and manage these new cyber risks.

Examples of these new cyber opportunities and cyber risks are included in Table 12.2.

TABLE 12.2 New cyber opportunities and risks

Cyber Opportunities	Cyber Risks
Instant access to a global audience to communicate and share information, ideas and business products and services in a direct, personal and highly cost-effective way.	Cyber bullying and extortion (also called 'online bullying'), when the Internet, e-mail, online games or any other kind of digital technology is used to threaten, tease, upset or humiliate another party.
Creation and dissemination of a vast upsurge of data and information that was previously unavailable about ourselves, our environments and surroundings and wider topics of interest.	Uploading and disseminating indecent or upsetting material online (eg 'revenge' pornography or offensive imagery).
New capabilities which can automatically connect, update, adjust, process, analyse and exploit this data at a scale and speed far beyond the capacity of human resources.	Malware, viruses, and distributed denial of service (DDOS) attacks.
The increased ability for businesses, organizations and individuals to harness this exploited data to obtain new knowledge, enhance their reputation and make better choices as a result.	Cybercriminal activities, including online fraud, espionage and theft of identity, money, data or intellectual property.
The expansion in levels of innovation, skills and jobs for businesses, organizations and individuals that cyber capabilities presents, leading in turn to increased prosperity.	Online reputational damage and corporate liability resulting from misuse of online social networks, hostile external stakeholders (eg pressure groups) and hostile internal stakeholders (also called 'insider threats').
New markets (eg online gaming, online education) and ways to expand 'traditional' markets (eg extending paper-based retail store catalogues to an online website) for businesses, leading in turn to increased prosperity.	Cyber terrorist attacks (eg large-scale online telecommunications infrastructure disruption).

According to the Institute of Risk Management (IRM, 2014), the threat actors behind these cyber risks tend to cover five broad areas: *activists, cyber-criminals, hostile spies, insider threats*, and *poor IT systems* within businesses and organizations. Although distinct and separate areas, they are often closely related to each other (see Figure 12.2 below).

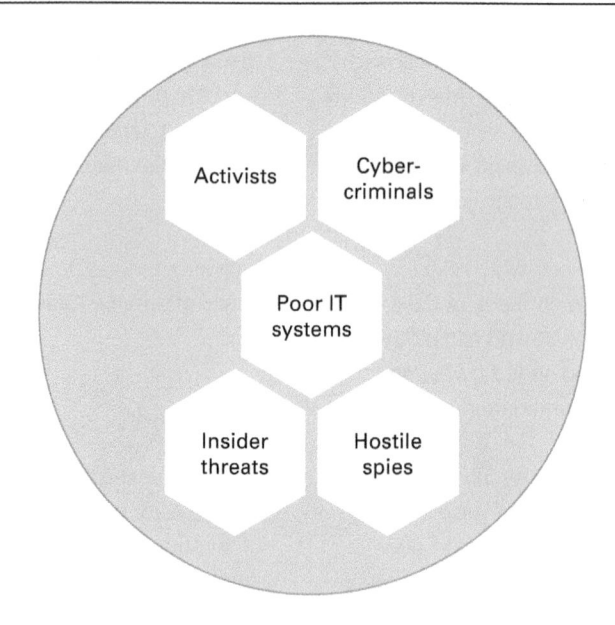

FIGURE 12.2 Close relationship between threat actors

- *Activists* (sometimes known as 'hacktivists') are often motivated by political viewpoints or beliefs, recognition and credibility from their peers, or simple curiosity. They can operate alone on basic IT systems at home or be part of a more sophisticated organized group (eg WikiLeaks). They usually are not motivated by financial gain.
- On the other hand, *cyber-criminals* are motivated by financial gain, and can be very well-organized and targeted in their approach by identifying businesses and not-for-profit organizations with high levels of online presence, customer data and financial trading. They often have more resources and more sophisticated techniques at their disposal than activists, and can be harder to detect and respond to.

- *Hostile spies* are funded and controlled by their governments with significant resources and skillsets at their disposal. Whilst they can cause all types of cyber risks, they are often motivated to steal intellectual property from businesses and not-for-profit organizations, to cause significant disruption by cyber warfare and damage to critical national infrastructure, or to illegally gain increased competitive advantage for their home nations.

- *Insider threats* come in many forms and are often hard to detect. They can vary from deliberately malicious staff who are disgruntled and wish to cause harm, staff who have good intentions but go against company rules through being manipulated or using workarounds and short cuts, staff who are ignorant or sceptical of cyber threats, or staff who simply commit errors online. It is important to note that addressing cyber risks through technology alone (eg patching and firewalls) is unlikely to mitigate this type of threat effectively.

- *Poor IT systems* within business and not-for-profit organizations can often be a cause of cyber risks, as they may be ineffective in their design, maintenance and support, leading to outdated software and infrastructure with significant vulnerabilities that all of the threat actors above can exploit. This is especially true if the IT systems are merged into another organization or are provided from outsourced third-party suppliers from overseas states with weak regulation and governance controls.

How is cyber risk managed?

Unless businesses and not-for-profit organizations completely dispose of online technology, it is very difficult and expensive to eliminate all the cyber risks in their risk portfolio. Indeed, given the increased levels of sophistication and evolving techniques of these threat actors, it could be argued that businesses and not-for-profit organizations should prepare and invest just as much for cyber incident responses as for preventative measures.

In addition to obtaining cost-effective insurance against cyber incidents where possible, the UK government guide on 10 Steps to Cyber Security (CESG, 2015) identified the following basic control areas that will address 85 per cent of all potential breaches for businesses and not-for-profit organizations:

- user education and awareness;
- home and mobile working;
- incident management;
- information risk management regime;
- managing user privileges;
- removable media controls;
- monitoring;
- secure configuration;
- malware protection;
- network security.

Organizations should also ensure that they:

- implement effective supply chain controls;
- develop clear policies for the business use of cloud services;
- develop clear policies for the use of social media.

For cyber risk managers, businesses and not-for-profit organizations should pay particular attention to the following techniques for managing cyber risks.

Developing a clear understanding of objectives for tackling cyber opportunities and risks

Many businesses and organizations may be unaware of their objectives, the trade-offs associated with their objectives, and what they are trying to protect. For example, some organizations may not be aware of valuable intellectual property that they hold, and how it might be stolen and exploited. Others may not be aware of different cyber risk areas, and may think that phishing and malware are the only online risks they face. As part of understanding the objectives for tackling cyber opportunities and risks, businesses and organizations may have to understand what their online assets are (ie what online factors really create value economically in the marketplace and how critical that value is to their continued success and prosperity) and then establish how attractive, and in what ways, those online assets are to cyber threat actors (eg would a cyber threat actor employ extortion or customer data theft to attack the organization?).

Agreeing a robust response to address cyber opportunities and risks, especially when they impact

Once these objectives and online assets are determined, responses for tackling the associated cyber opportunities and risks need to be clarified, agreed and communicated. However, a clear plan to respond to cyber opportunities and risks with SMART (specific, measurable, achievable, realistic and time-bound) objectives may not be in place, or may not have senior management endorsement. If this is the case, then the effectiveness of the responses in tackling cyber opportunities and risks will diminish. Whilst it may not be possible to know all the benefits and threats that cyber opportunities and risks present (unless these responses are clearly understood, defined, endorsed and communicated), then it is difficult to determine whether the impact and exposure organizations have to cyber risks will reduce. For nearly all businesses and not-for-profit organizations, it is inevitable that at some stage a breach of some type will occur. With this in mind, it is critical that an effective and pragmatic incident response procedure is in place to minimize adverse impacts (reputational and customer-focused) when this breach occurs.

Greater awareness of 'cost-effective' cyber opportunity and risk decisions

Many organizations may be investing in cyber opportunity and risk responses which are neither cost effective nor addressing the risk causes properly. For instance, investing in an expensive internal IT security upgrade is of limited use if an organization's sensitive data is held by an outsourced third-party company operating overseas with little or no regulation or governance. Chapman and Ward (2002, p. 239) state that 'a key source of uncertainty in most decision contexts relates to the identification of performance criteria together with relative priorities and trade-offs'. They identify a pure risk investment decision as having three interrelated decisions: how much it is worth spending to reduce a risk, to what extent it is worth reducing a risk, and which responses provide the most cost-effective solution. Once this takes place, a 'risk-efficient' decision can take place, where decisions at a point in time involve the minimum level of risk for any given expected level of performance. Unless these decisions and related trade-offs are made from an informed and well-thought-through process, then the impacts of cyber risks and their mitigation costs will be greater than they need to be.

An acknowledgement that there is no 'one size fits all' approach

Within the marketplace, there are different cyber risk profiles and risk appetites for different stakeholders. For example, a UK online gaming organization is likely to face a different set of cyber risks (such as extortion or online theft) than a US government department holding sensitive information (which may risk data or intellectual property theft). The risk appetite (defined as the amount of risk one is prepared to accept) of the UK online gaming organization may be high, and could recognize cyber threats as part of the trading environment. Conversely, the US government department may be highly risk averse, as it is sensitive to reputation damage. Therefore, understanding the environment and risk appetite of different stakeholders is key to determining the impact of cyber risks. By recognizing these different risk profiles and appetites for different stakeholders and industry sectors, risk management can be prioritized by focusing on the risks that can cause the most harm, and scarce resources can be allocated more effectively.

Recognition that cultural factors, not just IT factors, play a critical role in managing cyber risks

Traditionally, several technical ways have been identified for managing cyber risks (eg firewalls, encryption) and insurance considerations (eg privacy breaches) but often at the expense of cultural factors, such as board-level awareness and support, training and ownership. This suggests an overemphasis on technical solutions at the expense of cultural issues, which are arguably even more important in addressing cyber opportunities and risks. For instance, applying IT security policies and technical solutions within an organization will be of little use if employees are unaware of them, circumvent them or ignore them. Moreover, if an organization fosters cultural barriers to managing cyber risks (e.g 'senior management don't have time for this', 'cybercrime will never happen to us', 'this is just hype'), then the impact of cyber risks is likely to increase as they will be left unchecked (see Figure 12.3 opposite as an indicative high-level example). Therefore, understanding and managing cyber risk attitudes amongst stakeholders (eg managing motivations, translating attitudes into desired outcomes and understanding perceptions behind the attitudes) is critical.

Cyber Risk Management 207

FIGURE 12.3 Example of cyber risk perceptions

FATALISTS

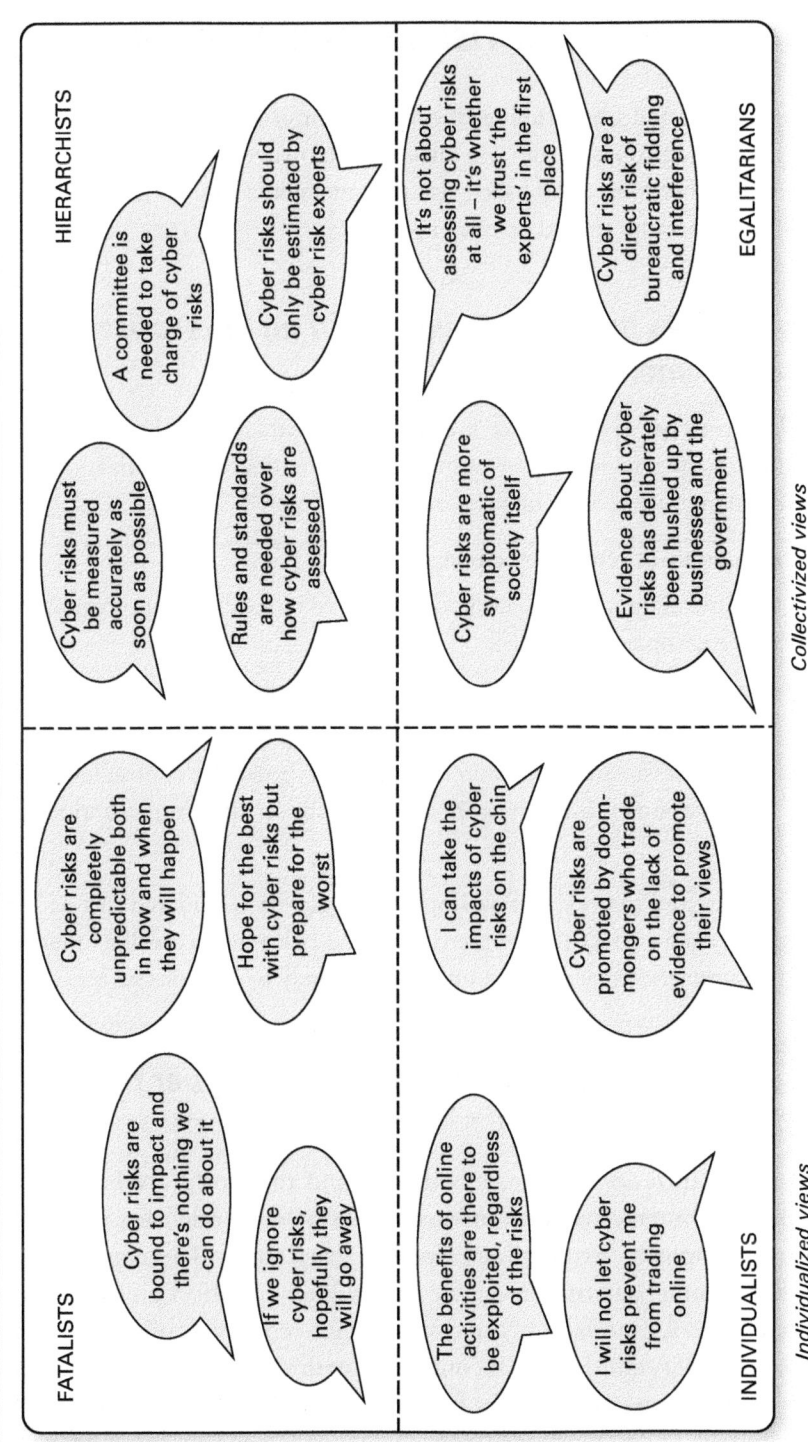

- Cyber risks are bound to impact and there's nothing we can do about it
- If we ignore cyber risks, hopefully they will go away
- Cyber risks are completely unpredictable both in how and when they will happen
- Hope for the best with cyber risks but prepare for the worst

HIERARCHISTS

- A committee is needed to take charge of cyber risks
- Cyber risks should only be estimated by cyber risk experts
- Cyber risks must be measured accurately as soon as possible
- Rules and standards are needed over how cyber risks are assessed

EGALITARIANS

- It's not about assessing cyber risks at all – it's whether we trust 'the experts' in the first place
- Cyber risks are a direct risk of bureaucratic fiddling and interference
- Cyber risks are more symptomatic of society itself
- Evidence about cyber risks has deliberately been hushed up by businesses and the government

INDIVIDUALISTS

- I can take the impacts of cyber risks on the chin
- Cyber risks are promoted by doom-mongers who trade on the lack of evidence to promote their views
- The benefits of online activities are there to be exploited, regardless of the risks
- I will not let cyber risks prevent me from trading online

Low levels of perceived control / High levels of perceived control

Individualized views / Collectivized views

How does cyber risk management fit?

Cyber risks and opportunities introduce unique benefits and challenges to individuals, businesses and organizations. However, they also augment and amplify other more established risk management areas. To manage this, the following factors should be put in place.

Cyber risks are considered within an Enterprise Risk Management framework

Whilst a cyber risk may have a direct cost, time or performance impact linked to a particular online event, it may also affect an organization from a wider perspective. Such impacts could include:

- significant reputation damage;
- cultural impacts (lowering of employee morale, a talent exodus from the company);
- business continuity and disaster recovery implications (recovering a compromised website within critical timeframes);
- a reassessment of outsourced third-party provider contractual obligations (how they store and transmit sensitive organizational data).

It is suggested that cyber risk impacts should be considered in relation to how they may affect these other enterprise risk areas as well as their individual impacts, as cumulative impacts are likely to be more severe.

A wider perspective is developed over cyber risk impacts

Most organizations and economies around the world are becoming increasingly interactive with and dependent on each other for trade, third-party suppliers, exports and wealth generation. Therefore, overseas cyber-criminal activities are increasingly likely to affect global economic stakeholders, especially in the cases of joint economic collaboration with other nations, multinational companies with several global bases, or outsourced third-party providers based overseas. These impacts will be more accurately understood and managed when placed in the context of a global stage.

Wider non-economic and social cyber risk impacts are assessed

As more cyber risks impact on legitimate organizations and economic activity, new risks with no direct financial impact may start to emerge. For instance, individuals may perceive the risk of online trading or banking as too high and cease online economic activity. Organizations may scale back their online presence (thus becoming potentially less competitive) or actually be encouraged to use cyber-criminal methods covertly to gain competitive advantage (thus exacerbating the problem). Furthermore, the increasing influence and wealth of cyber-criminals gained from economic stakeholders is likely to lead to non-financial risks impacting on individuals. For example, cyber-criminals may re-invest the profits of their activities in other illegal activities which do not have a direct financial impact (such as drug smuggling, human trafficking and terrorism). Not only will these risks impact the global economy from a revenue perspective (through less income generated from taxation) but they will also impact from a social perspective (through loss of jobs as companies close down and loss of disposable income through online theft).

A greater emphasis is given to cyber opportunity management

To date, the focus on cyber risk management has largely been on negative risk impacts rather than any opportunities that can be gained. For example, complying with online legal and regulatory requirements may present an opportunity for stakeholders to brand themselves as proactively dealing with cyber-criminal threats, therefore making their business a more attractive location to conduct online trading. Further opportunities could present themselves for organizations in gaining a reputation for cutting-edge good industry practice in responding to cyber-crime. A greater awareness of cyber risks and impacts also introduces opportunities for organizations to make themselves more attractive to their online customers. For instance, if a German organization is aware that some customers are more likely to be impacted by identity theft, then they can offer targeted advice and increased security to mitigate that specific risk. Employee awareness and skill sets can be significantly improved in reacting to cyber-criminal risks, which makes them more valuable assets to their organizations. This, in turn, makes organizations more attractive to their customers compared with the competition and provides them with a market advantage.

If cyber risk management is customer-driven as well as internally driven, then customers are more likely to award big contracts to those organizations that can offer understanding, reassurance and effective responses around cyber risks that specifically matter to them. As an example, a government department holding sensitive data may be more likely to give business to an organization that recognizes and can respond to risks associated with online customer data theft than ones that cannot. If the positive impacts of cyber risk management to organizations are determined, then they can use this as a competitive advantage and exploit the benefits it provides.

What's next?

As noted earlier, online and digital hot topics and objectives change at a rapid pace for businesses and not-for-profit organizations. The challenge in predicting what's next is that it may become outdated very shortly. However, the current emerging trends at the time of writing are as follows.

An increased and diversified use of online social media

This allows people to create, share or exchange information, ideas, and pictures/videos online in virtual communities and networks. This generates many benefits for organizations, facilitating communication internally with staff through corporate discussion boards and externally with customers and recruitment candidates through well-recognized social media tools such as Facebook or Twitter. Organizations can have instantaneous dialogue and rapport with these internal and external stakeholders, and subsequently build their knowledge, skills, brands and awareness of how they are being perceived. These benefits have to be assessed against the risks that social media generates, including the potential for staff and customers to be victims of cyber bullying and harassment, for inappropriate or offensive material to be accidentally or maliciously uploaded onto corporate platforms, and for potentially increased social engineering opportunities for stakeholders hostile to the organization.

The Internet of Things

This is described as 'connecting devices over the Internet, letting them talk to us, applications, and each other' (Kobie, 2015). Some of these devices are known as smart devices which can be controlled online by a remote end user, regardless of where that user is. As an example, a smart meter device could allow a user online in a Tokyo hotel to reduce his electricity consumption at his house in Ireland or a smart fridge to automatically order groceries online if it detects that a user has run out of stock. The opportunities are significant in that it can allow users and businesses to be far more mobile, efficient and informed in how they operate on a day-to-day basis. It is estimated that the number of smart or embedded devices is expected to increase to 50 billion by 2020. However, there are significant risks also associated with smart devices, with cyber-criminals potentially being able to hack into them and either obtain personal information or take remote control of them. For critical systems to users (eg electricity for emergency services and heating for homes in cold climates), the impacts of these risks could be loss of life.

IT consumerization

Many businesses and organizations now allow their employees to bring personally owned mobile devices (laptops, tablets and smartphones) to their workplace, and to use those devices to access privileged company information and applications. This brings many opportunities, including lowered costs for businesses to buy and maintain mobile devices, the convenience for employees to use one device which is familiar to them for both business and personal use, and the increased flexibility and agility of having the latest apps downloaded on these devices. In the IRM (Institute of Risk Management) cyber security survey (IRM, 2014), over 90 per cent of respondents said their organizations allowed the use of mobile devices for business use. Interestingly, this may be out of recognition that banning them would be pointless – through creative means, users will eventually use their own devices anyway regardless of whether the organization approves of this or not. Conversely, the business or organization may sacrifice their ability to manage and control these mobile devices as effectively as standardized IT devices, and users may not have the same security culture around their own devices when compared to organizational devices (eg neglecting to download the latest anti-virus software or using more 'work arounds' on their devices).

Cloud computing

This is defined by the US Department of Commerce's National Institute of Standards and Technology (NIST) as 'a model for enabling ubiquitous, convenient, on-demand network access to a shared pool of configurable computing resources (eg networks, servers, storage, applications, and services) that can be rapidly provisioned and released with minimal management effort or service provider interaction.' It has been compared to an online version of a water utility company – instead of drawing water from your own personal well, a water utility company will store, manage and provide the water to your house more efficiently and effectively. This creates many opportunities for businesses, including lowered IT infrastructure costs, the ability to store, process and analyse 'big data' sets more effectively, and the ability to transfer IT risks (eg security vulnerabilities and disaster recovery of data) to outsourced Cloud providers. On the other hand, organizations lose the direct control they have over their IT infrastructure should a risk impact their Cloud provider, both in terms of how it may perform (if the Cloud provider goes down, they may not be able to continue operating online) and how secure it may be (if the Cloud provider is hacked, they may not be able to react in the way they would like).

Find out more

Accenture (2015) Digital business era: stretch your boundaries [online] http://techtrends.accenture.com/us-en/downloads/Accenture_Technology_Vision_2015.pdf [accessed 26 July 2015]

Allsopp, W (2009) *Unauthorised Access: Physical penetration testing for IT security teams*, Wiley, Chichester

Cabinet Office (2011) The UK cyber security strategy: protecting and promoting the UK in a digital world [online] https://www.gov.uk/government/uploads/system/uploads/attachment_data/file/60961/uk-cyber-security-strategy-final.pdf [accessed 26 July 2015]

Center for Strategic and International Studies (2013) The economic impact of cyber crime and cyber espionage [online] http://www.mcafee.com/us/resources/reports/rp-economic-impact-cybercrime.pdf [accessed 26 July 2015]

CESG (2010) Good practice guide: online social networking [online http://www.cpni.gov.uk/Documents/Publications/2010/2010032-GPG_Online_social_networking.pdf [accessed 26 July 2015]

CESG (2015) 10 steps: a board level responsibility [online]https://www.gov.uk/government/publications/cyber-risk-management-a-board-level-responsibility [accessed 26 July 2015]

Chapman, C B and Ward, S C (2002) *Managing Project Risk and Uncertainty*, Wiley, Chichester

CISCO (2011) The Internet of Things: how the next evolution of the internet is changing everything [online] https://www.cisco.com/web/about/ac79/docs/innov/IoT_IBSG_0411FINAL.pdf [accessed 26 July 2015]

Department for Business, Innovation and Skills (2014) Cyber-security: balancing risk and reward with confidence [online] https://www.gov.uk/government/publications/cyber-security-balancing-risk-and-reward-with-confidence [accessed 26 July 2015]

Department for Business, Innovation and Skills (2015) 2015 information security breaches survey [online] http://www.pwc.co.uk/assets/pdf/2015-isbs-executive-summary-02.pdf [accessed 26 July 2015]

Dimensional Research (2014) The impact of mobile devices on information security: a survey of IT and security professionals, *Check Point* [online] https://www.checkpoint.com/downloads/product-related/report/check-point-capsule-2014-mobile-security-survey-report.pdf

Hadnagy, C (2011) *Social Engineering: The art of human hacking*, Wiley, Indianapolis

Harkins, M (2012) *Managing Risk and Information Security: Protect to enable*, Apress, New York

Hillson, D and Murray-Webster, R (2007) *Understanding and Managing Risk Attitude*, 2nd edn, Gower Publishing, Aldershot

Innovate UK (2015) Digital Economy Strategy 2015–2018 [online] https://www.gov.uk/government/uploads/system/uploads/attachment_data/file/404743/Digital_Economy_Strategy_2015-18_Web_Final2.pdf [accessed 26 July 2015]

Institute of Risk Management (2014) Cyber Risk [online] https://www.theirm.org/media/883443/Final_IRM_Cyber-Risk_Exec-Summ_A5_low-res.pdf [accessed 26 July 2015]

Jackson, J, Allum, N and Gaskell, G (2004) Perceptions of risk in cyberspace [online] http://www.academia.edu/217670/Perceptions_of_Risk_in_Cyber_Space [accessed 26 July 2015]

Kobie, N (2015) What is the Internet of Things? *Guardian* [online] http://www.theguardian.com/technology/2015/may/06/what-is-the-internet-of-things-google

Mitnick, K D and Simon, W L (2006) *The Art of Intrusion*, Wiley, Indianapolis

National Institute of Standards and Technology (2011) The NIST definition of cloud computing [online] http://nvlpubs.nist.gov/nistpubs/Legacy/SP/nistspecialpublication800-145.pdf [accessed 26 July 2015]

Oxford Economics (2014) Cyber attacks: effects on UK companies [online] http://www.cpni.gov.uk/documents/publications/2014/oxford-economics-cyber-effects-uk-companies.pdf?epslanguage=en-gb [accessed 26 July 2015]

Philpott, D R and Gantz, S (2012) *FISMA and the Risk Management Framework: The new practice of federal cyber security*, Syngress Media, Boston

Schneier, B (2000) *Secrets & Lies: Digital security in a networked world*, Wiley, New York

Singer, P W and Friedman, A (2014) *Cybersecurity and Cyberwar: What everyone needs to know*, Oxford University Press, New York

Taleb, N N (2007) *The Black Swan: The impact of the highly improbable*, Random House and Penguin, New York

PART TWO
Emerging trends

DR DAVID HILLSON

Chapter 1 launched our exploration of multidimensional risk management by outlining the basics of the topic, developing a first-principles definition of risk and a generic framework for the risk management process. These risk concepts formed the foundation on which subsequent Part One chapters could build, since every type of risk management is based on the same underlying idea of the nature of risk and how it can be managed.

We used the image of a prism to explain how the 'pure white' perspective of risk and its management could be split into a number of different dimensions, each derived from the original source, but every one having its own distinctive characteristics. The chapters in Part One describe a range of risk management dimensions, with each chapter covering the same ground for one of the risk management application areas, namely:

- the unique risk challenge addressed by this particular type of risk management;
- the key features of this form of risk management and how it differs from 'generic' risk management;
- the way that risk is specifically defined and understood in the particular context of this type of risk management, including any unique or specialized language, typical sources of risk, types of impact, common responses;
- the typical 'best-practice' risk management process in this area, including a process framework and commonly-used techniques;
- how risk management in this area interfaces with other business processes, with other types of risk management, and with enterprise-wide risk management (ERM);

- 'hot topics', current developments and future directions which are expected to occur in this area in the short/medium term (3–5 years);
- key references and recommended reading to find out more about this type of risk management.

Having described the main types of risk management in Part One, you might think that our exploration of the multiple dimensions of risk management is complete. However, returning to our image of pure white light passing through a prism, a different perspective emerges.

Those who can think back to their schooldays may know a simple way to remember the colours of the spectrum into which white light is split by a prism. The mnemonic 'Richard Of York Gave Battle In Vain' has helped countless children (and adults) to recall the fact that white light is refracted into seven main colours: Red, Orange, Yellow, Green, Blue, Indigo and Violet. These are of course also the colours of the rainbow. Each colour represents part of the visible light spectrum within a range of wavelengths, from red (630–700 nm) to violet (400–450 nm).

The truth of course is that light exists on a continuous spectrum, and the division of the visible portion of the spectrum into seven bands of colour is rather arbitrary, deriving from Isaac Newton's philosophy of the world (which regarded seven as a significant number: days in the week, notes in the musical scale, known objects in the solar system, etc.). The human eye can apparently distinguish up to 10 million different colours, and this is reflected in more modern versions of the spectrum (including the Munsell colour system).

Pursuing the analogy into our discussion of multidimensional risk management, we might expect that alongside the main types of risk management described in Part One, there could also be less well-known application areas to be discovered. And so it proves, with new types of risk management emerging for our consideration.

In Part Two we explore some of those developing trends in risk management, including some that are already becoming established and may soon enter into the mainstream, and other more novel application areas. While there are doubtless more niche areas of risk management that could be included, here we consider the following:

- country risk management;
- communicating uncertainty;
- risk-based decision making;

- risk leadership in complex organizations;
- resilience;
- organizational change management and risk;
- risk culture;
- social media risk;
- risk in development aid practice.

Including these emerging trends offers a richer understanding of the nature of risk management than is possible from examining only the main dimensions. Even this picture is incomplete of course, as there are many other risk perspectives that could have been included. But each of these new areas offers a unique risk-based perspective on the uncertain world we face, and each deserves consideration by anyone wanting to see the full picture.

Country risk management

DANIEL WAGNER

The ability to effectively manage country risk used to be considered something an international business may not need or could not afford, but the risk management landscape has experienced a transformation since the new century began. In our multidimensional, constantly changing and leaderless world, traders, investors and lenders no longer have the luxury of assuming everything will work out, or maintaining the mistaken belief that the horror stories that have happened to other organizations will not happen to them.

Conventional wisdom used to dictate that because everyone else is investing in a given country, it must be the right place to invest, the idea being that strength lay in numbers, and, surely, not everyone could be wrong. Yet, the 'herd' mentality and chasing the 'hot dollar' has got many companies into a lot of trouble. While global investors know that Mr. Putin's Russia is fraught with risks and that Brazil's economy consistently fails to perform even close to its potential, they continue to invest in both, believing that eventually things will get better, even though we know that is often not the case.

The importance of anticipation

To those who may think the world has become both more dangerous and complicated – you are right. The Great Recession of 2008 served to emphasize how much more interconnected countries, companies, and consumers are. The political change that has accompanied the recession, and the lingering impact of the Arab Awakening, are daily reminders that political change can be unforeseen and unpredictable, while its impact can be both long term and potentially devastating to a business.

Making matters worse, much of the impact of economic and political change is completely outside the control of a risk manager or decision maker. It has always been the case that acts of expropriation, currency restrictions, political violence, and embargos can arise at any time, but, given recent history, businesses must now also anticipate not only when such incidents may arise, but how many at one time.

The plethora of political and economic upheavals – particularly since 2008 – has made the need for anticipatory risk management essential, yet few small and medium-sized companies have the resources necessary to be able to address the problem. This chapter presents some guidelines for how to stay on top of country risk when trading or investing abroad in today's evolving landscape.

A sound cross-border risk management platform

To the extent that international companies devote any resources at all to understanding cross-border trade and investment climates (and most do not), they tend to over-rely on externally generated country risk analyses, which are more often than not produced generically and are not necessarily appropriate for specific transactions. This is perhaps the most common mistake risk managers make. They believe that because they may have some recent information about the general political and economic profile of a country, they have a true handle on the nature of the risks associated with doing business there.

What about gauging legal and regulatory risk, the country's friendliness toward foreign trade and investment, and other companies' experience there? Too often, companies get caught in an 'investment trap': they commit long-term resources to a country only to find that the bill of goods they were sold – or thought they understood – turned out to be something completely different. There are plenty of stories about companies whose investments turned into disaster because the regulatory environment changed, a legal issue arose, international sanctions affected their ability to operate, or they selected the wrong joint venture partner. After the investment has been made, it is often too late to pull out without incurring large losses and experiencing reputational risk once the story hits the press.

A sound cross-border-oriented risk management process will include certain basic elements that result in the creation of an environment conducive to effectively managing risk:

- adequate risk management policies and procedures;
- an accurate system for reporting specific country exposures;
- an effective process for analysing country risk;
- a country risk rating system;
- established country exposure limits;
- regular monitoring of country conditions;
- periodic stress testing of foreign exposures;
- adequate internal controls and an audit function;
- effective oversight by a well-informed board of directors.

Regardless of the extent to which your organization can fully comply with this 'ideal' checklist, given limited resources, it is important to establish clear tolerance limits, delineate clear lines of responsibility and accountability for decisions made, and identify in advance desirable and undesirable types of business. Policies, standards, and practices should be clearly communicated, and enforced, with affected staff and offices. Quarterly reporting should be imposed – more frequently if foreign exchange exposure impacts a given investment. It is naturally also important that analyses be adequately documented and conclusions communicated in a way that gives decision makers an accurate basis on which to gauge exposure levels, and that sufficient resources be devoted to the task of assessing risk.

Best practices

Best practices dictate that a number of actions should be taken to create an effective transactional risk management programme (that is, related to a single transaction). Among them:

- the risk management function should be centralized;
- risk guidelines should be established and widely disseminated;
- limits on exposure by country and sector should be established;
- a system to better delineate the severity of perceived risks should be established;
- quarterly transactional risk reporting should be implemented;
- maximal use should be made of internal information capabilities while incorporating a wide array of external information sources into analyses.

The ability to obtain primary knowledge through inputs from local offices, as well as by regular visits on the part of country risk officers, cannot be overemphasized. Banks, oil and gas companies, and mining companies tend to have in-house country risk teams, but most other forms of business do not, either because it is judged to be unnecessary or too costly. Best practice should encourage in-house assessments before relying on external sources of information in order to build internal rating applications.

In most organizations that have individuals tasked with managing country risk, the country risk function operates autonomously, as there tend to be diverging interests between the operating side of the business and risk management. It is therefore important for senior management to effectively oversee interaction between the two sides. The risk assessment decision chain should be transparent and independent of compromise by business unit practices.

Another common issue is that the lines of communication between risk management personnel, risk management and decision makers, or between decision makers is either bypassed, convoluted, or just plain wrong. Some examples are:

- risk management is given only cursory participation in the transaction approval process;
- sales teams bypass risk management entirely, or ignore risk management's recommendations, because they fear a transaction will be cancelled as a result of unacceptably high levels of risk;
- a CEO delivers a presentation to a board of directors that is false, but he believes it to be true, because the risk manager's staff said it was.

A risk manager may have the right information, but it is based on a short-term assessment of the risks. The long-term view may be completely different. In the absence of knowing what questions to ask and having clear lines of communication, the right information may not be taken into consideration. A board of directors often has no idea what questions they should be asking of corporate decision makers. Executive education on the subject of country risk can be invaluable to decision makers up and down the chain, and could save an organization millions of dollars through having a better ability to avoid costly mistakes.

Why every manager needs to be a country risk manager

While most risk managers and decision makers would probably say that they do not have any particular expertise in assessing and monitoring country risk, the truth is that they do so every day in an international business, whether they realize it or not. Since most businesses (apart from banks and natural resource companies) tend not to have country risk specialists on their staff, it is incumbent on risk managers and decision makers alike to become country risk managers.

This may appear as a daunting task – and it is. Country risk management is an art, not a science, and the average corporate manager will have had no formal training in the subject. Managing country risk is all about creating and understanding a mosaic of risk factors that form a unique risk profile for each transaction, whether it involves investing, lending or trading.

Country risk management isn't merely about considering obvious variables – such as the health of a country's economy and its political stability – but in addition to that, such things as the regulatory environment, developmental issues, environmental concerns, and socio-cultural considerations. Each transaction has a unique risk profile. To be effective as a country risk manager, the ability to identify what truly distinguishes one transaction from another, and their implied short- and long-term risks, is critical to making the decision to invest, and stay invested. Doing so requires ongoing monitoring, which can be rather time consuming.

The number of companies – including some of the largest and best-known names in business – that have no formal methodology or staff for assessing and monitoring cross-border risk is surprising. Their belief is that they are either so large, so well known, or have such a long operating history in a country that all they may need to do when a problem arises is send the CEO to 'solve' the problem. That is an obviously flawed approach and can have the opposite effect.

It is therefore incumbent upon every company doing business abroad to implement a meaningful approach to country risk management. Smaller companies may have no choice but to rely on third-party-produced reports. The problem with doing so is that these reports are often out of date as soon as they are published, and in general do not make recommendations about whether or how to proceed with a transaction.

Making an attempt to understand an investment or trade climate is better than no effort at all, but, by the same token, some companies become deluded into believing that because they may have a person or 'system' in place to monitor country risk, they are bullet proof. Too often, gaps and inconsistencies in the risk management process, the nature of the internal reporting system, or the manner in which senior management delivers information to the board, can itself be a significant problem. It is therefore recommended that organizations with significant international exposures devote the resources necessary to adequately address cross-border risk, which will only become a more important component of the risk management landscape with time.

Summary: staying ahead of the curve

Much of what determines whether a country risk manager can do a good job will ultimately be outside his or her control. No one, no matter how experienced, can know or anticipate precisely where a country is heading all the time. All we can do is make educated guesses based on what history teaches us, and what we have learned in the process. That said, to be effective, a country risk manager must have the tools necessary to do the job and have the backing of senior management to both integrate the country risk function into the decision-making process, and take that process seriously. Whether that occurs may also be outside the risk manager's control.

In the end, the ability to anticipate what the future will bring using a combination of knowledge, insight, and a healthy sixth sense, can make all the difference. Listening to your gut and sense of smell are, in the end, as important as all the other tools at one's disposal. A good risk manager knows when to listen.

References and further reading

Bremmer, I (2007) How to calculate political risk, *Inc. Magazine*, April

Kennedy, C (2008) Political risk management: a portfolio planning model, *Business Horizons*, **31** (6) pp 26–33

Matthee, H (2013) Political Risk Analysis, in *International Encyclopedia of Political Science*, ed. B Badie, D Berg-Schlosser and L Morlino, Sage Publications

Sottilotta, C E (2013) Political Risk: concepts, definitions, challenges, LUISS School of Government Working Paper Series

Wagner, D (1999) *Political Risk Insurance Guide*, International Risk Management Institute, Dallas, TX

Wagner, D (2000) *Defining Political Risk*, International Risk Management Institute, Dallas, TX

Wagner, D (2012) *Managing Country Risk*, Taylor and Francis, Abingdon

Wagner, D and Disparte, D (2016) *Global Risk Agility and Decision Making*, Macmillan, Basingstoke

Communicating uncertainty

14

DR VERONICA BOWMAN

Background

Clear communication of uncertainty is crucial for effective risk management, but is difficult to achieve in practice. Communications must be clear to experts and non-experts alike and must account for a lack of understanding of the definitions of both 'risk' and 'uncertainty'. This chapter provides an overview of the area; more detailed information can be found in two longer summary papers on communicating risk (Cabinet Office, 2011; Dept. of Health, 1997).

Risk

Risk cannot be considered in isolation. While a calculated risk is always the same, different people will perceive that risk differently. How 'risky' it is to walk on ice doesn't just depend on how likely you are to fall over, but also on the likelihood of injury, as well as your perception of the repercussions of that injury. A sprained ankle matters more if your livelihood depends on your ability to walk.

In finance, risk is defined as a 'measurable probability' involving future events (Knight, 1921) whereas uncertainty is defined as an unmeasurable quantity. However, this definition doesn't account for the risk's impact.

In risk assessment, consideration of impact has led to risk being defined as the 'probability of occurrence *multiplied* by the impact' (APM, 2004; IRM, 2002). Therefore, something that is unlikely to happen but has huge impact is as 'risky' as something that is likely to happen but has little impact.

These competing definitions should be appreciated; your audience will have differing understandings of what you mean by 'risk'.

Uncertainty

Uncertainty is often assumed to be a mathematical representation of variability (Oberkampf et al., 2002) and, as such, while it can't be measured, it can be calculated. There are two main types of uncertainty (Oberkampf et al., 2002; Der Kiureghian and Ditlevsen, 2009), which are calculated differently.

Aleatoric Uncertainty (also termed variability or a 'known unknown') is inherent in the random nature of the natural world and cannot be reduced by measurement improvement. For example, if you shoot two identical arrows from the same bow, the impact point will still vary due to meteorological turbulence.

Epistemic Uncertainty (also termed ambiguity or an 'unknown known') could be reduced if we had the theoretical ability to measure more accurately. For example, if we are measuring how heavy something is, but we can only measure to two decimal places, the exact weight is still uncertain. However, the more accurate our scales the less our uncertainty would be. If we had a perfectly accurate set of scales, the uncertainty would disappear completely.

Uncertainty can also be categorized by its source (algorithmic, experimental etc.); for further clarity see Kennedy and O'Hagan, 2001. However, even under these strict definitions, there is ambiguity when it comes to inference or prediction of the future, the so-called 'unknown unknowns'. Unfortunately, these have an impact on risk management as they tend to result in unplanned crises, like recessions.

Communication

Despite the nuances involved in the understanding of risk and uncertainty, there are common communication methods for both. Unfortunately, these methods focus on designing a strategy which is bespoke for each audience; there are no general guidelines, only examples of best practice. How people understand and act upon information about risk and uncertainty is still very much an open research question.

An effective communication strategy

The following five steps will help you to communicate uncertainty effectively:

- *Consider how you will communicate uncertainty early on* – this will inform the work that you do and ensure uncertainty presentation is not rushed.
- *Know your audience* – different audiences require different types of communication; ensure that you identify your audience.
- *Engage ahead of time* – the more that you can engage your audience in the development of your communication method, the more successful it will be.
- *Less is more* – keep outputs simple and clear, decide exactly what you are trying to convey and present only that.
- *Don't hide your uncertainty* – uncertainty is inevitable; don't try to minimize or hide it.

Consider how you will communicate early on

It doesn't matter how much effort you have put into a project or how good it is; if the output isn't understood then you have been wasting your time.

Many business professionals, analysts and researchers fall into the trap of spending most of their time analysing the problem, but then rushing the write-up in order to meet the deadline, reducing the impact of their work. When the results include uncertainty, which requires careful thought and preparation to present well, rushing the outputs can completely obscure the message. If you know at the start of a project how you will present the results and their associated uncertainty and to whom you are presenting, then there is both clear direction and an appreciation of the time required to produce the output. To ensure that the message is easily understood, and that all of the information clarifying the outputs is gathered, outputs must be planned in advance.

If you are presenting to an expert audience that has time to process the information and a good understanding of what uncertainty is, then, to some extent, your task is simplified; you can present results in complex ways and they will be understood. If, however, your results and the uncertainty associated with them need to be understood quickly or are produced for non-experts, then finding the most effective output format becomes a research problem in itself. The key is that you need to explain what your uncertainty is as well as impart the results to ensure the message is clear; it takes time and effort to present uncertainty well.

Know your audience

The more you focus your communication to your audience, the better it will be.

The way you present uncertainty to the general public differs from the way you would present it to a decision maker or senior management, not because they have any less capacity to understand but because they will *need the information for different reasons.*

When communicating to the public, they will be assessing your information for impacts on themselves and their families. They will be assessing the information you are giving them for *individual risk*. When communicating to a decision maker, they will be assessing your information for combined risks to a group of people, ie *societal risk*.

There have been a number of recent case studies looking at how best to communicate uncertainty to the public. One of the most effective efforts resulted in a new way of displaying risk via 'expected frequency trees', which are now widely used across the NHS. The development of these techniques via expert-led panels and workshops took months. However, the resultant information is readily accessible to everyone and the methods have wide applicability (see Forbes *et al.*, (2014) for a discussion of the techniques and their development). This demonstrates the level of effort required to produce simple effective communication of uncertainty, but also shows the broader benefits of the undertaking.

If your audience has a variety of skill levels, then communicate your results accordingly. There is no reason that the same results cannot be presented in varying levels of detail. This will allow an interested reader to find out more, but will also allow the non-expert who doesn't need the detail to understand the message. Similarly, even in oral presentations you can give a high-level overview and have additional detailed slides if your audience is interested. The skill is in providing the right level of detail to the right audience.

Engage ahead of time

If the way you communicate is familiar and well understood, the message will stand out clearly.

If images and data are unfamiliar then this can obscure the message and you may lose the audience; prior engagement makes all the difference. This could mean meeting your audience face to face and slowly working with them to explain the outputs and refine them into a format they understand. Alternatively, if the audience is a busy senior manager or a large group, prior engagement could be through focus groups or peer review.

Either way, prior engagement will result in your target audience being familiar with a presentation method, or at least able to readily understand it.

This ensures that even complex outputs with large uncertainties can be rapidly communicated, irrespective of the skill level of the audience.

In crisis situations, prior engagement is impossible. However, most risks are planned for and mitigation strategies are developed. This is the time when information sources and formats can be familiarized and research into communication methodologies can be undertaken. Within reason, if there is no time to expose an audience to a new way of communicating, use one they are familiar with, even if it is slightly less clear, so that the message is not obscured.

Less is more

Do not overcrowd images or complicate messages; several simple pictures or details are better than one long or complicated one.

Uncertainty is calculated numerically, comes from numerous sources and can have a multitude of effects. This can lead to an assumption that graphics and tables have to contain all of the relevant information, thus making them busy and unclear. Do not overcrowd images; several simple pictures are better than one chart with many messages.

Development of clear and simple graphics is an obvious way of communicating uncertainty. From spaghetti plots and fan plots (see Figure 14.1) showing future paths, to simple bar charts, there are a multitude of ways to get your message across. A good overview of the various types of graphics can be found in Spiegelhalter, 2011. The key is to pick a single graphic to illustrate each point and not to try and put too much information on each image.

FIGURE 14.1 A spaghetti plot shows several possible realizations of a function, allowing an appreciation of the spread of the data, particularly useful if the data is non-normal. For normal data, a fan chart shows a mean and three standard deviations. If the data become less certain over time then the colour can fade – a useful technique

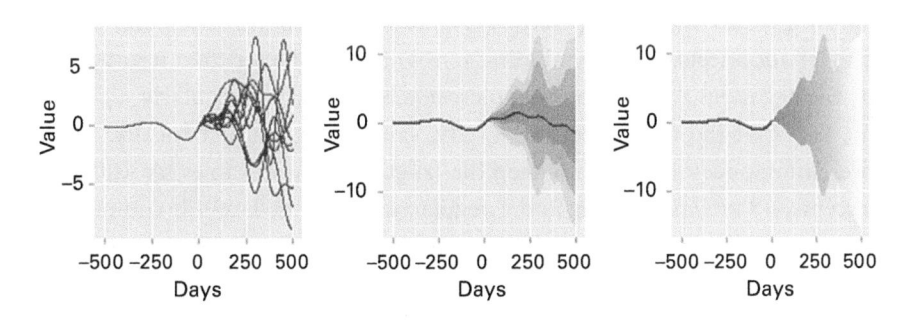

Don't hide your uncertainty

Simply stating that there is little uncertainty or, worse still, that you have assessed the uncertainty and associated risk and there is nothing to worry about can lead to disaster.

Every individual has different values and assesses risk differently, and no one likes to be patronized. If you have a very large uncertainty on an output, then state this and describe your reasoning process, otherwise you risk mistrust and ridicule if, subsequently, your assessment does not match reality (weather forecasters are told they can't predict the weather, when actually they simply don't present the uncertainty). Even simple charts can include uncertainty, as in Figure 14.2.

FIGURE 14.2 A bar chart should include associated uncertainties. For normal data error bars are used, but for non-normal data this is misleading and a box-plot is preferable, as demonstrated. Each chart shows the same data

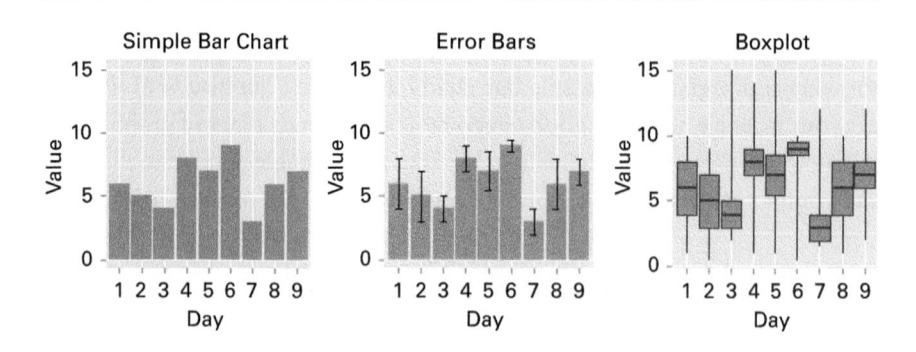

Be careful with language. There are scales that have been developed to guide language use when dealing with uncertainty (IPCC, 2010) and it is worth being familiar with them. Equally, be careful how you frame results. Human nature dictates that if you positively frame a statement (for example, '99 per cent of adolescents are law abiding'), it will sound better than if you focus on the negatives ('1 per cent of adolescents break the law regularly'), despite the fact that the two sentences say the same thing mathematically. When presenting uncertainty, try to keep the language neutral ('In every 100 adolescents, 99 are law abiding and 1 regularly breaks the law'). If you need to present one fact or the other, match your language to the information. If you need to present the information about the law breakers then 'Only 1 per cent of adolescents break the law regularly' changes the tone and indicates to the reader that 1 per cent is a small proportion of the whole with the addition of a single word.

Summary: case study

The following case study illustrates the points outlined above. The UK government works to ensure they are prepared for an accidental or deliberate release of a pathogen (disease), and one of the key tasks is to decide how the hazard area might be displayed to decision makers and the public.

In this circumstance there is considerable uncertainty involved, from the potential size and location of the release, to the meteorology (weather) which will spread the hazard, to the effect of the treatment. It is important that this uncertainty is conveyed. However, it is also crucial that the audience has confidence in the results and can act quickly on any information.

To produce visualizations that would meet these criteria, the following steps were undertaken:

1 At the outset, a test set of visualizations and information tables were produced for a fictitious scenario.

2 A panel of stakeholders, users and subject matter experts (SMEs) was identified.

3 The visualizations were presented to the panel during a simulated incident, the methodologies were critiqued and the benefits of each method discussed.

4 The agreed techniques were further developed into a set of outputs.

5 A series of focused discussions were held with key personnel to refine those outputs.

6 The panel was reconvened and the final outputs were again tested in a simulated scenario.

7 Further improvements were made following the panel and an agreed set of outputs were finalized.

This process took around six months to complete; however, the benefits of taking this time were considerable, as we will see below.

Before this work started, hazard areas were presented as a set of templates (see Figure 14.3). However, hard lines between hazard levels where no hard cut offs exist and unclear values (dosages with no indication of effect) caused confusion.

FIGURE 14.3 A hazard prediction with a standard hazard level output; each hazard level represents a specified dosage level of hazardous agent

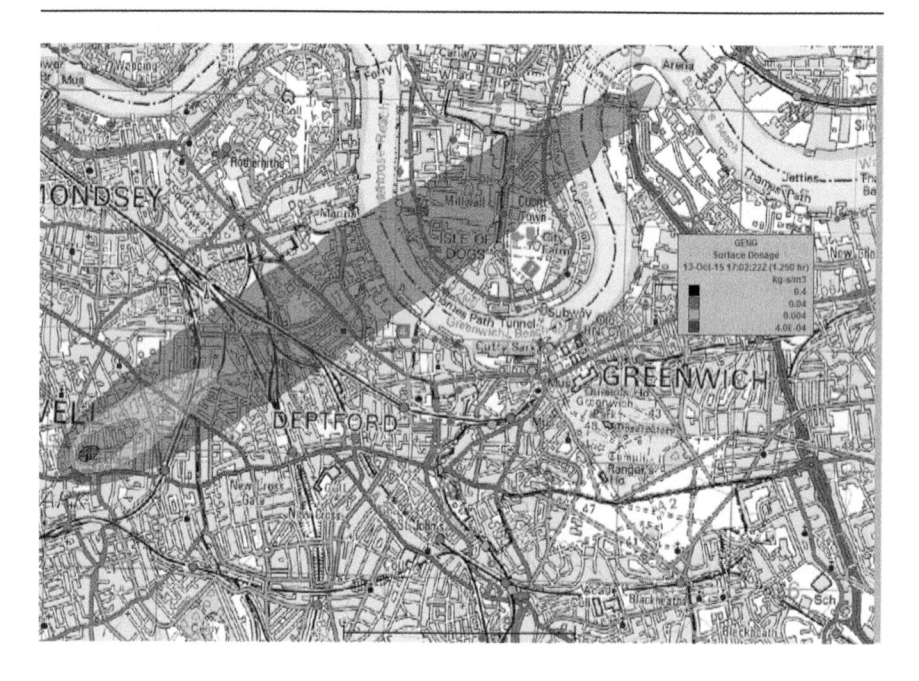

Initially the audience was resistant to any efforts to convey uncertainty, feeling that it clouded an already complicated picture. However, as better visualizations were developed, the benefit of including the information became clearer. The panel became familiar with the types of output they would receive and the ramifications of the uncertainty on decisions was better understood.

Eventually the outputs shown in Figures 14.4 and 14.5, and in Table 14.1 were developed. All encapsulate uncertainty but each represents a different level of detail, allowing users to interrogate outputs further as and when they need to. In particular, complex calculations were undertaken to provide probability of affect for the hazard plot to reflect what was expected by the viewer. These outputs are easier for the decision maker to act on and are widely accepted by the user community.

Communicating Uncertainty 233

FIGURE 14.4 Hazard level data is presented as an improved hazard plot

SOURCE: Map © OpenStreetMap, under the Open Database Licence, www.openstreetmap.org/copyright

Emerging Trends

FIGURE 14.5 Hazard level data is presented as a postcode plot detailing areas to be treated in priority order

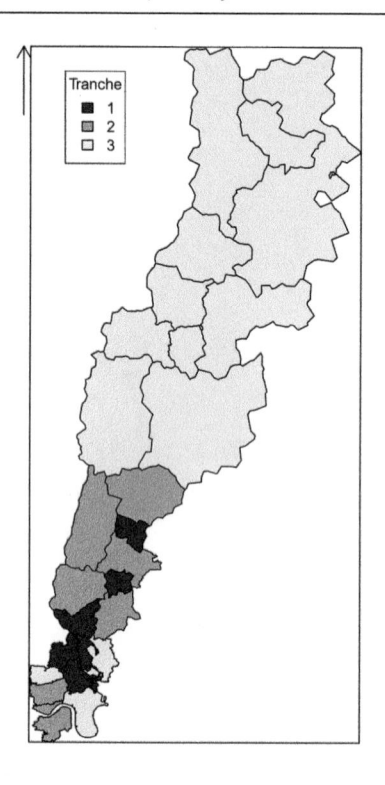

TABLE 14.1 A representation of the final tables developed for the fictitious scenario. This table is a reduced form of the one developed for classification reasons

Postcode district	Fatalities without treatment	Uncertainty range	Fatalities with treatment	Uncertainty range
ABC 1	100	(85,115)	3	(2,4)
ABC 2	95	(90,105)	2	(1,2)
BCD 10	120	(90,140)	4	(1,5)
BCD 11	50	(45,55)	1	(0,2)

SOURCE: © Crown copyright (2015), Dstl. This material is licensed under the terms of the Open Government Licence except where otherwise stated. To view this licence, visit http://www.nationalarchives.gov.uk/doc/open-government-licence/version/3 or write to the Information Policy Team, The National Archives, Kew, London TW9 4DU, or email: psi@nationalarchives.gsi.gov.uk

References

Association for Project Management (APM) (2004) *Project Risk Analysis and Management (PRAM) Guide*, 2nd edn, APM Publishing, Buckinghamshire, UK

Berger, J and Berry, D (1988) Statistical analysis and the illusion of objectivity, *American Scientist* **76** (2), pp 159–65

Cabinet Office (2011) Communicating Risk [online] http://www.cabinetoffice.gov.uk/sites/default/files/resources/communicating-risk-guidance.pdf

Casella, G (2008) *Bayesians and Frequentists: models, assumptions, and inference*, ACCP 37th Annual Meeting, Philadelphia, PA [online] http://www.stat.ufl.edu/archived/casella/Talks/BayesRefresher.pdf

Department of Health (1997) *Communicating about risks to public health: pointers to good practice* [online] http://www.bvsde.ops-oms.org/tutorial6/fulltext/pointers.pdf

Der Kiureghian, A and Ditlevsen, O (2009) Aleatory or epistemic? Does it matter? *Structural Safety* **31** (2) pp 105–12

Forbes L J et al. (2014) Offering informed choice about breast screening, *Journal of Medical Screening*, **21** (4), 194–200

Institute of Risk Management (IRM) (2002) *A Risk Management Standard*, IRM, London

Intergovernmental Panel on Climate Change (IPCC) (2010), guidance note for lead authors of the IPCC fifth assessment report on consistent treatment of uncertainties [online] https://www.ipcc.ch/pdf/supporting-material/uncertainty-guidance-note.pdf

Kennedy, M and O'Hagan, A (2001), Bayesian calibration of computer models, *Journal of the Royal Statistical Society B*, **63** (3), pp 425–64

Knight, F H (1921) *Risk, Uncertainty and Profit*, Dover, New York, NY

Oberkampf, W L et al. (2002), Error and uncertainty in modeling and simulation, *Reliability Engineering and System Safety*, **75**, pp 333–57

Spiegelhalter, D (2011) Visualising uncertainty about the future, *Science*, **333** (6048) pp 1393–400

WikiBook (2014) *A Look at the Bias and the Fallacy [online]* https://en.wikipedia.org/wiki/Book:A_Look_at_the_Bias_and_the_Fallacy [accessed 17 November 2015]

Risk-based decision making

15

DR KEITH SMITH

Introduction

Like risk assessment, risk-based decision making has been the subject of research for many years, but the findings have generally remained within academic circles. However, it is now recognized that in this increasingly complex and highly connected world (IRM, 2014), a few poorly taken decisions can launch an organization on an irretrievable journey to disaster (Nutt, 2002, pp 1–22).

It is not possible to exhaustively cover such a large and complex topic in a single chapter, so the goal here is to highlight a few areas where significant improvements in decision-making skills can be made. You will also find some practical tips on how systemic problems in risk-based decision making can be tackled by adopting appropriate processes.

The decision maker's conundrum

Given an identified cause leading directly to a limited and identifiable set of outcomes (a simple problem), decision making is relatively easy. This of course excludes decisions where all of the outcomes are considered unacceptable. Unfortunately though, we now live in a world where organizations are dependent on other organizations to deliver their goods and services into a global marketplace (PWC, 2008). This means the decisions we take cannot always be isolated from the complexity of the relationships held with these other key organizations. This, along with the increased complexity embodied in contracts to support these relationships, and the multitude of consequences that can stem from such organizational structures, means organizations face an increasing number of complex decisions (IRM, 2014). The characteristics of such complex decisions and how they may be approached, is therefore quite different from simple decisions, as Figure 15.1 illustrates.

FIGURE 15.1 Simple and complex decisions have different characteristics and must be managed with different management styles

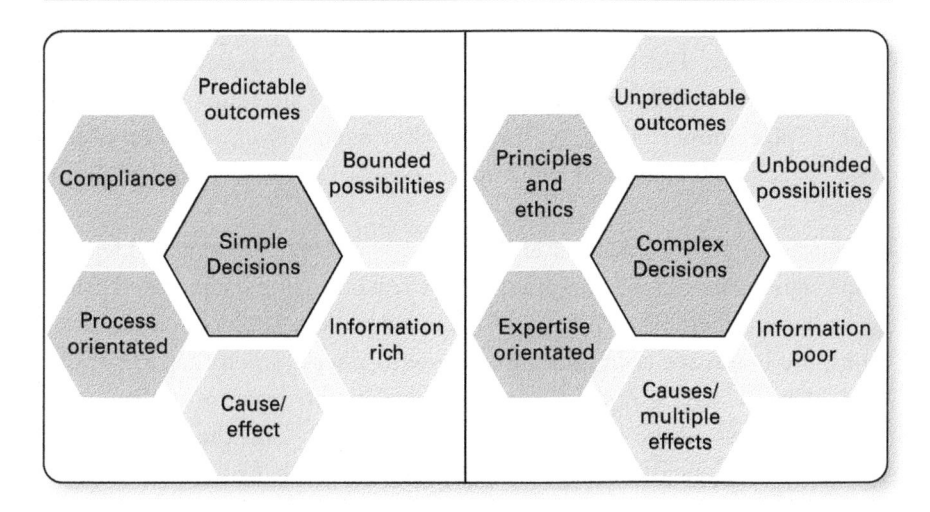

![Figure 15.1: Two hexagonal diagrams comparing Simple Decisions (Predictable outcomes, Compliance, Bounded possibilities, Process orientated, Information rich, Cause/effect) and Complex Decisions (Unpredictable outcomes, Principles and ethics, Unbounded possibilities, Expertise orientated, Information poor, Causes/multiple effects)]

Compounding the situation of decision making in a complex environment, with highly connected risks, we find we are frequently data rich but information poor (Obeidat *et al.*, 2015). We are also called upon to make these decisions in tighter timeframes as the 'Clockspeed' (Fine, 1998) of our industrial society increases (Smith, 2011a, b).*

Understanding how decisions are made

The first step to improved decision making comes with a psychological understanding of how decisions are actually made. You cannot improve that which you do not understand. Given that we all make decisions from an

---

* One of the key selling features for computers when Fine wrote his book was the rate at which the microprocessor could handle instructions. The term 'Clockspeed' had been used to describe this key feature, as instruction processing is determined by the clock chip used. By adopting the term for his book, Fine tapped into the rich similarity between computers processing data and industry processing business.

early age simply to survive, it may seem strange that we do not have this depth of understanding already. Actually, as you venture into a position of understanding how decisions are made, it soon becomes apparent that our brains are designed to hide some of the limitations and inconsistencies of our decision-making processes.

The first important point arises from the work of Herbert Simon with 'Bounded Rationality' (Simon, 1982). Simon remarked that the human brain is only capable of so much processing. It is therefore not surprising that the brain uses techniques and shortcuts to conserve energy, reduce processing time and free up resources. This is the background behind heuristics and biases, most famously investigated by Amos Tversky, the Nobel Prize winner Daniel Kahneman (Kahneman *et al.*, 1982) and latterly by others (Gigerenzer and Gaissmaier, 2011; Gigerenzer and Todd, 1999).

Heuristics and biases are useful in many ways, but they can also lead to some significant systemic errors. For this reason their existence and effect must be considered by the serious decision maker. Understanding heuristics, the biases we hold and indeed how to 'check' when they are about to mislead us are important tools in the decision maker's toolbox. We cannot address all the heuristics and biases known (and there are many), but addressing one of the top decision biases can perhaps signpost a direction of study.

Confirmation Bias is a name given to a variety of behaviours for preferentially seeking information that supports the desired or expected outcome. This includes decisions that have already been made, whether the decision maker knows it or not! Not only is this a common bias, but it is a particularly important one which is difficult to avoid (Wason and Johnson-Laird, 1972).

To add balance to the argument, heuristics can be beneficial. Indeed, a trained mind is a powerful tool when dealing with risk-based decisions.

Managing this kind of bias requires the systematic surfacing and weighing up of both sides of the argument objectively. An organization can operationalize these principles by adopting a good process methodology, preferably one that is proven in the field already. A good example would be the one popularized by Charles Kepner and Mat-thys Fourie (KEPNERandFOURIE™). This methodology includes a construct (CauseWise) which forces consideration on what is driving the decision (it is a confirmed cause), but provides equal consideration to that which is not the cause (something that could be a cause, but is ruled out by an identified fact). The construct is further framed by forcing justification with 'why not' validating the logic of the whole construct. Decision makers adopting such structured methodologies will inevitably be less prone to poor decisions caused by this kind of systemic bias. The act of forced mindfulness can also be an advantage (see dual processing below).

Other common heuristics and biases decision makers should address are:

- *Anchoring*, where an initial value, arising within the context of the issue, becomes a seed solution from which the decision maker estimates the final answer.
- *Representativeness*, where two or more situations look the same but have important differences.
- *Availability*, which is where people favour attention on issues most recently brought into clear mindful focus.

These three may be investigated further through the various works by Kahneman and Tversky (Kahneman *et al.*, 1982; Kahneman, 2012). Also consider optimism bias (Sharot, 2011; Sharot *et al.*, 2007) which makes us look favourably on positive information with obvious consequences for objective decision making.

Dual processing

Beyond Simon's Bounded Rationality, there are many other important psychological underpinnings to decision making, but few are as important as the theory of dual processing (Epstein, 1994; Sloman, 1996). The basis of the theory, explained in some detail by Evans (2003, 2007), identifies two dominant modes of problem solving. The first is associated with the subconscious and is considered as instinct and other deep-rooted learned behaviours. A decision based on this mode is characterized by speed and feeling. The second dominant mode in dual processing is where we apply thoughtful rational consideration to a decision. In other words, we consciously and mindfully think about it, but that takes time and effort.

Dual processing causes several issues for decision makers. The first problem is that the first processing we do on anything we face is to 'feel it' (Slovic and Peters, 2006; Zajonc, 1980). If our subconscious brain thinks it has a solution, it may not even engage the higher thoughtful mode.

To see this dual processing in action, think about whether you have ever made a decision you almost instantly regretted as you become aware of the consequences. Did that happen when you were angry or under intense time pressure? Anger and other emotions are also important, as these change our risk-taking and decision-making profile (Heilman *et al.*, 2010; Loewenstein *et al.*, 2001).

Clockspeed vs velocity

By far the most commonly referred-to properties of a risk are its impact and its likelihood. More recently people have started to consider other properties of risks such as velocity, which is the speed at which the risk event is approaching. Velocity, however, is not the best way to look at the timing of a risk.

Given that the first reaction any human has to a subject is to 'feel it' with the faster subconscious mode, if time with the right information is short, this fast mode is the dominant mode under which the decision will be made. If on the other hand, time with the relevant information is sufficient, we may then engage our rational thinking mind to process the information. So this is not so much a 'speed of risk approaching' issue, as an 'information availability and processing' issue. This is the Risk Clockspeed view, extending the terminology adopted by Fine into the world of risk-based decisions (Smith and Borodzicz, 2008; Smith, 2011a, b).

If the information needed to quantify and manage a risk is available sufficiently ahead of time to plan, execute and manage mitigating actions, then use that time and process the information with the experience residing in your team to arrive at a good decision. This is Slow Risk Clockspeed.

If the information needed to quantify and manage a risk is emerging in or close to real time, then the assessment and decision must be made by someone with a trained subconscious. We have a name for this kind of person: 'an expert'. Using experts is how you manage risk-based decisions in a Fast Risk Clockspeed environment. The question is, how many organizations allow their experts to take the final decision, particularly when these experts struggle to explain how they arrived at that decision? In the lighthearted illustration (Figure 15.2), the expertise clearly needs to be with the driver, irrespective of his position in the hierarchy.

FIGURE 15.2 Fast decisions in a complex environment require expertise

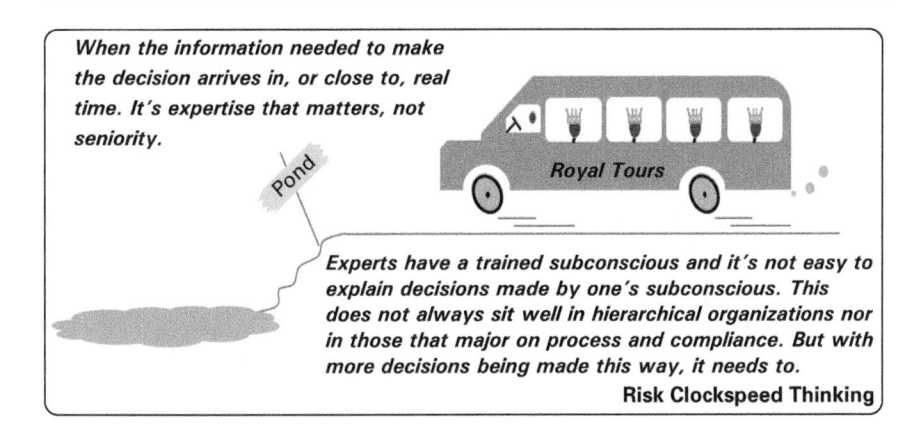

> When the information needed to make the decision arrives in, or close to, real time. It's expertise that matters, not seniority.
>
> Pond
>
> Royal Tours
>
> Experts have a trained subconscious and it's not easy to explain decisions made by one's subconscious. This does not always sit well in hierarchical organizations nor in those that major on process and compliance. But with more decisions being made this way, it needs to.
>
> Risk Clockspeed Thinking

Situation awareness and decision making

There is a field of risk-based decision making which is very relevant to the problem of Fast Clockspeed Risk in a complex environment. Naturalistic Decision Making (NDM) is a field of risk-based decision making founded by its most prolific author, Gary Klein (Klein, 1999, 2008; Zsambok and Klein, 1997). The emergency services and specifically the fire services, who frequently make such decisions, make extensive use of Klein's work, particularly his work on Recognition Primed Decision Making (RPDM) (Klein, 1993).

RPDM is where the decision maker uses a current situation assessment to subconsciously compare against previously experienced situations for a suitable response. When a candidate is found with enough similarities to the current situation, the associated solution is recalled and the decision is made. But implementing this recalled solution is not necessarily the optimal decision so much as one that will do. This is a process called 'Satisficing'. Of course the problem is, the decision taken may not be right for long (Dekker, 2011).

Decision controls

Some exciting work has recently been undertaken in the UK Fire Service by a team led by DAC Dr Sabrina Cohen-Hatton of London Fire Brigade (Cohen-Hatton, 2014a, 2014b; Cohen-Hatton *et al.*, 2015) to improve the quality of decisions made by incident commanders.

Emerging Trends

Cohen-Hatton found that commanders managing at an incident were undertaking situation assessment and in most cases rapidly moving to a decision on how to tackle an incident. She found little evidence of 'plan formulation', the stage anticipated in the original fire service decision-making model. As with Klein's RPDM, this incident-based decision may not have been the best, as much as a workable decision for the moment. However, if the decision compromised future decisions, or did not fully align to the goal set for the current incident, then the decision was questionable. By introducing carefully selected decision controls, applied just before the decision maker followed through with implementation, Cohen-Hatton demonstrated that significantly improved decisions could be made. Figure 15.3 illustrates the old and the new models for clarity.

FIGURE 15.3 Illustration of old and revised decision models used in the UK Fire and Rescue Services for Incident Command

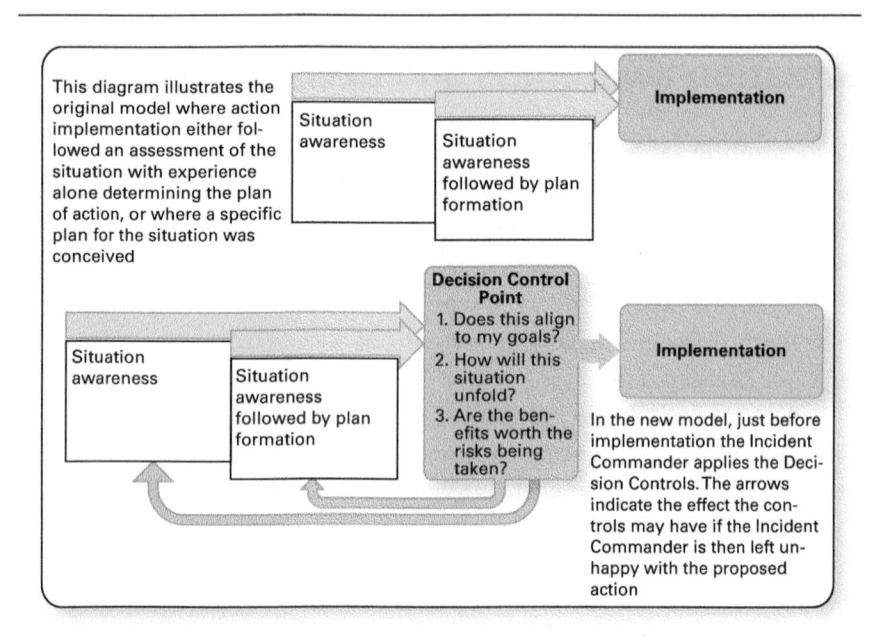

Perhaps more surprisingly, the work also revealed that decision controls of this type led to improved situation awareness.

There is nothing exclusive to the situation of decision making by incident commanders. If decision controls can make such a difference to the quality of real-time decisions made at an incident, their use within any organizations operating in a fast-moving environment could be equally transformational.

Summary

Good decision making is increasingly important to organizations, but as discussed in the opening paragraphs of this chapter, good decisions are becoming harder to make. Furthermore, the solution is not always a matter of simply gathering more data. By understanding how decisions are made, decision makers can gain insight into systemic errors they may be making. For this reason, interest in human limitations, heuristics and biases and how these affect our decisions needs to become popular reading.

While process may not always be the answer, processes designed to tackle systemic issues certainly have a role to play in better decision making. Some of these methods are already available and have proven track records, so organizations do not have to reinvent the wheel each time.

Our scope of risk-based decisions includes an increasing number where the necessary management information emerges in or close to real time. This type of risk-based decision needs to be made by empowered experts provided with appropriate decision support. Risk Clockspeed thinking is a tool to help organizations adapt their risk management approach to accommodate the timing of information availability.

The new work on decision controls is particularly interesting. Traditional decision controls are a set of financial hurdles, or milestones for a project to meet. This new type of decision control, applied in real time, is aimed at psychological validation and material improvement of the final decision. The results obtained from recent field trials of these decision controls has proven their usefulness and now it is up to organizations to translate this kind of thinking into daily practice.

Acknowledgement

Kepner and Fourie methodology is provided by Thinking Dimensions. KEPNERandFOURIE™ is a registered trademark of Thinking Dimensions and it is used with kind permission.

References

Cohen-Hatton, S R (2014a) The psychology of incident command decision making trials, *Fire Magazine*, October, pp 16–18

Cohen-Hatton, S R (2014b) Psychology of incident command: the research results, *Fire Magazine*, July/August, pp 46–49

Cohen-Hatton, S R, Butler, P C and Honey, R C (2015) An investigation of operational decision making in situ incident command in the UK fire and rescue service, *Human Factors: The Journal of the Human Factors and Ergonomics Society*, **57** (5), pp 793–804

Dekker, S (2011) *Drift into Failure: From hunting broken components to understanding complex systems*, Ashgate Publishing, Ltd, Farnham

Epstein, S (1994) Integration of the cognitive and the psychodynamic unconscious, *American Psychologist*, **49** (8), pp 709–24

Evans, J (2003) In two minds: dual-process accounts of reasoning, *Trends in Cognitive Sciences*, **7** (10), 454–59

Evans, J (2007) Dual-processing accounts of reasoning, judgment, and social cognition, *Annual Review of Psychology*, **59**, pp 255–78

Fine, C H (1998) *Clockspeed: Winning industry control in the age of temporary advantage*, Perseus Books, Reading, Massachusetts

Gigerenzer, G and Gaissmaier, W (2011) Heuristic decision making, *Annual Review of Psychology*, **62**, pp 451–82

Gigerenzer, G and Todd, P M (1999) *Simple Heuristics that Make Us Smart*, Oxford University Press, New York

Heilman, R M, Crisan, L G, Houser, D, Miclea, M and Miu, A C (2010) Emotion regulation and decision making under risk and uncertainty, *Emotion*, **10** (2), p 257

IRM (2014) *Extended Enterprise Managing Risk in Complex 21st-Century Organisations*, Institute of Risk Management, London

Kahneman, D (2012) *Thinking, Fast and Slow*, Penguin Books, London

Kahneman, D, Slovic, P, and Tversky, A (1982) *Judgment under Uncertainty: Heuristics and biases*, Cambridge University Press, Cambridge

Klein, G A (1993) *A Recognition-primed Decision (RPD) Model of Rapid Decision Making*, Ablex Publishing Corporation

Klein, G A (1999) *Sources of Power: How people make decisions*, MIT Press, Massachusetts

Klein, G (2008) Naturalistic decision making, *Human Factors: The Journal of the Human Factors and Ergonomics Society*, **50** (3), pp 456–60

Loewenstein, G F, Weber, E U, Hsee, C K and Welch, N (2001) Risk as feelings, *Psychological Bulletin*, **127** (2), pp 267–86

Nutt, P C (2002) *Why Decisions Fail: Avoiding the blunders and traps that lead to debacles*, Berrett-Koehler Publications

Obeidat, M, North, M. Burgess, L. Parker, R and North, S (2015) DRIP data rich, information poor: a concise synopsis of data mining, *Universal Journal of Management*, **3** (1), pp 29–35

PWC (2008) *11th Annual CEO Survey*, PWC, Belfast

Sharot, T (2011) The optimism bias, *Current Biology*, **21** (23), R941–R945

Sharot, T, Riccardi, A M, Raio, C M and Phelps, E A (2007) Neural mechanisms mediating optimism bias, *Nature*, **450** (7166), pp 102–105

Simon, H (1982 *Models of Bounded Rationality, Volume 1: Economic analysis and public policy*, MIT Press

Sloman, S A (1996) The empirical case for two systems of reasoning, *Psychological Bulletin*, **119**, pp 3–22

Slovic, P and Peters, E (2006) Risk perception and affect, *Current Directions in Psychological Science*, **15** (6), pp 322–25

Smith, K (2011a) The affective risk management organization, *EDPACS, The EDP Audit, Control, and Security Newsletter*, **43** (6), pp 1–11

Smith, K (2011b) *People, Fortunes, Systems and Clockspeed*, University of Portsmouth, Portsmouth

Smith, K and Borodzicz, E (2008) Risk Clockspeed: A new lens for critical incident management, *Systemist*, **30** (2), pp 354–71

Wason, P C and Johnson-Laird, P N (1972) *Psychology of Reasoning: Structure and content*, Harvard University Press, USA

Zajonc, R B (1980) Feeling and thinking: preferences need no inferences, *American Psychologist*, **35** (2), pp 151–75

Zsambok, C E and Klein, G A (1997) *Naturalistic Decision Making*, Lawrence Erlbaum

Risk leadership in complex organizations

16

DR RICHARD BARBER

Introduction

For senior leaders, the risks that matter are not the relatively well-understood tangible, visible risks that we see in traditional risk registers. What really matter are risks that are not documented, understood or managed. It is such risks that most often lead to failure.

The answer may seem to be to build better, bigger and more complete risk registers, but that would not work. Important sources of risk to organizational success are often sensitive, intangible or multi-faceted. These types of risk are difficult to manage using traditional forms of risk recording and reporting (Barber, 2003).

Significantly, these risks are also often interrelated, subtle, systemic and emergent. That is, they influence multiple functions of the organization and have emergent properties over time. Unmanaged, they have implications for capability, performance and strategic performance.

For risk management, the key implication of such risks is that traditional process-based approaches are inadequate. This is illustrated in Figure 16.1.

Leaders who can find, understand and manage complex, systemic, and sensitive risks gain advantages for their organizations. The challenge is how to do so.

Getting the assumptions right

Leaders may understand the need to find the deeper, hidden drivers of risk to performance, yet may not have effective, practical tools for doing so in real time and within normal resources. Some leaders call in consultants in

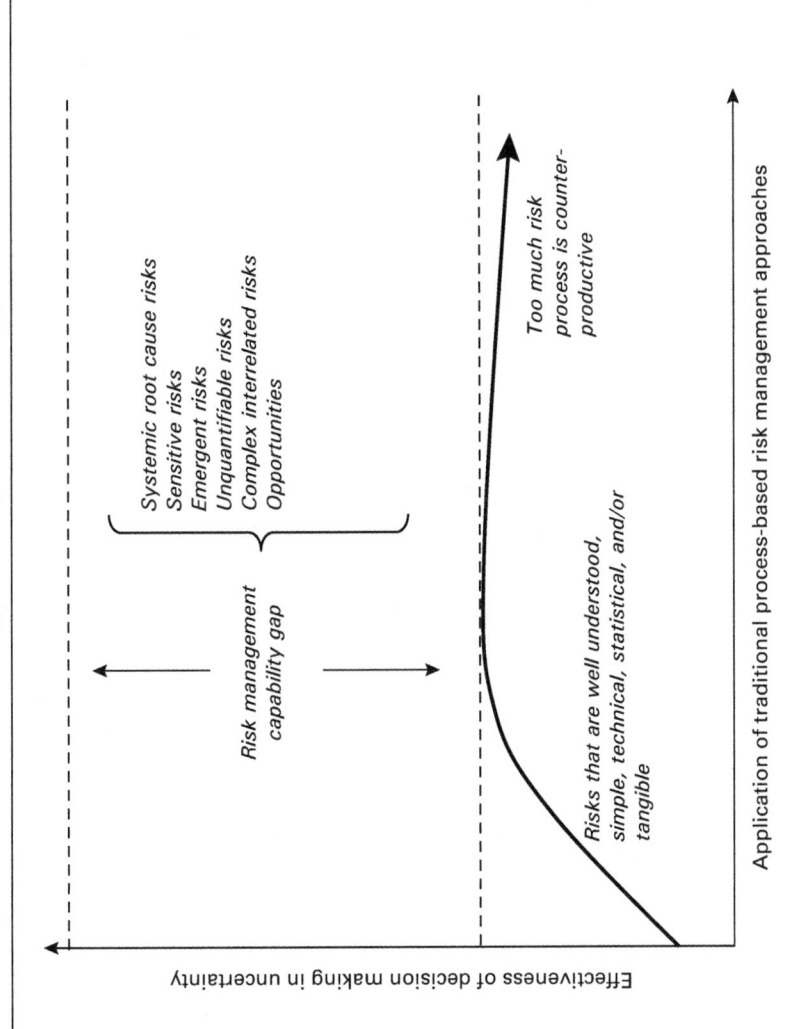

FIGURE 16.1 Traditional risk management fails when dealing with complex forms of risk

the hope of lifting thinking and practice to a new place. However, most consultants are part of the status quo; their products and services vary in detail, but not in their underlying assumptions about risk.

This is hardly surprising, since world-wide, traditional risk management approaches are very similar. They assume that we can safely work on risks one at a time and should focus on those with higher risk ratings, even though this is not a reasonable assumption when dealing with complex, interrelated systemic risks (Cantle, 2012).

To avoid more of the same thinking it is possible to re-invent risk management, using assumptions that better reflect the reality of our complex, uncertain world. For example the following three assumptions are simple but important observations about risk mindset:

Assumption 1. When working on risk our objective is to ensure that leaders understand the uncertainties involved when making decisions.

It is the quality of decision making that determines performance. Risk management work must serve the needs of decision makers or it has no point.

Assumption 2. Our aim should always be to achieve the best possible outcomes aligned to our purpose.

This implies that risk work must be focused on maximizing and improving – not, as is usually the case, focused on threat first and then (perhaps) on opportunities.

Assumption 3. The word 'risk' can be used in many different ways even by the same people, but there is a pervasive sense that it has negative connotations.

We need to find a way to deal with all kinds of uncertainty, including opportunities, without trying to force people to think of risk as positive.

The following additional assumptions arise from the dynamic nature of every human organization and its environment:

Assumption 4. Important organizational risks may be complex, intangible, interrelated and even 'wicked'.

We need to be prepared to analyse, understand and respond to complex, wicked uncertainties. Simplistic risk management approaches lead to false confidence and perverse unforeseen outcomes.

Assumption 5. Every organization faces important risk factors that are too sensitive to be properly documented in risk registers or risk reports.

Effective approaches to risk management must be sophisticated enough to deal with all kinds of risk, including those that are difficult to acknowledge, work on and document. A 'risk register'-based approach cannot be enough by itself.

Assumption 6. Emergence is an important risk characteristic of complex human systems.

It is not possible for us to identify and understand, even as possibilities, some of the things we don't yet know. Our approach to performance in uncertainty must deal effectively with unknowable future possibilities.

We can use the above assumptions as the basis for a set of risk management principles for leaders to apply when working in and on uncertainty.

Useful principles for leaders working in and on uncertainty

Principles should be of practical value as tests we can apply to behaviours, policies and processes. The following principles have been tested in practice by the author over the last 10–15 years:

Principle 1: Effective approaches to risk management should focus on the quality of decision-making processes in uncertainty.

Identifying, understanding and cataloguing risks does not help if decision processes are inconsistent, lack rigour, are biased or don't ensure that uncertainties are explored, analysed and then taken into account. Although even the best decisions cannot guarantee success, the quality of the work done when making decisions is fundamental to successful risk management.

Principle 2: Dealing with uncertainty should be built into our business systems so that it becomes business as usual.

Policies, rules and processes should accommodate uncertainty. Decision processes should inherently require that uncertainties are analysed and understood. Working in and on uncertainty is then experienced by people as their core work – rather than as a separate activity. The overall effect is to simplify and reduce the number of formal risk management processes and to make risk work more directly valuable to those involved.

Principle 3: A focus on the quality and value of responses to risk as a whole creates better outcomes than focusing on the 'biggest' risks.

The best outcomes are achieved by finding those responses to risk that create the best 'benefit for cost and effort' as a whole for the organization. Expressed another way, we should focus on risk management outputs and outcomes, not on inputs.

Principle 4: Inquiry, networking and dialogue with stakeholders is fundamental to performance in uncertainty (and to the management of risk).

The best and perhaps only effective approach to dealing with uncertainties that are hidden, sensitive, complex or emergent is shared dialogue and collaborative work across the whole system of organization. This is not limited to obvious roles, structures and functions. It includes all factors and all actors with an influence on the organization's ability to deliver on its purpose and its objectives.

Principle 5: The sophistication and quality of inquiry and analysis must match the nature and complexity of the risk environment.

Complex, systemic, intangible, interrelated risks cannot be understood or managed without the use of soft systems thinking (Jackson, 2003) methods and tools. Such methods (eg risk mapping, risk relationships analysis, risk treatment pattern analysis) can enable decision makers to work on sets of complex, intangible risks as a single whole, in real time and within real resource constraints. At the same time, we should not overcomplicate problems. Quantitative risk analysis and simple risk-by-risk approaches should be used where they can be effective.

Principle 6: Management of systemic, interrelated risks requires systemic, interrelated, integrated responses.

Systemic causes of risk and risks that are complex and interrelated will tend to react in unpredictable and even perverse ways if risk responses are transient or simplistic. To achieve a sustained risk benefit, responses to systemic risks must become an integral part of the risk dynamics.

Principle 7: The key risk work of senior leaders is to create an organization that is alert, responsive, proactive and resilient in the face of uncertainty and change.

Senior leaders should be involved in finding, understanding and managing strategic risks. They create even greater value when they build structures, systems, processes and cultures that support awareness, agility and resilience. Ultimately, building these capabilities is the only effective response to strategic uncertainty.

Systemic risk leadership in practice

The assumptions and principles described above are more than rhetoric. Working from them, tools and techniques can be developed in order to better support decision making. Effective risk leadership requires the judicious use of tools such as those used by the author, including:

- **Risk Mapping.** Complex risks can be represented using simple techniques in the form of influence and impact risk maps. Such maps are powerful tools for complex risk review, dialogue, identifying response options and managing risks over time.
- **Risk Relationships Analysis.** A many-to-many risk matrix can be used to analyse the ways in which a set of risks are interrelated. Instead of simply working on the 'biggest' risks, decision makers can decide where best to apply leverage on the set of risks as a whole.
- **Risk Treatment Pattern Analysis.** This method uses a tabular review process to find hidden patterns in possible risk treatments (responses). It is possible to find new options for systemic interventions – often in counterintuitive ways.
- **Systemic Risk Analysis (SRA).** SRA combines the techniques described above to establish a focused, strategic and system-wide response to risk. Working with the executive, this can be extended further using synthesis, to generate genuinely new, powerful insights for decision and action.
- **Systemic Risk Responses Registers.** This form of risk register is simpler in its form than traditional risk registers, yet represents many-to-many relationships between sources of risk and proposed system-wide risk responses (treatments). This makes it an ideal tool for executive and board review of risk management strategies and their value as a whole rather than risk by risk.

The above tools are powerful and practical. However, the greatest benefits accrue when the six assumptions and seven principles are combined into a single overall approach to performance in uncertainty. An example of this is the Organizational Risk Leadership Framework shown in Figure 16.2.

This framework for thinking and practice includes the use of simple, list-based risk management tools and methods when applicable as part of a

FIGURE 16.2 Organizational Risk Leadership Framework

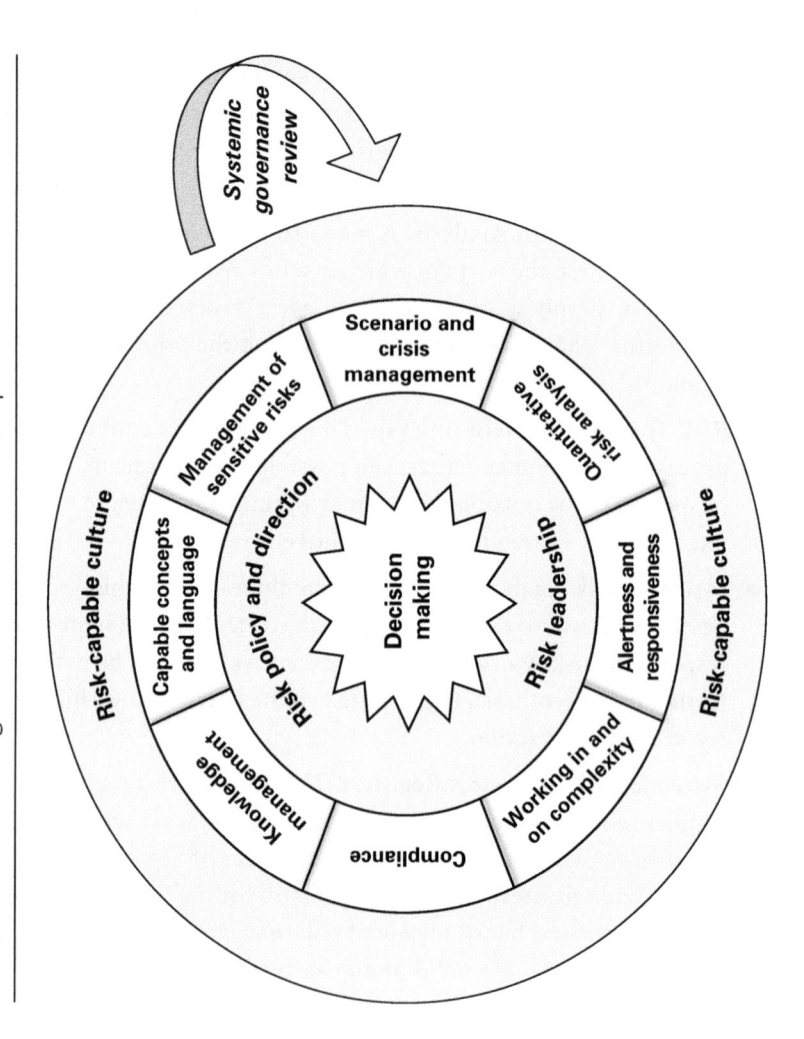

much larger, more complete and more capable way of thinking about and working on complex risk environments. Its core characteristics include:

- it is focused on enabling effective decision making in uncertainty;
- it includes the requirement for effective risk policy (direction);
- culture underpins everything;
- it includes ways of dealing with sensitive risks, complex risks and risks that are emergent;
- systemic risk analysis:
  - provides feedback on framework implementation;
  - provides leaders with unique 'whole of system' insights on interrelated risks and how best to approach them for best overall outcomes.

There is an additional benefit that is not directly visible in Figure 16.2. Through Principles 1, 2 and 4 in particular, applying this framework leads to a risk management process that is less separated from normal work. By improving key business process and by applying systemic risk thinking, leaders and staff are able to focus on their core work. Risk management work still happens, but most of it occurs as part of routine business processes. This is a non-trivial outcome in its own right, if only because it supports a positive culture about risk work and its value.

Summary: what this means for leaders of organizations

It is clearly necessary to rethink how we approach risk in organizations. A soft systems thinking approach to risk management is necessary in order to ensure that decision makers are armed with new, powerful insights about complex uncertainties and the best options for response. At the same time, risk management as a separate set of activities is reduced and is replaced by a focus on capable business systems, quality of decision making and on maximizing outcomes.

Applying systems thinking to the challenges posed by complex uncertainty is non-trivial. It requires us to avoid superficially simple tools and instead to tackle the more difficult root causes below the symptoms of risk. Some will struggle with this – either because we are uncomfortable stepping away from simple, easy processes or because it forces us to confront sensitive and difficult issues that we might prefer to avoid.

References

Barber, R B (2003) The dynamics of internally generated risks in organisations, Proceedings of the ANZSYS Conference, November 2003, Monash

Cantle, N (2012) Systems thinking and risk management, *The Actuary Magazine*, 9 (2), April/May, pp 19–23

Jackson, M C (2003) *Systems Thinking: Create holism for managers*, John Wiley & Sons, Chichester

Resilience

17

DR ERICA SEVILLE

In an increasingly complex world, organizations face a broad spectrum of risks arising from both natural and man-made causes. In such a world, one of the greatest assets an organization can have is the ability to survive disruption and to capture the opportunities that come from change and uncertainty.

Resilience as a concept has been around for many years, being used in the fields of ecology, disaster recovery, engineering and economics to name just a few. Over the past decade there has been increasing interest, both in academia and practice, in how to create more resilient organizations.

This chapter explains what a resilience approach is, how resilience fits with a risk management approach, and proactive ways to build an organization's resilience.

What is a resilience approach?

Resilient organizations are those that are able to survive adversity and to thrive in a world of uncertainty.

The study of organizations facing crisis includes an array of literature examining why organizations fail. Researchers have analysed major accidents, developed models of crisis causation and management, and have also explored how the structure and operation of organizations can prevent or lead to crises occurring (see for example seminal works by Reason, 2000; Pearson and Clair, 1998; Turner, 1976; Perrow, 1999).

Less attention has traditionally been given to what makes organizations succeed despite adversity. The organizational resilience literature is beginning to fill this gap, focusing on the characteristics of organizations that survive and thrive (Corey and Deitch, 2011; Kendra and Wachtendorf, 2003; Seville *et al.*, 2008, Lee *et al.*, 2013).

Resilience is a multidimensional, socio-technical phenomenon that addresses how people, as individuals or groups, manage uncertainty. Organizations respond to uncertainty in many ways: they centralize internal controls (Pfeffer, 1978), they learn (Carroll, 1998; Weick *et al.*, 2005), they are creative (Kendra and Wachtendorf, 2003), and they adapt (Vogus and Sutcliffe, 2008). Resilience is often characterized using notions of bouncing back, robustness, absorption, and surviving and thriving.

In recent years there have been efforts to develop a suite of indicators for identifying resilience within an organization, in advance of a crisis (McManus *et al.*, 2008; Lee *et al.*, 2013; Kachali *et al.*, 2014). Thirteen indicators of resilience (Figure 17.1) have been identified, and grouped under three attributes: (1) the adaptive capacity of an organization that is created by its leadership and culture; (2) the internal and external networks and relationships that an organization can draw on for support; and (3) how the organization strategically positions itself to be change ready (Resilient Organisations, 2015).

FIGURE 17.1 Resilience indicators

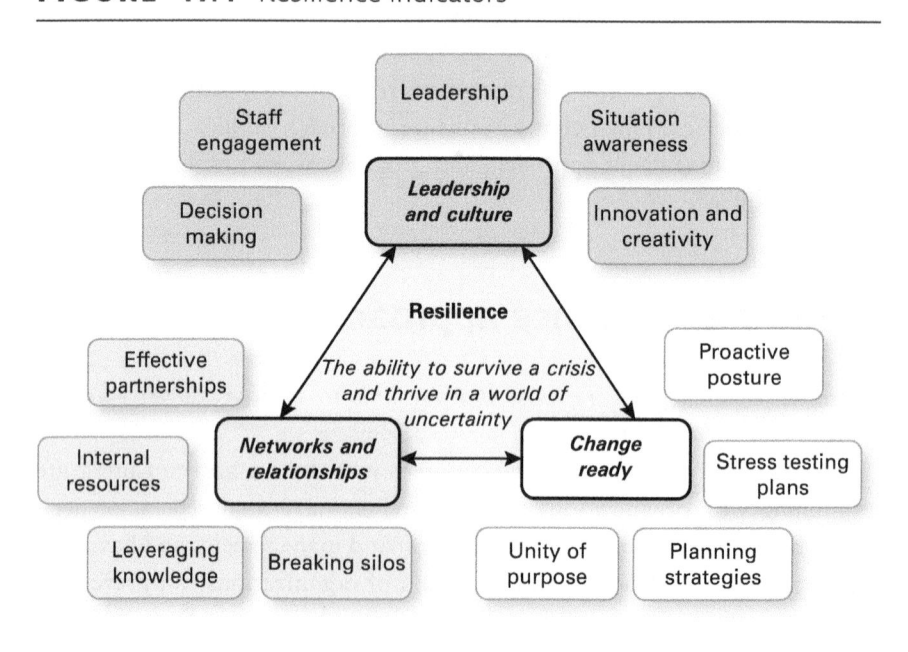

Resilience and risk management

It is important to understand how resilience and risk management interrelate. Risk management provides a framework for organizations to proactively think about and manage uncertainty. A resilience perspective provides a different, yet complementary lens on how to position an organization to manage uncertainty. Rather than focusing on the source and nature of risk for an organization, a resilience approach focuses on the capability of the organization to perceive and manage risks intelligently and to be able to deal with any situation that unfolds.

Resilience requires both planned and adaptive capabilities (Lee et al., 2013). Effective risk management, alongside other business planning processes, provides an important foundation for enhancing an organization's planned resilience capability, with the organization consciously developing, in advance, the capability and capacity to deal with particular situations. Adaptive resilience capabilities come to the fore when an organization faces a situation it hasn't anticipated, needing to develop new capabilities as the situation evolves. This adaptive resilience capability provides real value for organizations in helping to address risks where traditional risk management is less effective. Examples include:

- risks that have not been previously identified and are therefore not on any risk register;
- risks where we have very limited knowledge of risk source, scale, failure routes, or chains of causality;
- risks where the likelihood of occurrence is so low that they are not deemed a sufficient priority for treatment;
- risks where there is an adversary, and therefore estimations of likelihood and consequence change dynamically;
- complex system risks where the level of interdependency means it is very difficult to anticipate the consequences that may cascade from an initial event;
- risks where ownership and/or responsibility for managing that risk is unclear so the risk essentially remains 'unmanaged'.

Rather than focusing on the mechanism of disruption, resilience requires a suite of capabilities to be in place for when disruption occurs, encouraging the investment in adaptive management strategies. Resilience is more than just business continuity or crisis management though, in that it focuses on developing an innate capacity within an organization to deal with adversity – a capacity that goes beyond a small crisis response team, and becomes baked into the organization's culture and values, and in doing so offers 'business-as-usual' benefits as well.

Summary: proactive ways to develop resilience

Seville *et al.* (2015) provide seven principles for improving organizational resilience:

1 *Make adaptive capacity a core competency.* Competitive advantage rests with organizations that have the capacity to manage disruption – whether unforeseeable or merely unforeseen. Adaptive capacity is built from an organization's risk intelligence, flexibility, and readiness to change.

2 *Develop leaders that people want to follow.* The way in which people throughout an organization – from the CEO to call centre employees – demonstrate leadership influences resilience. To encourage the development of leaders that people will want to follow in times of crisis, invest in building leadership skills throughout the organization in times of relative calm.

3 *Become a learning organization.* A learning enterprise is able to evolve with continuously changing risk environments. Resilience requires an organizational structure that encourages new ideas, spreads them across the organization, and embeds them in business strategies.

4 *Build social capital.* Social capital represents the networks and resources available to people through their connections to others; it is essential to any successful venture. Build high-trust relationships to produce 'thicker' information exchange between staff, yielding strengthened staff engagement, improved process and product innovation, enhanced resource sharing, and 20/20-level situation awareness.

5 *Practise resilience as a team sport.* No organization is an island; the resilience of an organization is directly related to the resilience of the other organizations on which it depends (customers, suppliers, regulators, and even competitors). Reach out to help others also become more resilient.

6 *Design resilience into operational excellence.* Simple, standardized, and sustainable operating disciplines greatly increase the chances of surviving and thriving in times of disruption. Incorrect or missing data, gaps in process knowledge by workers, and inconsistent

operating discipline are the genesis of hazards and incidents – potentially turning disruption into disaster. Invest in creating a good operational discipline.

7 *Look beyond risks to see opportunities.* Organizations that actively manage their capability to deal with disruption forearm themselves with the capability to be future-ready. The same systems that enable organizations to flex in times of crisis also allow them to take on new risks deliberately. Disruption creates windows of opportunity for implementing change, such as the ability to redesign systems and processes, to rethink how facilities are utilized, or to create new collaborations or partnerships. Research has also shown that organizations that manage their crises well can actually grow their share value (Pretty, 2002). Always look for the opportunity that comes hand in hand with adversity.

Over the past five years there have been a number of initiatives to help organizations operationalize the concepts of resilience. For example, the Australian Attorney General's Department have created a free to access resource called the Resilience Healthcheck (REAG, 2015). The Healthcheck facilitates conversations within an organization about how it is performing against the 13 indicators of organizational resilience. This tool is an excellent starting point for anyone wanting to introduce the concept of organizational resilience to their organization.

Taking these ideas a step further, there are also a number of research-based tools available for benchmarking an organization's level of resilience (Stephenson *et al.*, 2010; Lee *et al.*, 2013; Whitman *et al.*, 2013; Resilient Organisations, 2015). Benchmarking can be used for identifying resilience strengths and weaknesses and for tracking progress in resilience improvements over time. These tools are useful for generating conversations between organizations about how to move resilience agendas forward. For example, in New Zealand a group of 18 critical infrastructure providers used resilience benchmarking to identify common gaps in resilience capability which they then, collectively, set out to address (Brown *et al.*, 2014). Similarly, in Australia, a cluster of five water companies, each considered to be sector leaders in resilience, undertook a resilience benchmarking project to stretch their thinking and encourage even more resilience improvement (Vargo *et al.*, 2012).

Resilience provides an important perspective on how well an organization is positioned to manage uncertainty and the unexpected. Well-managed risks and effective planning need to be coupled with great leadership and a culture of teamwork and trust which can respond effectively to the unexpected. The concept of resilience provides a framework for incorporating these aspects, which are rarely addressed on an organization's risk register.

References

Brown, C, Seville, E and Vargo, J (2014) Bay of Plenty lifelines group resilience benchmark report, Resilient Organisations Research Report 2014/06, September

Carroll, J S (1998) Organizational learning activities in high-hazard industries: the logics underlying self-analysis, *Journal of Management Studies* 35 (6), pp 699–717

Corey, C M and Deitch, E A (2011) Factors affecting business recovery immediately after Hurricane Katrina, *Journal of Contingencies and Crisis Management* 19 (3), pp 169–81

Kachali, H, Whitman, Z, Stevenson, J R, Vargo, J, Seville, E and Wilson, T (2014) Industry sector recovery following the Canterbury earthquakes, *International Journal of Disaster Risk Reduction*, doi:10.1016/j.ijdrr.2014.12.002

Kendra, J M and Wachtendorf, T (2003) Creativity in emergency response to the World Trade Center disaster, in *Beyond September 11th: An account of post-disaster research*, Natural Hazards Research and Information Centre, Univ. of Colorado, CO

Lee, A, Seville, E and Vargo, J (2013) Developing a tool to measure and compare organizations' resilience, *Natural Hazards Review*, 14 (1) pp 29–41

McManus, S, Seville, E, Vargo, J and Brunsdon, D (2008) A facilitated process for improving organizational resilience, *Natural Hazards Review* 9 (1), pp 81–90

Pearson, C M and Clair, J A (1998) Reframing crisis management, *Academy of Management Review* 23 (1), pp 59–76

Perrow, C (1999) *Normal Accidents: Living with high risk technologies*, 2nd edn., Basic Books, New York

Pfeffer, J (1978) *Organizational Design*, Harlan Davidson, Arlington Heights, IL

Pretty, D (2002) *Risks That Matter*, Oxford Metrica, Oxford

REAG (2015) Organisational Resilience Healthcheck, Resilience Expert Advisory Group, Australian Attorney General's Department, Australia [online] http://www.organisationalresilience.gov.au/HealthCheck/Pages/default.aspx

Resilient Organisations (2015) www.resorgs.org.nz [accessed 5 October 2015]

Reason, J (2000) Human error: models and management *British Medical Journal*, 320, pp 768–70

Seville, E P, Brunsdon, D, Dantas, A, Le Masurier, J, Wilkinson, S and Vargo, J (2008) Organisational resilience: researching the reality of New Zealand organisations, *Journal of Business Continuity & Emergency Planning*, **2** (2), pp 258–66

Seville, E, Van Opstal, D, and Vargo, J (2015) A primer in resiliency: seven principles for managing the unexpected, *Global Business and Organizational Excellence*, **34**, pp 6–18, doi: 10.1002/joe.21600

Stephenson, A, Vargo, J and Seville, E (2010) Measuring and comparing organizational resilience in Auckland, *Australian Journal of Emergency Management*, **25**(2), pp 27–32

Turner, B A (1976) The organizational and inter-organizational development of disasters, *Administrative Science Quarterly* **21** (3), pp 378–97

Vargo, J, Sullivan, J and Parsons, D (2012) Benchmarking resilience: organizational resilience in the Australian water industry, *Resilient Organisations* [online] http://www.resorgs.org.nz/images/stories/pdfs/OrganisationalResilience/sw_resilience_scorecard.pdf [accessed 29 Feb 2016]

Vogus, T J and Sutcliffe, K M (2008) Organizational resilience: towards a theory and research agenda, IEEE International Conference on Systems, Man and Cybernetics, Montreal

Weick, K E, Sutcliffe, K M, and Obstfeld, D (2005) Organizing and the process of sensemaking, *Organization Science* **16** (4), pp 409–21

Whitman, Z, Kachali, H, Roger, D, Vargo, J and Seville, E (2013) Short-form version of the Benchmark Resilience Tool (BRT-53), *Measuring Business Excellence*, **17** (3), pp 3–14

Organizational change management and risk

18

DR RUTH MURRAY-WEBSTER

'I have to change to stay the same.' This quotation from the Dutch expressionist artist Willem de Kooning provides the context for this chapter. Whatever the strategy and objectives of your organization, the one thing that is certain is that you will need to change if you are to remain relevant in your field. To change the way that people in your organization interact with systems, processes and other people to deliver products and services effectively and efficiently is challenging. It is also full of uncertainty with the potential to make your change management performance soar, or sink. Change and risk: risk and change – these can be argued to be two sides of the same coin. This reciprocal relationship between the management of change and the management of risk is explored in this chapter.

Why is change risky?

There is a vast body of research and experience that shows that organizational change is ubiquitous and always messy. This is not surprising. It is easy for an individual to make a choice, weigh up the pros and cons/opportunities and threats associated with that choice and then implement it. If the choice is something that a collection of people need to make and implement, be that in a family, a social club or a workplace, then the complexity of the task increases the more people are involved. In our organizations we mitigate this complexity by having structures, roles, hierarchies and networks that seek to simplify decision-making processes and control the implementation of our choices, but we cannot get away from the fact that every person in that organization and every stakeholder in the wider context of the organization will have a point of view that could be pivotal to making or not making the desired change.

There is lots of advice available for leaders and practitioners of planned organizational change. Table 18.1 summarizes this and is drawn from the literature referenced at the end of the chapter.

Implicit in this advice, but often not explicitly outlined is the need to understand change from the perspective of the recipients of change (Murray-Webster, 2014; Murray-Webster and Maylor, 2012, 2014).

TABLE 18.1 Success factors for planned change, derived from Murray-Webster (2014)

'Success factors' for planned change	Synthesized from the following literature
Have clear and realistic objectives • The business case must be aligned with corporate strategy, understood in terms of measurable benefits, and be championed and funded by sponsors at the most senior level. • A powerful vision and set of key performance indicators of how the organization will look following the change must be developed and communicated to all stakeholders.	Kotter, 1995 Buchanan and Boddy, 1992 Armenakis and Harris, 2002 Nutt, 1986
Inject speed into the process • The first steps into the transition must be understood and made easily accessible, with a sense of urgency created to help overcome any inertia. • The first steps must include some quick wins in order to ensure continued investment in the change and to motivate people to want to continue with the transformation.	Kotter, 1995 Beckhard and Harris, 1987

(Continued)

TABLE 18.1 *(Continued)*

'Success factors' for planned change	Synthesized from the following literature
Communicate with and encourage people • Change leaders must be appointed who are skilled in engaging people's hearts and minds. • The performance gap between the 'as is' and 'to be' states must be understood and communicated, to prevent inertia and to spread dissatisfaction with the current situation.	Kotter, 1995 Kotter and Schlesinger, 1979 Burnes, 2004 Buchanan and Boddy, 1992 Beckhard and Harris, 1987 Armenakis and Harris, 2002 Pideret, 2000 Ford *et al.*, 2008 Deetz *et al.*, 2000
Have a dedicated team to manage the change • Appoint visionary, creative and empowered leaders to drive the change. • Create a powerful, guiding coalition and supporting governance arrangements to ensure that decision making is focused moving the organization forward towards its goals.	Kotter, 1995 Buchanan and Boddy, 1992
Continuously sustain momentum of change • Put in place a change management plan that maps out activity along the whole transition curve. The plan must include activities to re-energize the change work if/when inertia strikes, to learn from experience, plans for consolidating improvements and plans for institutionalizing new approaches during the 're-freeze' stage. • Ensure that attitudes to change are continually understood and addressed to respond to any resistance and to overcome any complicity.	Kotter, 1995 Kotter and Schlesinger, 1979 Buchanan and Boddy, 1992 Brady and Maylor, 2010

Figure 18.1 shows in a simple form the underpinning relationship between the explicit organizational goals and plans for change, the implicit

thoughts, feelings, beliefs and intentions related to the change held by the people involved, and the resulting actions (or lack of action) from those people that lead to observable changed, or unchanged outcomes.

FIGURE 18.1 Organizational and human influences during planned change

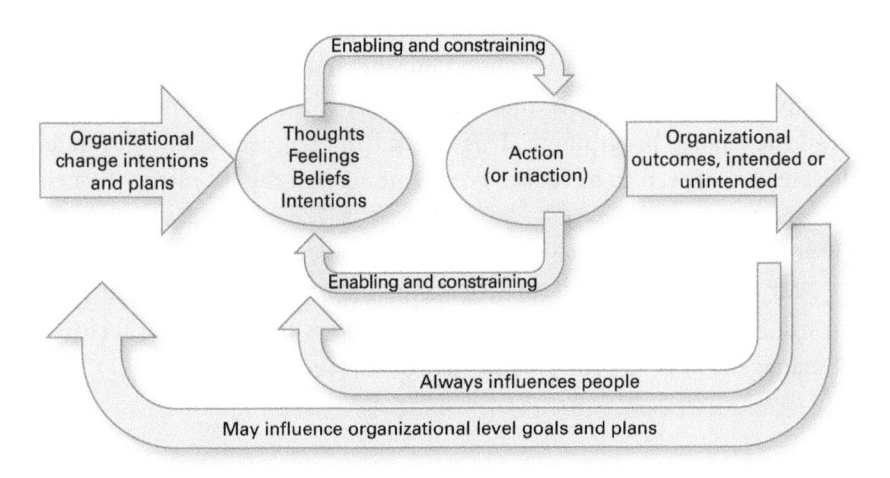

```
                    Enabling and constraining
                    ┌─────────────────────┐
                    ↓                     ↓
  Organizational    Thoughts                         Organizational
  change intentions Feelings      Action             outcomes, intended or
  and plans         Beliefs       (or inaction)      unintended
                    Intentions
                    ↑                     ↑
                    └─────────────────────┘
                    Enabling and constraining

                    Always influences people
        May influence organizational level goals and plans
```

SOURCE: Derived from Murray-Webster, 2014 (with permission)

This chapter cannot deal with the detail of this relationship and how to design change programmes to deliver more of the intended, rather than unintended consequences, but it does deal with the vital role of risk analysis and management in this process. In a nutshell, the biggest killer of organizational change is not resistance, as is often believed. The biggest killer is apathy because there is no data available to know what thoughts, feelings, beliefs and intentions exist, and so no control of actions and outcomes. Inclusive risk identification is one way to challenge apathy and gain better control of the change effort.

Why is risk analysis and management vital during change?

At its heart, risk analysis requires stakeholders (people) to share their perceptions of uncertainties that would affect objectives should they occur, so they can be prioritized.

All self-respecting change managers will have a risk register, log or database of some sort and will attempt to assess the likelihood and size of impact of uncertainties on objectives. Such risk logs are often of poor quality (poorly described risks, biased prioritizations etc.) and provide no confidence to senior leaders that the risk information is adding value. Improving the quality of risk information is one thing that often needs to change in an organization. A larger, underlying challenge though is that the risk identification step of the process does not facilitate the sharing of perceptions and perspectives from enough of the people who have the power to materially change outcomes. Perceptions that risk analysis is a bureaucratic, tick-box exercise often limit the time and energy that is given to really understanding the uncertainties with the power to enable or de-rail the change programme. This is not helped if people in risk-related roles are, or are seen to be focused on avoiding bad things, rather than enabling performance.

If you believe that change is risky and that risk management, done well, is a vital element of change management, then the following eight-point plan will be of interest. The eight points all address critical success factors if risk management is to add value to change management.

Critical success factors if risk management is to help change management

1. **Understand how much risk you are willing to take:** improved understanding of change objectives and the tolerance for risk taking in pursuit of those objectives (Hillson and Murray-Webster, 2012).
2. **Engage stakeholders:** be inclusive, design ways to really engage people to share perceptions and identify risks (Pullan and Murray-Webster, 2011).
3. **Don't forget the upsides:** what are the uncertainties that would result in beneficial outcomes? Think about how to creatively unlock thoughts on this as well as on downsides with the potential to cause problems.
4. **Build trust so people will share:** take people seriously, acknowledge their points (even if you don't agree), seek to understand, say thank you, be a role model for the behaviours you want others to follow.
5. **Measure the right things, or don't measure at all:** measuring the value of risk management is tricky in performance terms as it's

hard to demonstrate the value of managing something that may never have happened. Process measures, however, such as 'how many risks on the risk register' drive the wrong behaviours. If you're going to measure, be sure you incentivize what you want to happen.

6 **Be prepared to challenge, with respect:** learn how to question, clarify and hold others to account assertively but not aggressively, manage upwards and sideways as well as downwards.

7 **Know the difference between a stretch target and delusional optimism:** keep focused on 'plan A' while having well developed 'plan Bs' in place, don't 'shoot the messenger'.

8 **Take risks, but with your eyes open:** all change is risky; you can't manage all the risk so you need a keen understanding of which risks matter the most. Manage those and deal with the rest if and when they happen.

Summary

Most collective human endeavours are risky, ie there are many things that might happen that would matter if they did. This is particularly the case when pursuing benefits from organizational change as accomplishing intended benefits is always reliant on bringing the people on the journey with you.

Engaging those people on whom change success depends and enabling them to share their perceptions of risk on change objectives, good and bad, is a brilliant way of showing that you are interested to understand people's viewpoints and that you are willing to act to deal with those risks with the potential to materially influence outcomes.

The benefits of serious engagement of stakeholders in risk identification extend beyond the boundaries of having a better analysis of risk than you might otherwise have achieved and greater preparedness for dealing with unexpected or unwanted situations. Risk identification is also an ideal way to start and maintain meaningful dialogue with stakeholders about the change itself and for the change team to learn which levers they need to address in order to be successful.

Change and risk go hand in hand so need to be considered together and the reciprocal nature addressed. Do this and accomplishing change can become a whole lot easier.

References

Armenakis, A A and Harris, S G (2002) Crafting a change message to create transformational readiness, *Journal of Organizational Change Management*, **15** (2), p 169

Beckhard, R and Harris, R (1987) *Organizational Transitions*, Addison-Wesley, USA

Brady, T and Maylor, H (2010) The improvement paradox in project contexts: a clue to the way forward? *International Journal of Project Management*, **28** (8), p 787

Buchanan, D A and Boddy D (1992) *The Expertise of the Change Agent*, Prentice Hall Europe, UK

Burnes, B (2004) Kurt Lewin and the planned approach to change, *Journal of Management Studies*, **41**(6), p 977

Deetz, S, Tracy, S and Simpson, J (2000) *Leading Organizations through Transition: Communication and cultural change*, Sage Publications, USA

Ford, J D, Ford, L W and D'Amelio, A (2008) Resistance to change: the rest of the story, *Academy of Management Review*, **33** (2), p 362

Hillson, D A and Murray-Webster, R (2012) *A Short Guide to Risk Appetite*, Gower Publications, Hampshire, UK

Kotter, J P (1995) Leading change: why transformation efforts fail, *Harvard Business Review*, **73** (2), p 59

Kotter, J P and Schlesinger, L A (1979) Choosing strategies for change, *Harvard Business Review*, **57** (2), p 106

Murray-Webster, R (2014) What does it take for organizations to change themselves? The influences on the internal dynamics of organizational routines undergoing planned change, Cranfield University School of Management Doctoral Thesis

Murray-Webster, R and Maylor, H (2012) How a well-managed change programme yielded no change and what this tells us about change and control: a structuration perspective, *Proceedings of the 28th European Group for Organization Studies (EGOS) Colloquium*

Murray-Webster, R and Maylor, H (2014) Too close for comfort? Organizing across temporary/permanent boundaries during planned change to organizational routines, *Proceedings of the 30th European Group for Organization Studies (EGOS) Colloquium*

Nutt, P C (1986) Tactics of implementation, *Academy of Management Journal*, **29** (2), p 230

Pideret, S K (2000) Rethinking resistance and recognizing ambivalence: a multidimensional view of attitudes towards an organizational change, *Academy of Management Review*, **25** (4), p 783

Pullan, P and Murray-Webster, R (2011) *A Short Guide to Facilitating Risk Management*, Gower Publications, Hampshire, UK

Risk culture

19

ALEX HINDSON

What is risk culture and why is it important?

Enterprise Risk Management (ERM) has been under the spotlight since the 2008 financial crisis, particularly in the financial services sector. The question is often asked, 'Where was ERM?' This reflects a concern that the focus has been on implementing ERM processes but that it has failed to engage people's hearts and minds, leading to a significant increase in regulation, process and governance. There is, however, no guarantee that all this regulatory attention will drive a change in staff behaviours. This requires a change in risk culture.

Culture in many ways is what staff in your organization do when you are not watching them. It is values-based and ethically driven. You can create ever-stronger processes and controls, but if your staff do not understand or buy in, these will only be paper thin and will probably not stand up to scrutiny in a future crisis.

The pressure is increasing to address risk culture head on. For example, in 2014 the Financial Stability Board (FSB) issued specific guidance to regulators on evaluating an organization's risk culture (Financial Stability Board, 2014). This provides 35 targeted questions that can be used in appraising an organization's risk culture.

The FSB document provides a range of detailed questions covering four major themes: Tone at the Top, Accountability, Effective Communication, and Challenge and Incentives. These themes are in turn broken down into 12 specific issues. An extract is provided in Table 19.1, showing the six questions associated with the issue of 'Leading by Example' under Tone at the Top.

Emerging Trends

TABLE 19.1 Financial Stability Board guidance

Area	Question
Tone at the Top – leading by example	1. The board and senior management have a clear view of the risk culture to which they aspire for the financial institution and of the behavioural and organizational consequences of this culture, systematically monitor and assess the prevailing risk culture, and proactively address any identified areas of weakness or concern.
	2. The board and senior management, consistently within their specific roles and responsibilities, promote through behaviours, actions and words, a risk culture that expects integrity and a sound approach to risk management as well as promoting an open exchange of views, challenge and debate.
	3. The board and senior management promote healthy scepticism that encourages and supports openness to challenge by providing alternative points of view that may result in a better decision, ensuring that all directors have the tools, resources and information to carry out their roles effectively, particularly their challenge function.
	4. The board and senior management are committed to establishing, monitoring, and adhering to an effective risk appetite framework, supported by appropriate risk appetite statement(s) that underpin the financial institution's risk management strategy, and is integrated with the overall business strategy.
	5. Mechanisms are in place, such as talent development, succession planning, and confidential 360-degree review processes, to ensure that decision making is not dominated by any one individual or small group of individuals in a manner that is detrimental to the interests of the institution as a whole.
	6. Senior management is subject to the same expectations for integrity, risk governance, and risk culture as all other employees; that is, mechanisms are in place to subject them to incentive structures, which may include impacts on compensation, role and responsibilities, or termination.

SOURCE: FSB (2014)

The Institute of Risk Management (2012) produced a series of papers on risk culture and offered the following working definition:

> The values, beliefs, knowledge and understanding about risk shared by a group of people with a common purpose, in particular the employees of an organization or of teams or groups within an organization.

This is based on the IRM Risk Culture Framework outlined in Figure 19.1. This shows risk culture as a complex outcome of a series of concentric and interacting factors. At the core of all individuals in an organization is a set of personal predispositions to risk taking, which are deeply held attitudes shaped by formative experiences. These are overlaid with personal ethics, the anchors that drive people's values. These aspects of people's personalities are not readily visible but their behaviours can be observed and measured. Collective behaviours, 'the way we do things round here', form an organization culture, and this in turn influences an organization's collective risk awareness and approach to risk taking in decision making.

FIGURE 19.1 IRM Risk Culture Framework

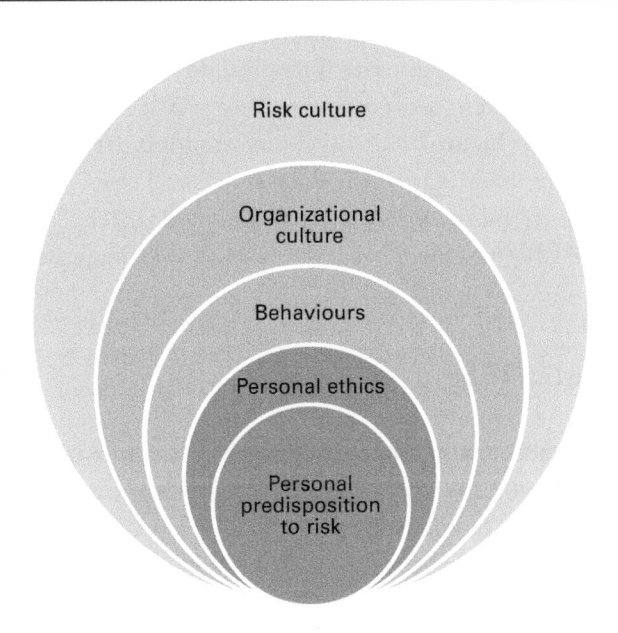

[Concentric circles diagram showing from outer to inner: Risk culture, Organizational culture, Behaviours, Personal ethics, Personal predisposition to risk]

SOURCE: © 2012 The Institute of Risk Management. From IRM (2012), used with permission

How to approach risk culture

The first thing to realize is that risk culture is a complex issue. It is possible to glimpse it through different aspects of a prism but it would be foolhardy of anyone to claim to fully understand it or be able to control it.

The second important point is to understand that any work an ERM function might want to undertake with respect to risk culture will become a change management programme applied to a complex social system. As such risk professionals need to be humble enough to recognize that they are not always equipped with sufficient understanding of psychology and sociology to tackle this alone, and they should reach out to others to partner on this topic. Human Resources and Communications can be key allies in seeking to drive organization change and they may have their own objectives in terms of driving certain behavioural changes.

Diagnosing risk culture

Although risk culture is complex to grasp and difficult, if not impossible, to measure, it is possible to diagnose and understand aspects of risk culture.

Tools and methodologies exist for sampling the risk culture of an organization, and different tools can be used to test at different layers of the 'onion' diagram in Figure 19.1. Psychometric tools are for example particularly useful in investigating the innermost two layers, whereas surveys and interviews are more appropriate for the outer layers. The IRM guidance (IRM, 2012) gives further advice on available diagnostic tools.

Risk awareness

One important facet when thinking about the risk culture of your organization is to reflect on how best to implement an ERM programme successfully. ERM needs to be implemented in a different manner depending on how an organization operates more generally. Figure 19.2 provides a simple model for considering what type of organizational culture you might be dealing with.

'Systems of Control' define the extent to which activity is governed by formal processes which staff are expected to comply with. The other extreme

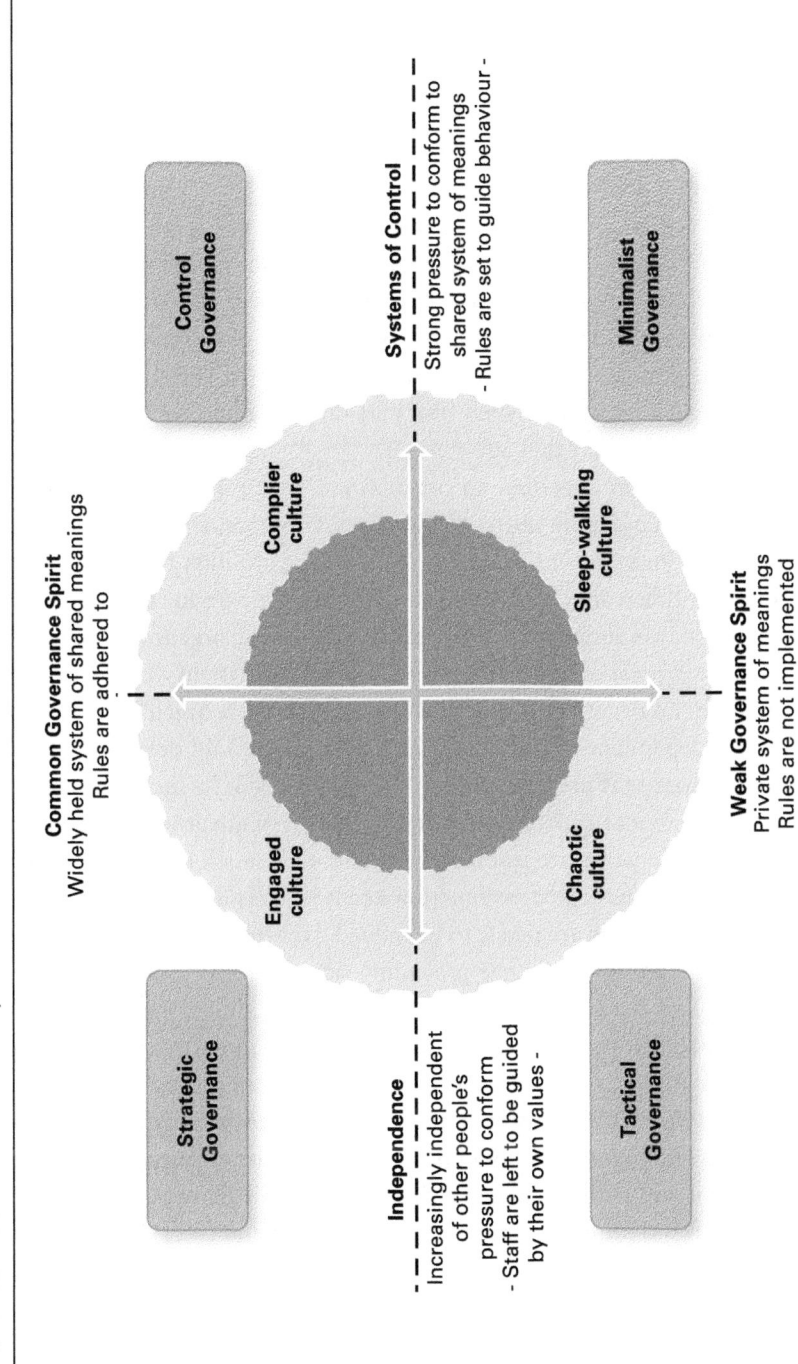

Risk Culture 273

FIGURE 19.2 IRM Risk Aspects Culture Model

Common Governance Spirit
Widely held system of shared meanings
Rules are adhered to

Weak Governance Spirit
Private system of meanings
Rules are not implemented

Systems of Control
Strong pressure to conform to shared system of meanings
- Rules are set to guide behaviour -

Independence
Increasingly independent of other people's pressure to conform
- Staff are left to be guided by their own values -

Complier culture
Sleep-walking culture
Engaged culture
Chaotic culture

Control Governance
Minimalist Governance
Strategic Governance
Tactical Governance

SOURCE: From IRM (2012), used with permission

('Independence') describes an organization where staff make their own decisions based on their values. If a 'Common Governance Spirit' exists together with Independence, an *Engaged Culture* results where people tend to 'do the right thing' because they firstly understand the context and they share common values. A Strategic Governance approach means that in an engaged culture it is important to understand that ERM needs to be sold to people; they need to understand the benefits to them personally and to the organization as a whole.

In other organizations with a strong rules focus and weak spirit, a *Sleep-Walking Culture* might have been created. People tend to blindly follow the rules they have been given without engaging with broader objectives. A Minimalist Governance approach is warranted in this situation to prevent the controls and processes being counter-productive. The danger is that if procedures are too complex then staff may take the opportunity to not think sufficiently about what they are doing.

Complier Culture describes an organization where there is a strong alignment of understanding in terms of 'Common Governance Spirit' as well as a preference for 'Systems of Control'. In such an organization rules are not only welcomed but they are closely followed. There is a desire for Compliance, although this may in some ways stifle creativity. In such an organization a governance approach predicated on a strong internal control system would work well.

Finally in an organization with 'Weak Governance Spirit' and a preference for independent thinking, a *Chaotic Culture* could develop with few rules and those that are in place not being followed. In such an organization, a very Tactical approach needs to be taken to governance where only the essential elements are implemented and very much on a needs basis.

Clearly a risk management function needs to consider both the extent to which the current culture needs to be moved over time, but a pragmatic perspective needs to start from the prevailing situation.

Ultimately if the goal is to create a risk-aware culture, where people are able to make informed decisions based on a clear understanding of the threats and opportunities associated with business opportunities, then they need to be informed, empowered and encouraged to actively consider risk.

A risk-aware organization will potentially be more attuned to its external environment and its internal capabilities, and it will also be more agile and resilient in responding to rapidly changing circumstances. A culture where staff are encouraged to consider the threats and opportunities around their business activities will potentially grasp the implications of changes sooner, identify and harness opportunities, and be better able to organize its resources in a joined-up manner.

Changing or influencing risk culture

So how does one approach this? Influencing an organization's risk culture is clearly a significant change management initiative. The IRM offer guidance in terms of the Risk Aspects Culture Diagnostic (IRM, 2012). Eight distinct areas of risk culture are described. The five aspects outlined in pale grey in Figure 19.3 relate to the governance-related or 'hard' aspects of culture dealing with leadership roles and functional responsibilities, reporting and disclosure. By contrast the three dark grey aspects covering societal-related or 'soft' aspects of culture deal with skills, remuneration and handling bad news.

By considering these eight aspects, it is possible to design a series of interventions to allow culture change to be initiated. The following case study illustrates how this might be approached.

FIGURE 19.3 IRM Risk Aspects Culture Diagnostic

Tone at the Top	Risk leadership	Informed risk decisions	Decision making
	Dealing with bad news	Reward	
Governance	Accountability	Risk resources	Competency
	Transparency	Risk skills	

SOURCE: From IRM (2012), used with permission

Case study

This case study describes a UK-based financial institution where the risk function proposed a risk culture programme to the Board Risk Committee. The risk function captured the aim and approach for a risk culture study in a one-page terms of reference, and the Risk Committee agreed to sponsor and steer the programme.

The drivers for the study were related to providing assurance to the Committee that risk culture, as demonstrated by day-to-day operations, was aligned to the core values espoused and promulgated by the organization. The need for this assurance was prompted by three converging trends:

- First there was increased focus by the UK Financial Conduct Authority (FCA) on culture and values in financial institutions (Financial Conduct Authority, 2015).
- Second, this was supported also by the Financial Stability Board (FSB) issuing guidance to supervisors on how to approach the analysis of risk culture (Financial Stability Board, 2014).
- Third, the Financial Reporting Council (FRC) guidance on Risk Management confirmed the board's accountability for defining 'the culture it wishes to embed in the company, and whether this has been achieved' (Financial Reporting Council, 2014). The FRC further anticipated that companies would provide information on progress in achieving their desired culture within their Annual Reports.

The scope of the project included a pilot study within one specific operating division to test the value of the process and consider how it might be rolled out later to the rest of the organization.

The project was planned over three phases. Phase 1 involved completing a high-level gap analysis using the IRM Risk Aspects Culture Diagnostic (see Figure 19.3). This was completed by the risk function and identified some initial areas to investigate further.

The second phase involved constructing a diagnostic tool based around the 35 questions within the FSB publication (Financial Stability Board, 2014), and sought to capture and score evidence of how the organization matched up to these expectations. The rationale for adopting this approach was to ensure that an internal evaluation was done, prior to any possible regulatory intervention. This phase was implemented by interviewing a small number of senior managers within the Reward, Talent Management, Compliance, Company Secretarial and Internal Audit functions.

The outcomes of the first two phases were presented back to the Committee and senior management as a checkpoint prior to agreeing priorities for the detailed third phase of work. Several key areas for further analysis and action were highlighted, particularly related to performance and talent management processes.

This last phase involved completing over 30 structured interviews with a cross-section of staff within the selected division to supplement an online survey issued to over 500 members of staff. The online survey used the 'Moral DNA' psychometric test, which is validated with over 100,000 completed profiles, and which had previously been used by peer organizations to evaluate their corporate culture.

The overall outcome of the project was a report, presented to senior management and the Committee outlining areas of strength and weakness in terms of the alignment of culture with corporate values, and a number of proposed improvement actions, aligned to the eight risk aspects, that could be sponsored by the Committee. The report specifically helped the Committee articulate the risk culture it was seeking to engender and areas where this was not currently being translated into practice.

By investigating and analysing the current risk culture, identifying significant trends, and in some cases delivering difficult messages, it was possible to guide directors on a journey whereby they were able, by reacting to the current situation, to articulate their cultural objectives. This then enabled a cross-functional team involving Communications, Human Resources and others to put together a structured change management plan to guide the organization towards this culture goal. Further analysis along the journey would enable progress to be determined and adjustments made to the programme.

Summary

Risk culture is very important for organizations to grasp, under increased scrutiny by external stakeholders such as regulators and shareholders, but it is also not an easy aspect of ERM to master.

Creating or shaping a more risk-aware culture is, however, potentially the greatest value a risk function can bring to the table in terms of preparing their organization for the challenges of uncertain and fast-changing environments.

An organization with a risk-aware culture is one that is more resilient to external influences and better able to adapt. The principal benefit of a strong risk culture comes from enhanced and timely decision making. An agile organization is able to reach decisions in terms of the risk and reward of different opportunities more quickly and in a more informed manner. Fewer unenforced errors arise from a risk-aware organization able to learn from previous events and mistakes and improve its processes in a timely manner. Finally these benefits in turn improve the external perception of an organization by its stakeholders such as investors, analysts, credit rating agencies and regulators. So ultimately a risk-aware culture is about protecting corporate reputation.

References

Financial Conduct Authority (2015), Business Plan 2015/2016 [online] http://www.fca.org.uk/static/channel-page/business-plan/business-plan-2015-16.html [accessed 29 September 2015]

Financial Reporting Council (2014), *Guidance on Risk Management, Internal Control and Related Financial and Business Reporting*, Financial Reporting Council, London, UK

Financial Stability Board (2014), *Guidance on Supervisory Interaction with Financial Institutions on Risk Culture*, Financial Stability Board, Basel, Switzerland

Institute of Risk Management (2012), *Risk Culture: Resources for practitioners*, Institute of Risk Management, London, UK

Moral DNA (2015) What's your moral DNA? [online] http://moraldna.org [accessed 18 September 2015]

Power, M, Ashby, S and Palermo, T (2013) Risk culture in financial organisations: a research report, *London School of Economics* [online] http://www.lse.ac.uk/accounting/CARR/pdf/final-risk-culture-report.pdf [accessed 29 September 2015]

Social media risk

DR GREG KER-FOX

Introduction

Social media platforms refer to software applications that are deployed through websites or downloaded to smart devices. These applications enable people to participate in online social networking: communicating, creating and sharing content, collaborating and building communities. In little more than a decade, the industry has grown exponentially to 2 billion active social media accounts (Statista, 2015). While many of the related risks are not new, social media technology magnifies exposures and can result in extensive widespread damage in a short space of time.

The social media business model

Social media platforms create an audience by enticing users with a valuable service, for which no direct fee is charged. These services include:

- building social and professional networks (one-to-one relationships);
- building audiences (one-to-many relationships);
- publically interacting with friends and colleagues through online posts;
- privately interacting with friends and colleagues, or user-defined groups through internal messaging systems;
- publically interacting with audiences and followers;
- publishing opinions and promoting content, in the form of blogs (long text) or micro-blogs (short text);
- publishing and sharing content such as videos, audio, photos, papers, articles and PowerPoint presentations.

People wishing to utilize the social media platform must first create a user profile. This may include a username, avatar (personal image), background information and an e-mail address or mobile phone number for authentication. User profiles and their activity on the application, such as 'Liking' a new music album or viewing the artist's page, provide personal information and an indication of current interests. This enables the platform to develop more detailed consumer profiles for each user. These consumer profiles indicate the types of products and services the user may be receptive to. The profiles are further refined by the platform through information collected from subsidiary applications on user's devices, as well as the user's activity on subsidiary websites and those belonging to the platform's clients and partners (Facebook, 2015a).

Social media platforms sell the user's attention and consumer profile to advertisers, who wish to market products and services to the user with the objective of making a sale or furthering an agenda (Facebook, 2015b). Advertisers also use the consumer profiles and social media to better understand their markets, which directs product development. Much like print and televised media, revenue is generated primarily from advertising. However, when it is used well, social media can provide a far more focused and measurable impact on the target audience than traditional advertising.

Current understanding of risk includes the dual concept of opportunity (upside risk), and threat (downside risk), and social media creates both opportunities and threats for business. These are detailed in the following two sections.

Opportunities created by social media for business

Direct marketing

Social media platforms are well suited to direct marketing for consumer-facing organizations with short sales cycles. Marketing is targeted at individuals based on their consumer profile. Under these conditions, an individual user may decide whether or not to purchase the product or service they are being exposed to.

Building reputation capital

Company pages can be used to build reputation capital and brand awareness with subscribers by publishing positive company news, such as significant achievements, capacity, capability and corporate social investment activities.

Recruitment

Social media can be used to build professional networks. This provides a vehicle for employers to engage with prospective employees, to build skills databases and advertise vacancies.

Communication

Social media provides a means for employers to communicate with their employees. Staff working far from home use social media as a cost-effective way of maintaining contact with friends and family.

Customer support

Social media provides a platform for customers and members of the community to communicate publicly with the organization. This may include complaints about poor service, product quality or inappropriate staff behaviour, reports of fraud, technical assistance and requests for product and service enhancements.

Education and training

Platforms enabling users to share videos are becoming a convenient and effective way for people to acquire knowledge. This media is being applied in areas such as induction of new employees, safety, health, quality, ethics and compliance.

Threats associated with social media for business

Reputation risk

Social media provides public platforms for users, both informed and uninformed, to share opinions and broadcast negative events and crises. The speed with which news can spread, difficulty in ensuring commentary is fair and accurate, and global reach makes this form of risk challenging to mitigate.

Loss of productivity

Facebook's Q2 2015 earnings report indicates that their 968 million daily active users spend 46 minutes on average per day on Facebook, Messenger and Instagram (Facebook, 2015c). This equates to more than 271 billion man hours a year consumed by these three applications alone. Assuming that a significant number of users are employed, and that a portion of time spent on social media by employees may be during working hours, the cumulative cost (due to lost productivity) of social media to the global economy could be hundreds of billions of pounds annually.

Legal and regulatory risk

Laws that specifically address the unique issues presented by social media are being developed. However, much reliance is still placed on case law to set a precedent for interpreting existing laws in a social media context. Companies may unknowingly be guilty of legal and regulatory non-compliance through actions relating to social media (Bowman Gilfillan, 2014) such as:

- gathering applicant information using social media as part of the recruitment process, such as to establish religious or political affiliation, which would be unconstitutional;
- staff responding to customer complaints on the company's social media pages with proposed solutions which may be entering the company into binding contracts, without the necessary authorization;
- breaches of intellectual property law through copyright infringements;
- vicarious liability for employee misconduct on social media, while using company devices during working hours;
- misrepresentation by not removing misleading remarks made by third parties on the company's pages.

Non-compliance with legal and regulatory frameworks may lead to penalties and even loss of trading licences.

Security breaches

Hackers use a range of techniques to gain unauthorized access to users' devices, company networks and data servers. Social media is providing many new opportunities for unscrupulous people to achieve this. Personal devices, such as smartphones and tablets, generally have lower levels of security than work stations. This enables users to install third-party applications from unsecure sites. Devices used to interact on social media using public networks are particularly vulnerable. Staff using personal devices on the company network increases the organization's exposure.

Traceability

Social media platforms generally require some form of authentication for new user registrations. However, a profile created on a third-party device (such as at an internet café), on a public network, using an anonymous web browser, authenticated with an unregistered mobile phone number or disposable e-mail address, would be difficult to trace. Therefore the username, avatar and profile content may bear no resemblance to the actual account holder.

Identity theft

Hackers may create fake accounts to impersonate a company, or hack into official accounts and post content that furthers their own agendas.

Terrorist attacks

Mobile phones contain global positioning system (GPS) technology to establish the whereabouts of the device. This is used by social media to localize advertising. A terrorist or stalker who was able to access their victim's smartphone would be able to keep track of their exact whereabouts.

Malicious attacks

Hackers gain access to a user's account with the intention of viewing content that is restricted from public view. They may also wish to defame the user by posting malicious content such as text, images and video.

Abuse of stakeholders

Staff may post offensive comments about colleagues, clients or partners, which reflects negatively on the company. This type of record is legally admissible in many jurisdictions (Phillips and Littlefair, 2015) and can be used as evidence in disciplinary processes.

Industrial espionage

Malware is software that is designed to disrupt or damage a computer system. This type of software can be executed by injecting code into credible social media sites and e-mails (Federal Bureau of Investigation, 2015). Spyware is a type of malware that enables a hacker to gain unauthorized access to a device, with the intention of collecting information by transmitting data covertly. This can be used to record keystrokes, collecting passwords and usernames. It could also be used to remotely activate the device's built-in microphone or camera, providing traders and competitors with price-sensitive confidential information.

Recruitment fraud

People seeking employment can be identified from their comments on a prospective employer's pages. A fraudster, with a plausible false profile, can make contact with the job seeker through the platform's internal messaging system. They then request personal details and an upfront administrative fee, in return for placement that never materializes.

Damage to employer of choice profile

Job seekers regularly review prospective employers on social media, to get a sense of the company culture and staff morale. Negative posts from disgruntled current or former employees will negatively impact the company's ability to attract new talent.

Publicizing bad service

Some platforms offer the facility for third parties to review the company, product or service, and give a rating. This information is useful when choosing a restaurant. However, organizational stakeholders may place limited value on positive reviews, but be negatively influenced by a few unvetted negative or emotional comments and ratings.

Data misuse

Hackers may gain access to the social media site's servers and steal their registered users' data, including banking details and activities on the site. If made public, this could reflect badly on individuals and even place them at risk of harassment (Brewster, 2015).

Loss of intellectual property

The objective of gaining unauthorized access to devices and servers may be to illegally retrieve confidential information and intellectual property.

Companies may also suffer this kind of loss by being unaware of the terms of use of data transfer or storage services offered by many social media platforms. These conditions of use may give the service provider a worldwide licence to reuse the content (Google, 2014).

Exploiting social media opportunities

Businesses using social media can take a number of measures to exploit the opportunities associated with it. These are discussed below.

Data mining

Data mining service providers can analyse the vast amounts of data that flow through the Internet daily. This is useful for better understanding target markets, product development and designing directing marketing campaigns.

Communicating with audiences

Company social media profiles can attract significant levels of traffic. This provides an opportunity for the company to communicate with interested parties. There are different ways of promoting a profile, such as including links on main company websites, posting blogs with useful or interesting information that may draw an audience, including sharing buttons on blogs, using multiple social media sites, using hash-tags of trending topics, and tagging popular people and sites, which may result in them sharing your comment with their audiences.

Crisis communication

A crisis often results in a significant amount of attention being focused on affected parties. This intense focus can be devastating if the crisis event is managed ineffectually. However, a robust response, with meaningful, timeous feedback and decisive action, can actually build reputation capital. Social media provides invaluable platforms for companies to keep affected stakeholders informed of developments and progress with mitigating the consequences of the crisis. Just as is the case with threats created from negative commentary, these platforms provide businesses with a form of communication that has no boundaries, is instantaneous and is provided at no cost.

Increasing revenue

As discussed under the business model section, social media generates income by assisting clients to increase sales through direct marketing. Consumer-facing organizations are particularly well suited to this type of marketing campaign. However, by profiling key decision makers, even business-to-business organizations can use social media to grow revenue. This is done by exposing the decision maker, such as a design engineer or procurement manager, to the company's capabilities, services and products, while they are conceptualizing designs, preparing tender specifications and drawing up lists of invited bidders. In this way, the company will be given the opportunity to submit proposals to fulfil the client's requirements.

Mitigating social media threats

Businesses using social media can take a number of measures to mitigate the likelihood or severity of threats arising from its use. These are discussed below.

Social media plan

A company social media plan indicates the social media platforms to be used. Official company social media profiles should be maintained regularly, with timely response to comments. Unofficial or auto-generated profiles should be deactivated, as these can draw traffic and commentary with no response from the company.

The plan indicates how the profile pages will be used (publishing company news, customer support, recruitment or marketing), and what is to be achieved (brand building, increased sales or product development).

A social media policy indicates what company information can be shared online, who is authorized to formally represent the company online and what type of social media behaviour impacting the company is acceptable.

Reputation risk

Much of the damage to reputation occurs in the aftermath of a crisis, and includes the way in which the organization responds (or doesn't). Social media can enable the organization to contain further damage by keeping affected stakeholders informed of the status of the crisis, and progress with corrective action. Different stakeholders, such as clients, customers, staff and shareholders, may be inclined to use different forms of social media. Communication channels to access the various stakeholders can be defined as part of the crisis communication plan.

Listening posts

A negative comment on social media with no response from the affected party, can cause damage to reputation. Data mining service providers can provide insight into areas where the company is receiving attention, trending topics, traffic volumes, duration and demographics. This will ensure that the company is aware of and can responding to exposures, such as news articles, customer complaints, public commentary and staff activity.

Page guidelines

All company social media profiles should include a legally compliant 'Page guidelines' section, setting out the purpose of the page, acceptable activity and the owner's rights to moderate or remove non-compliant posts.

Staff personal devices

Where there is a case to give personal devices access to company networks, this must be done in compliance with the company network's security protocols. Consideration could be given to free distribution of effective anti-virus software for personal devices, to provide additional protection for the company network.

Industrial espionage

All mobile devices with access to the Internet should be powered off during sensitive meetings, to prevent remote activation of microphones and cameras. Controls should be in place to prevent the installation of third-party applications that may contain malware and spyware.

Staff training

Educate staff on the personal and business risks associated with social media, and the potential negative impact of their online activity on the company. Guidelines should be given on reducing the chances of having their credentials stolen, reducing personal and professional vulnerability and the safe use of public Wi-Fi networks etc. Any action required on e-mails, such as accepting a friend request, should be treated with caution. Login credentials should only be captured on websites that start with https// (indicating that they are secure).

Managing access to social media sites

Where access to social media is provided on company devices, this should be done to limit security risks and loss of productivity. Video streaming and online gaming can be disabled and access to social media sites restricted to less productive times of the day.

Safety

Many social media applications request access to the user's contact list, microphone, camera and GPS locator. These requests should be denied unless the user is comfortable with the application and its parent company utilizing this information to refine their consumer profile.

Terms and conditions of use

Continued use of a social media platform implies acceptance of their terms and conditions, including any changes. Companies must understand these terms and ensure their willingness to utilize the technology under imposed conditions.

Regulatory compliance

Organizations need to understand and ensure compliance with the laws and regulations governing social media in all the jurisdictions in which business is conducted.

Summary

Social media technology significantly increases related risk exposure, and simply ignoring social media in no way mitigates the associated risk. However, companies willing to confront the exposures can manage them proactively and benefit from the powerful business opportunities created by this medium.

Acknowledgement

Some of the material in this chapter is based on content written by the author for the Engineering and Construction Risk Institute (ECRI) and is used with permission.

References and further reading

Bowman Gilfillan (2015) Social media and the law [online] http://www.bowman.co.za/Social-Media-Law/Index.asp

Brewster, T (2015) Ashley Madison CEO steps down after catastrophic attack, *Forbes* [online] http://www.forbes.com/sites/thomasbrewster/

Engineering and Construction Risk Institute (2015) Social Media Risk best practice [online] http://www.ecrionline.org

Facebook (2015a) Facebook Data Policy, 30 January [online] https://www.facebook.com/policy.php

Facebook (2015b) Facebook's Statement of Rights and Responsibilities, 30 January [online] https://www.facebook.com/legal/terms

Facebook (2015c) Second Quarter 2015 results presentation [online] http://investor.fb.com/results.cfm

Federal Bureau of Investigation (2015) Internet Social Networking Risks [online] https://www.fbi.gov/about-us/investigate/counterintelligence/

Google (2014) Google Terms of Service, 14 April [online] https://www.google.com/intl/en-GB/policies/terms/

Phillips, M and Littlefair, B (2015) Keeping It Social, *RM Professional, CPL* [online] http://portfolio.cpl.co.uk/RMProfessional/2015-autumn/cyber-security/

Statista (2015), Number of worldwide social network users [online] http://www.statista.com/statistics/

Stelzner, M (2015) 2015 Social Media Marketing Industry Report, *Social Media Examiner* [online] http://www.socialmediaexaminer.com/SocialMediaMarketingIndustryReport2015.pdf

Risk in development aid practice

21

MAGDA STEPANYAN

Risk consideration is nothing new to development aid practice, including both development policy making and programming (within this chapter reference to development aid includes both development and humanitarian organizations). However, with the growing complexity and uncertainty of the development context, it is important to critically revisit the application of risk in development aid. Since its origin, the notion of risk has undergone an extraordinary extension, which is only partly reflected in the concept of risk adopted and practised in development aid. This chapter explores if and to what extent the evolution of 'risk' is reflected in development aid policies and programming.

The conceptualization of the notion of risk, starting from its origin at the end of the Middle Ages, has seen four main qualitative shifts (Ewald, 1993; Beck, 1992; Lund Declaration, 2009):

- Risk as an objective danger that resides in nature. Originating at the end of the Middle Ages, this notion of risk is similar to that of hazard: natural disasters, famine, etc.
- Risk as an accident associated with human fault, an accident that is inevitable in the quest for economic progress. Gaining momentum in the 19th century, this notion of risk embraces industrially produced dangers and hazards and examines human fault as the cause of potential losses and damages.
- Risk as a social phenomenon that resides in the relations between human beings. By the end of 19th century, risk is understood as no longer a phenomenon external to people (like hazard), nor is it

misconduct; instead, it resides among human beings and in their decisions. 'Risks... presuppose decisions' (Beck, 1992). Such risk is hard to rationalize and accurately define in terms of probability, consequences, compensation and accountability.

- Risk as a global 'grand challenge' including mega risks that have a potential to affect the whole of humanity, jeopardize sustainable development, and even endanger our existence; for instance, climate risk, tightening supplies of energy, water and food, ageing societies, public health, etc.

Even though there are no clear-cut comparisons, some parallels can be drawn between the way risk is conceptualized and implemented in development aid practice and the four qualitative shifts in the notion of risk. These are discussed below.

Risk as an external danger

The downside of risk has been actively explored in development practice, particularly since the adoption of the Hyogo Framework for Action (HFA, 2005) in 2005. In 2015 the Sendai Framework that succeeded HFA reiterated the importance of disaster risk management and set the goals for disaster risk reduction by 2030. The importance of assessing the risk of natural disasters and providing adequate response has governed a large volume of DRM (Disaster Risk Management) and DRR (Disaster Risk Reduction) interventions worldwide. These activities span the whole spectrum of the disaster risk cycle, from preparedness and prevention through response to recovery and reconstruction. The HFA has been championed by organizations such as the United Nations (particularly the Development Programme (UNDP) and the Office for Disaster Risk Reduction (UNISDR)), the World Bank (largely through the Global Facility for Disaster Reduction and Recovery (GFDRR)), the European Union (largely through Humanitarian Aid and Civil Protection), as well as many national development agencies (USAID, SIDA, DFID, JICA, etc.), International Non-Governmental Organizations (INGOs) such as COOPI, Save the Children International, IFRC, and national emergency response structures (MSB in Sweden, etc.).

The downside of risk is also explored for technological hazard and man-made conflicts, with the latter being more strongly addressed in development and humanitarian programming. Safety and development considerations go hand in hand: safety is necessary for development, while development ensures safety. Through the Inter-Agency Standing Committee (IASC) global and country-level clusters are set up among UN agencies and International NGOs to ensure effective response and recovery to 'bounce back better' after shocks such as natural disasters or humanitarian crises.

Among relatively recent developments is the process of national risk assessment (within the EU and OECD member states) aimed at all-hazard and all-of-society risk assessment, including issues on safety (natural and technological hazards) and security (malicious attacks and man-made conflicts). Identification and assessment of such risks precedes the capability planning of response agencies to ensure safety and security of societies. Also from this perspective, risk is perceived as a negative phenomenon that is predictable, preventable, and avoidable. Even though this process of national risk assessment is not considered as a development process per se, it is quickly gaining interest in developing countries and has huge potential to strengthen countries' sustainable development.

An indivisible component of the risk of natural and man-made disasters is 'vulnerability' that can be explained in terms of the level of exposure, susceptibility to risk (in such domains as social, economic, cultural, etc.) as well as the lack of resilience capacities (specifically, capacities to anticipate, cope, and recover from a shock) (Birkman et al., 2013). This is an important conceptualization as it explains the multidimensional characteristic of disaster risk and the understanding that risk response cannot be confined to one policy area. Moreover, acknowledging the importance of connecting the different policy communities working on different types of risks, resilient development is quickly becoming a new paradigm that requires integrated consideration of various risks of individuals, communities, states, and their institutions. However, in the absence of a shared understanding of the concept of resilience, there is also large disarray in practice.

Risk as an accident associated with human fault

In development aid practice the conceptualization of risk as a potential deviation from a norm (ie budget, work plan, or the quality of deliverables) partly due to human fault can be explained in terms of Enterprise Risk Management (ERM) or corporate risk profiling. This type of risk too is predictable, can be calculated and avoided. Many large development and humanitarian organizations have designed ERM strategies, including but not limited to UNDP, UN Women, World Bank, NGOs, etc. The purpose is to systematically identify, assess, and respond to existing and emerging risks for an organization and its interventions. However relevant this is, the ERM processes are not yet deeply rooted in development aid practices, being an exception rather than a shared practice in the sector. Consider the following example: the 2015 Report on the Current State of Enterprise Risk Oversight (Beasley *et al.*, 2015) reveals that organizations (including not-for-profit ones) continue to struggle to integrate their risk oversight efforts with their strategic planning processes. For example, in 2013 the UNDP Office of Audit and Investigation (UNDP, 2013) concluded that the UNDP ERM system is unsatisfactory. There are requirements towards risk assessment at the organizational and project/programme level; however, the challenge remains to ensure that risk assessment and response is institutionalized, systematized, and informs decision-making processes within the organization and its interventions. Here is where development and humanitarian organizations fall short.

Exploring futures can further strengthen strategic and operational planning, but without understanding and managing existing and emerging risks it could be of little value. Instead, future thinking and foresight programmes are becoming more and more attractive for development (UNDP, 2014) and humanitarian organizations (such as Humanitarian Futures) often at the expense of adequate risk management. Yet it is the fundamental right of the beneficiaries and benefactors of both humanitarian and development organizations to demand the accountability of these organizations regarding the risks they are facing and the risks they are managing. Risk disclosure is quickly becoming an important governance, accountability, and transparency requirement.

Risk as a social phenomenon

This is the least explored notion of risk in development aid practice. From this perspective, risk is perceived as socially constructed and politically loaded, as an uncertainty that can have either positive or negative impact on the risk bearers. The application of this notion of risk in development aid practices should be equally concerned with the downside and upside of risk, in order to avoid and minimize negative consequences and to maximize benefits. Risk no longer resides outside human society, but it is not just an unfortunate consequence of human error either. Instead risk is an integral part of human life: the multiplicity of uncertainties that surround us as individuals, organizations, or societies shape the landscape of threats and opportunities we face (ie the risk landscape). Without taking into account the risk landscape of its beneficiaries, development intervention misses the correlations and interdependencies between various risks. As a result it can potentially heighten some of the threats while aiming to minimize the others, or it may miss opportunities through not being able to adequately identify and respond to them. For example, while investing in capacity development of civil servants in developing countries, quite often development intervention accelerates already present high mobility within governmental agencies. This is explained by the fact that with improved capacities people become more competitive in the labour market and can find better-paid jobs elsewhere. With such intervention, the risk landscape of a civil servant is altered: if prior to an intervention it was an opportunity for a civil servant to be employed by the Government, after an intervention it could be a limitation, as an opportunity would be to follow the economic benefits. Ultimately, the goal of strengthening state institutions could be potentially missed.

Development aid practice could benefit from application of some simple principles:

1 Understand the 'initial' risk landscape of the target beneficiaries prior to any development intervention.

2 Set the priority objectives for the intervention as a 'desired' risk landscape of primary beneficiaries. This would imply careful consideration and explicit reference to the potential challenges and desired opportunities that an intervention would trigger for its beneficiaries. Also, this implies consideration of connections among various risks (networked risks) and account for the risks that could be triggered for the larger cycle of the indirect beneficiaries.

3 Design the monitoring and evaluation system so that it provides feedback loops on both the progress made (retrospective view) and the emerging risks (forward-looking perspective).

4 Create room for prospective learning alongside the implementation to embrace the newly emerging changes and navigate through these changes towards the most desired ones.

Understanding of opportunity management in development aid is growing (World Bank, 2014) and it is important to consider the dynamic correlation between both threats and opportunities. This requires adequate understanding of the concept of risk, as well as availability of methodologies and tools for effective risk management, which is a largely untapped area. Probably, closest to this notion of risk is the resilience system analysis developed by OECD.

Another very important dimension of this notion of risk is that risk is subjective: different stakeholders (communities, states, private sectors, donors, etc.) have different risk perceptions, whereby the threat for one can be an opportunity for the other. This subjectivity depends on the whole set of risks faced by the person, community, organization, or society at large, ie the risk landscape. That same risk landscape becomes the reference for varying risk perceptions and explains the risk response pattern. For instance, in some cases limited capacities of state in service provision might require outsourcing, which is an opportunity for the private sector.

The importance for development partners while designing and implementing their interventions is to clearly address the question: whose threats and whose opportunities to prioritize? The choices are inevitably ethical since any development intervention alters the 'risk landscape' of its beneficiaries, leaving some better off and the others worse off vis-à-vis their situation prior to the intervention. This has to be acknowledged, and become a central part of the development ethics. It is especially relevant considering the risks that have cross-border or international character. Yet, there is a clear risk governance deficit in ensuring that risk management is inclusive and accounts for various risk perceptions.

Risk as a global 'grand challenge' or mega risks

The term 'grand challenge' implies two important prerequisites: global consensus on the nature of the challenge, and a broad-based mobilization in response. This is a novel dimension of risk management, yet to be explored. However, some of the grand challenges are already being addressed within development aid; for instance, climate change, renewable energy supply, and food security.

Understanding and responding to mega risks is inevitably linked to such characteristics as disruption of cause-effect relationships. In our globalized and highly interdependent society, such disruption occurs in various dimensions – across generations, geographic areas, sectors, institutions, etc. – and this can lead to a 'butterfly effect' that often escapes our attention. A recent example is the financial crisis that triggered a large wave of cascading risks across geographic regions, sectors and industries. Understanding the 'butterfly effect' could help us to understand how risk propagates across borders, sectors, generations, and help to identify early signals of potential mega risks.

Summary

Development cooperation is a combined effort of development partners to influence the risks of millions by creating opportunities and preserving them from negative shocks. Yet the importance of risk management is hardly articulated in development aid practice. This has led to a risk governance deficit in the development sector, which is largely explained by the lack of understanding of the concept of risk, as well as the absence of methodologies and tools for adequate risk management for development.

References

Beasley, M, Branson, B and Hancock, B (2015) 2015 report on the current state of enterprise risk oversight [online] https://www.aicpa.org/interestareas/businessindustryandgovernment/resources/erm/downloadabledocuments/aicpa_erm_research_study_2015.pdf

Beck, U (1992) *Risk Society: Towards a new modernity*, Sage Publications, Thousand Oaks, CA

Birkmann *et al.*, (2013) Framing vulnerability, risk and societal responses: the MOVE framework, *Natural Hazards*, 67 (2), pp 193–211

Cooperazione Internazionale (COOPI) http://www.coopi.org/en/home/

Department for International Development (DFID): https://www.gov.uk/government/organisations/department-for-international-development

European Commission (2015) Disaster risk management: echo factsheet [online] http://ec.europa.eu/echo/files/aid/countries/factsheets/thematic/disaster_risk_management_en.pdf

Ewald, F (1993) Two Infinities of Risk, in *The Politics of Everyday Fear*, ed. B Massumi, University of Minnesota Press

Global Facility for Disaster Reduction and Recovery (GFDRR): https://www.gfdrr.org

Humanitarian Aid and Civil Protection: http://ec.europa.eu/echo/

Humanitarian Futures: http://www.humanitarianfutures.org

Hyogo Framework for Action (2005) *UNISDR* [online] http://www.unisdr.org/we/coordinate/hfa

Inter-Agency Standing Committee: https://interagencystandingcommittee.org

International Federation of Red Cross and Red Crescent Societies (IFRC): http://www.ifrc.org

Japan International Cooperation Agency (JACA): http://www.jica.go.jp/english/

Lund Declaration: Grand Challenges (2009) [online] http://www.vinnova.se/upload/dokument/Verksamhet/UDI/Lund_Declaration.pdf

The Organisation for Economic Co-operation and Development (OECD): http://www.oecd.org/gov/risk/

OECD (no date) Risk and Resilience [online] http://www.oecd.org/dac/risk-resilience.htm

Save the Children International: https://www.savethechildren.net

Swedish International Development Cooperation (SIDA): http://www.sida.se/English/

Swedish Civil Contingency Agency (MSB): https://www.msb.se/en/

United Nations Development Programme (UNDP): http://www.undp.org

UNDP (2014) Foresight as a strategic long-term planning tool for development countries [online] http://www.undp.org/content/undp/en/home/librarypage/capacity-building/global-centre-for-public-service-excellence/Foresight.html

UNDP Office of Audit and Investigation (2013) Audit of UNDB enterprise risk management system [online] http://audit-public-disclosure.undp.org/view_audit_rpt_2.cfm?audit_id=1181

United Nations Office for Disaster Risk Reduction (UNISDR): http://www.unisdr.org

US Agency for International Development (USAID): https://www.usaid.gov

World Bank (2014) World Development Report 2014: Risk and opportunity management for development [online] http://siteresources.worldbank.org/EXTNWDR2013/Resources/8258024-1352909193861/8936935-1356011448215/8986901-1380046989056/WDR-2014_Complete_Report.pdf

Epilogue
The future of risk management

DR DAVID HILLSON

Risk is everywhere

Based on more than three decades of direct personal involvement with risk management, two quotes seem apposite. The first is the opening line of the novel *The Go-Between*: 'The past is a foreign country; they do things differently there' (Hartley, 1953). But the French proverb is also true: 'Plus ça change, plus c'est la même chose.' Much has changed in the world of risk management, although a lot is still the same.

Seen from a certain perspective, this is not surprising, since risk is everywhere. The world we inhabit is unpredictable, strange, incomprehensible, surprising, mysterious, awesome, different, other. This is true from the macro level of galaxies to the exotic nano-realm of subatomic particles, and everywhere in between. Irrefutable evidence forces people to accept the truth that we neither know nor understand everything, and we cannot control everything.

Consequently, the word 'risk' has become a common and widely used part of today's vocabulary, relating to personal circumstances (health, pensions, insurance, investments etc.), society (terrorism, economic performance, food safety etc.), and business (corporate governance, strategy, business continuity etc.).

And it seems that mankind has an insatiable desire to confront risk and attempt to manage it proactively. Many of the institutions of human society and culture could be viewed as frameworks constructed to address uncertainty, including politics, religion, philosophy, technology, laws, ethics and morality. Each of these tries to impose structure on the world as it is experienced, limiting variation where that is possible, and explaining residual uncertainty where control is not feasible. Sense making appears to be an innate human faculty, seeking patterns in apparent randomness. People apply a variety of approaches, both overtly and subconsciously, to reach an acceptable degree of comfort in the face of uncertainty.

Risk management is everywhere

As a result, not only is risk everywhere, but so is risk management. Perhaps it is not too far-fetched to describe risk management as offering an integrative framework for understanding many parts of the human experience, if not all. Just as the presence of risk is recognized and accepted as inevitable and unavoidable in every field of human endeavour, so there is a matching drive to address risk as far as possible. This has led to a proliferation of areas where the phrase 'risk management' is used to describe efforts to identify, understand and respond to risk, particularly in various aspects of business.

There seems little doubt that risk management has been part of human activity for a very long time, even when it was not recognized or labelled as such, and it is today a vital component of business. As a result, anyone asking the simple question, 'What is risk management?' will not find a simple answer. Even the most cursory exploration reveals a huge variety of differing perspectives, all claiming to represent the best way to address risk.

In fact risk management is not a single subject at all, as we have seen throughout this book; risk management is a family of related topics. These business applications range from project or Operational Risk Management through reputation or supply chain risk management up to governance and enterprise-wide risk management, with many other disciplines also included under the risk management umbrella.

Earlier chapters have demonstrated that many common elements are shared by these different types of risk management, but each has its own distinctive language, methodology, tools and techniques. They vary in scope from the broadest application to very specific areas of risk. They are at different levels of maturity, with some types of risk management being quite recent developments while others measure their history in decades or longer. But each is important in its own way, representing part of the response of business to the uncertain environment within which it operates.

Our two-part exploration of multidimensional risk management has covered the main application areas through which businesses and organizations currently seek to address risk (Part One of this book), as well as a number of emerging risk management approaches that are becoming more prominent (Part Two). In some ways it has been hard to make a clear distinction between the topics in 'current best practice' and those in 'emerging trends', and it seems likely that some readers will debate the presence of one or more types of risk management in the two parts. Some may feel that an area included in Part One as a main application area is in fact rather marginal in their organization or their experience; others will consider that something we have labelled in Part Two as 'emerging' is for them a mainstream area of focus. Some readers may believe that a key aspect of risk management is missing altogether, or that something has been included that does not deserve to feature in this volume.

This illustrates the dynamic nature of the risk challenge faced by business today and tomorrow. What was indispensable today may become obsolete tomorrow. A topic considered as part of the exotic fringe until recently may emerge in the near future as a fundamental element in theory and practice. This is what makes risk management interesting of course.

What next?

Having surveyed the current state of risk management in terms of both best practice and emerging trends, what is coming next? Each of the chapters in Part One has closed with some suggestions on how that particular area of risk management might develop in the short term. But in a broader sense, where is risk management heading? Can we use our risk-based skills in exploring and assessing future scenarios to make any reasonable predictions?

Three potential futures seem worth considering: expansion, contraction and cycle. These alternative options are outlined below.

Expansion

The first possibility is that the scope of risk management will continue to expand, encompassing more elements of business life (as well as encroaching into personal and societal areas), adding new dimensions of application along the way until 'everything is just risk management'. Ultimately all decisions will be taken in the light of the identification and assessment of relevant uncertainty. This expansionist view is exemplified by some risk management practitioners whose slogan is 'Manage the risk = manage the business'.

This implies that normal planned activity needs no special attention, and all that is required is management of variations from the plan. By looking ahead to identify potential variations, both positive and negative, and focusing management attention on addressing just these aspects, proponents of this position claim that success is ensured.

While the 'Expansion' option emphasizes the importance of risk management, it is an extreme position that doesn't match reality. The risk element is not the whole picture in a business (or in life), and concentrating wholly on managing risk to the exclusion of other aspects would be detrimental and counter-productive.

Contraction

It is probably true that the scope and influence of risk management will continue to expand, at least in the short term, as more areas of application are found for risk-based approaches. But is such expansion limitless, or will some critical point be reached when further growth is unsustainable, to be followed by contraction? Might risk management as a distinct discipline even disappear altogether? There are two ways in which this conceivably might happen.

Firstly, it is possible that risk management might just be the latest management fad, although admittedly it is already rather more long-lasting than most. The recent emphasis on risk management started in the 1970s, and though it shows little sign of reducing, it is conceivable that our future colleagues might place less emphasis on risk than we do today. If risk management goes the way of other fads, it could disappear from the scene very quickly, becoming just a memory or a footnote in the annals of management history.

There is a second way in which risk management might disappear, rather than fading away into oblivion. If risk management becomes all pervasive to the point where it is intrinsic to the nature of business at all levels, it could become absorbed into 'normal management practice' and so cease to exist as a separate discipline. If everyone naturally and habitually 'thinks risk' and manages it as a normal part of daily life, then it might no longer be necessary to have a special function called 'risk management', since this would be accepted and practised by all. Risk management could vanish as a result of its own success, leaving risk specialists and practitioners as outdated purveyors of a universally recognized self-evident truth.

Cycle

A third option for the future of risk management is possible, combining expansion and contraction into a cyclic phenomenon, alternating between periods of high visibility and times where risk management is less prominent. A review of the broader story of risk management across the span of human history reveals periods when it had a higher profile than at other times.

Social commentators suggest that advances in technology, law and religion can be seen as human responses to uncertainty, seeking to make sense of the ineffable, and attempting to impose control wherever possible. If this is true then the major changes in civilizations might be interpreted as cycles of risk management, though not within the same process-driven framework we see in modern business. And maybe the expansion of risk management we are witnessing in the business world today is merely part of the latest cycle, reflecting wider societal trends.

Where now?

Only time will tell whether we will see indefinite **expansion** of risk management until it encompasses everything, or whether a turning point might be reached to be followed by a **contraction** leading to the disappearance of risk management as a distinct discipline, or whether some ongoing **cycle** of growth and decline might occur.

The reason that risk management is such a fascinating topic is precisely because it is constantly changing. New approaches and application areas emerge, new dimensions of risk management are discovered, and new insights into the meaning of risk are revealed. Like everything else about the future, the way that risk management will develop in the coming years remains uncertain. But as risk practitioners we should expect nothing less!

References and further reading

Bernstein P L (1996). *Against the Gods: The remarkable story of risk*, J Wiley, New York, USA

Centre for Tomorrow's Company (2015) *Tomorrow's Risk Leadership: Delivering risk resilience and business performance*, Centre for Tomorrow's Company, London, UK

Cleary, S and Malleret, T (2007) *Global Risk: Business success in turbulent times*, Palgrave Macmillan, Basingstoke, UK

del Cano, A and de la Cruz, M P (1998) The past, present and future of project risk management, *International Journal of Project & Business Risk Management*, 2 (4), pp 361–87

Dembo, R S and Freeman, A (1998) *Seeing Tomorrow: Rewriting the rules of risk*, J Wiley, New York, USA

Gardner, D (2008) *Risk: The science and politics of fear*, Virgin Books, London, UK

Hartley, L P (1953) *The Go-Between*, Hamish Hamilton, London, UK

Hillson, D A (1998) Project risk management: future developments, *International Journal of Project & Business Risk Management*, 2 (2), pp 181–95

Hillson, D A (2003) Risk management: best practices and future developments, Presented at II Congreso Nacional de Gerencia de Proyectos, Universidad Nacional de Ingenieria, Lima Peru, 24–25 October 2003 [online] http://risk-doctor.com/pdf-files/rm1003.pdf

Hillson, D A, ed. (2012) *Project Risk Management, Past, Present and Future*, Association for Project Management, High Wycombe, UK (available online for APM members from https://www.apm.org.uk/news/project-risk-management-past-present-and-future)

Taleb, N N (2007) *The Black Swan: The impact of the highly improbable*, Allen Lane/Penguin, London, UK

INDEX

Note: The index is filed in alphabetical, word-by-word order. Within main headings, numbers are filed as spelt out in full and acronyms filed as presented. ISO standards are filed in numerical order. Page locators in *italics* denote information contained within a Figure or Table.

action plans 82, 119
activists 97, 98, 202
activity BIA 151–53
adaptive capacity 256, 258
adaptive resilience 257
addition, of risks 65–66
advanced measurement approach (AMA) 63–64
advertising 113, 280, 283
AES 100
aggregated loss distribution 59–61
aleatoric uncertainty 226
alliances 88, 90–91
ambiguity 226
analysis *see* risk analysis
anchoring 91, 239
Anderson, Richard 36
Association for Federal Enterprise Risk Management (AFERM) 19
Association for Project Management (APM) 77, 186
assurance reviews 83
attentional bias 168
attitudes 111, 118, 169, 173, 177
    see also risk attitudes
audience 201, 227–28, 229, 279–80, 285
audit function 29, 30, 31, 103, 120, 137, 221, 276, 293
audits 25, 97, 145, 158
availability bias 239
awareness 191–92
    see also risk awareness; situation awareness

bandwagon effect 168
banks 19–20, 24, 50, 52, 56, 57, 59–61, 63–64, 67–68, 222
    see also International Basel Committee of Banking Supervision
bar charts 229, 230
benchmarking 42, 259
bias 43, 91, 166, 168–69, 189, 238, 239
board engagement 16, 18, 20–21, 31, 41, 44, 118–20, 134, 222, 270

bounded rationality 238
BP 99–100
branding 24, 111, 116, 117, 123, 195, 286
bribes 96, 98
British Organizational Resilience Standard BS65000 142
bureaucratic weakness 98
Business Continuity Institute 123, 132, 158
Business Continuity Management (BCM) 125, 141–63
Business Continuity Management System (BCMS) 143, 144–46, 158–59, 160, 161
business continuity plans 132, 135, 156
business continuity policy 145
business impact analysis (BIA) 148–55, 160
business language 170
businesses 22–23, 69–70, 89–90, 103, 195–96
butterfly effect 295

capability model (OCEG) 39–41
capacity development 294
capital 24, 27, 55–56, 62
    see also reputation capital; social capital
cash flow 24
categorization 66
causal network modelling 62
CauseWise 238–39
change management 45, 262–68, 272
change management plans 264, 277
change teams 264, 267
chaotic culture 273, 274
climate change 15, 77, 110, 291, 295
cloud computing 211–12
Code of Ethics (Conduct) 183, 184, 186
Committee of Sponsoring Organizations of the Treadway Commission (COSO) 19, 38, 43, 126, 136
common governance spirit 273, 274
Commonwealth Games 111
communication 7, 8, 28–29, 58, 78–79, 170, 173, 198, 225–35
    lines of 222

Index

social media 281, 285
see also language; terminology
communication plans 79, 156, 175, 287
communications function 272, 277
competitive advantage 9–10, 21, 124, 134, 209, 210, 258
complex decisions 236–37
complex organizations 246–54
compliance 34–49, 52, 103, 274, 282, 288
complier culture 273, 274
conditions 77
conduct risk 47, 68, 69
confirmation bias 168–69, 238
conflict of interest 186
conflict sensitivity 101
consensus estimate 118
construction projects 81–82, 88, 104
consultants 109, 115, 246, 248
consultation 25, 28–29, 78–79, 174, 178
consumers 115–16, 128, 280
see also customers
context 6, 8, 9, 20–21, 24–26, 46, 78, 79–80, 111
contraction 301, 302
contractors 82, 86–87, 90
contractual liability 87
Control Risk Self-Assessment (CRSA) 57
controls 31, 40, 46, 52–53, 81–82, 221, 256
see also systems of control
conversion, data 65
convolution distribution methods 59
coordination 34, 35, 45, 46–47, 112, 113–14
copula techniques 63–64
corporate affairs function 113
corporate communications function 113
corporate social responsibility (CSR) 100–01, 102, 110, 113, 178
corruption 98, 100, 101, 103
cost effectiveness 53
cost estimates 88
country risk analysis 220–21
country risk management 102, 219–24
credibility 117, 170, 181
Credit Lyonnais 59
crisis communication 285, 287
crisis management 109, 114, 156, 159, 161, 177, 229, 252, 257
cross-border risk management 220–21, 223
CRSA (Control Risk Self-Assessment) 57
CSR (corporate social responsibility 100–01, 102, 110, 113, 178
culture 96, 104, 125, 166–67, 169

see also chaotic culture; complier culture; engaged culture; organizational culture; risk culture
customer relationship management (CRM) 177–78
customers 24, 110, 115–16, 209–10, 281, 282
see also consumers
cyber bullying 201, 210
cyber criminal activities 201, 202, 208–09, 211
cyber opportunities 201, 204–05, 209–10
cyber risk 69, 197–203, 207, 208–09
cyber risk management 194–213
cyber terrorist attacks 201
cyclic phenomenon 301–02

dashboards 28, 67
data 53–54, 57, 62–63, 65–66, 155, 201
data mining 285, 287
data misuse 284
decision controls 241–42, 243
decision making 205, 236–43, 249, 252, 253, 264
decision trees 62
Delhi Commonwealth Games 111
development aid practice 290–97
direct marketing 280, 286
disaster risk management (DRM) 290, 291–92
disaster risk reduction (DRR) 291
disruption 122–24, 128–31, 141, 159
distributed denial of service (DDOS) attacks 196, 201
distrust 98, 99, 100
see also trust
diversification inter (& intra) risk 56
diversity 169
dual processing 239–40

economic conditions 34–35, 209, 220
EDMF (ethical decision-making framework) 183–84
EITI (Extractive Industries Transparency Initiative) 101
emergence 249
emerging markets 94–95, 96, 97, 98, 100, 101, 104, 120
employees 116–17, 188, 198–99, 209, 211, 282, 284
see also personnel (people)
employer brand equity 116
engaged culture 273, 274
engagement *see* board engagement; engaged culture; prior engagement
enterprise risk assessment 22–23

Index

Enterprise Risk Management (ERM) 15–32, 35, 43, 106, 126, 133, 134, 136–37
enterprise-wide risks 22–23
epistemic uncertainty 226
ethical decision-making framework (EDMF) 183–84
ethical dilemmas 182, 183–84, 189
ethical leadership 47, 189, 191
ethical risk 185–87, 189
ethical risk management 116, 180–93
ethical risk profile 186–87
ethics assessment tool *see* Santa Clara Alternative
ethics quick test 185
event agnostic 141–42, 159
event trees 62
exercise scenarios 156–57
expansion 300–01, 302
expected frequency trees 228
exposure *see* potential exposure; risk exposure
external affairs 102
extortion 99, *201*, 206
extractives companies 101, 104
Extractive Industries Transparency Initiative (EITI) 101
extreme events 52, 61–62

Facebook 111, 210, 280, 281–82
fan charts *229*
fast decisions 240–41
fault trees 61, 62
Financial Conduct Authority (FCA) 276
financial performance 123–24, 133–34
Financial Reporting Council (FRC) 276
financial services 30, 31, 50, 52, 55–56, 67–68, 117–18, 275–77
see also banks; insurance companies
Financial Stability Board (FSB) 269–70, 276
financing options 120
Fourier transforms 59
fraud 53, 68, *201*, 284
frequency distribution 59, *60*
front-end loading (FEL) 75
frontier markets *see* emerging markets
functional distortion 43

G4 Guidelines of Global Reporting Initiative (GRI) 185
gender factors 169–70
generational diversity 169
Glasgow Commonwealth Games 111
global 'grand challenge' risk 291, 295

global portfolio management 96
globalization 15, *35*, *95*, 106–07, 208
good will 24
governance 20, *30*, 31, 34–49, 54, 67, 83–86, *273*, 274
governments 97–98, 101, 105, 171, 195, 206, 210, 294
GRC (Governance, Risk and Compliance) 34–49
'grey swan' risks 128
groupthink 168

hacking ('hacktivists') 202, 211, 282, 283, 284
Harvard Business Review 112, 209
hazard data presentation 231–34
heatmaps 65, 186
Henley Business School 109
heuristics 238–39, 243
high loss risk situations 53
hostile spies *202*, 203
human fault risk management 290, 292–93
human resources (HR) function 102, 113, *137*, 178, *198*, 272, 277
Hyogo Framework for Action (HFA) 291
hyperbolic discounting 168

ICT readiness, business continuity 152–53, 161
identity theft 209, 283
IEC 62198 76, 77
'Illustrated Series' guides (OECG) 43
impact measurement 54–55
implementation 7, 26–27
  barriers to 43–45
in-house risk assessment 103, 222
Incident Command, UK Fire and Rescue 241–42
incident data 65
incident plans 156
indicators *see* key risk indicators (KRIs); resilience indicators
individual risk 21, 65, 87, 194, *195*, 196, 228
industrial espionage 283–84, 287
information dissemination 67, *201*
information exchange 258
information gathering 40, 68–69, 148, 151, 229, 282, 284
infrastructure projects 91, 92, 97–98, 104, 259
innovation 18, 122, *201*
insider threats *201*, 202, 203
Institute of Risk Management (IRM) *8*, 35–36, 44, 200, 202, 211, 271, 272–73, 275

Index

insurance 19–20, 31, 52, 56, 61, 67
   cyber risk 196, 203, 206
   supply chain risk management 131–32, 136
   see also Zurich Insurance Group
integration 41–43, 51–52, 89–90, 127
integrity 189, *270*
intellectual property 74, 195, 203, 204, 282, 284–85
Inter-Agency Standing Committee (IASC) 292
internal controls-based risk management 31, 46, 221, 256
International Alert 101
International Basel Committee of Banking Supervision 54
international risk appetite 96
internet 109, 118, 194, *201*, 287
Internet of Things 210–11
interviews 272, 276
Investment Approval Committee 85, 86
investment governance 84–86
Investment Review Committee 85, 86
investment trap 220
investor relations function 79, 113
Iranian Revolution 99, 103
IRM (Institute of Risk Management) 8, 35–36, 44, 200, 202, 211, 271, 272–73, 275
ISO22301 29, 145, 150, 155, 158–59
ISO22313 145, 146–47
ISO25999 132
ISO26000 100
ISO27031 152, 158–59
ISO31000 8, 9, 16, 20, 29, 38, 45, 100, 126, 136, 184
IT operations (systems) 68, *202*, 203

key risk indicators (KRIs) 28, 65, 66–67, 68
Knight, F 2
knowledge 23
knowledge-based trust 181
known unknown 226

language 170, 230–31
   see also terminology
leadership 44, 144, 148, 189, 192, 258, *263*
   see also risk leadership
learning organizations 258
legal risk *30*, 103, 282
liquidity 24
location 73, 96, 104, 111
lognormal distribution 59
loss aversion 168

loss data 57, 62–63
Loss Distribution Approach (LDA) 58–61, 62–63
loss measurement 54–55
loyalty 110, 116

macro stress testing 62
major project risk management 70
major risks 89
malware 194, *201*, 204, 283–84, 287
managed risk 21–22, 27, 31–32
management *see* board engagement; risk managers; senior management; tone from the top; top (level) management
management meetings 83
   see also risk committees
market expansion *201*
market-perceived relative quality 115
market sentiment 117–18
marketing function 113
Marks, Norman 35, 46–47
mathematical theory 2
maximum allowable outage (MAO) 150, 155
maximum data loss 155
measurement 54–55, *81*, 266–67
   see also advanced measurement approach (AMA); metrics
mega-projects 91–92
mega risks 291, 295
meta-competences 191
metrics 52–53, 55, 135
   see also measurement
micro stress testing 62
minimalist governance *273*, 274
minimum business continuity objectives (MBCO) 150, 155
mining industry 99, 222
mis-selling 53, 61, 68
misrepresentation 282
mobile (personal) devices 211, 287
modelling 53–54, 57, 58–63, 125
monitoring 7, 28, 82–83, 92, 105, 173–74, 175
   see also reviews
Monte Carlo simulations 59, 61, 87
moral DNA psychometric test 276–77
Morgan Stanley 24
motivation 40, 144

national diversity 169
national risk assessment 292
natural resources 15, 17, 18, 97, 223
naturalistic decision making (NDM) 241

Index

NCSU report (2015) 16, 29–31
near-term bias 168
negative bias 189
neuro-linguistic programming (NLP) 44–45
new business models 69–70
non-executive directors (NEDs) 120
non-governmental organizations (NGOs) 101, 112, 291
normal distribution 59
not-for-profit organizations 115, 194–96, 199, 200, 202–05, 293
nuclear industry 23

objective setting 3, 39, 161, 294
objectives 4, 5, 6, 9, 30, 39, 47, 50–51
   cyber security 197, 204
   organizational change 263
   P3 risk management 76, 77
   see also recovery point objective (RPO); recovery time objective (RTO)
OGC M_o_R 8
oil companies 56, 104, 222
   see also BP
online activities 194–95, 199
online assets 204
online bullying 201
Open Compliance and Ethics Group (OCEG) 34, 35–36, 37, 39–41, 43, 46
operating discipline 258–59
operational level continuity 155
operational losses 62–63
operational risk 54, 55–56, 63
Operational Risk Management (ORM) 50–71
opportunities 5, 7, 25, 28, 259
optimism bias 168, 239
organizational change management 262–68
organizational context 20–21, 24–26, 46
organizational culture 16, 25, 36, 39, 41–43, 110, 117, 144, 200, 206–07
organizational design 45, 47
organizational ecosystem 147
organizational resilience 50, 142, 158–162, 250, 255–61
organizational risk leadership framework 251–53
organizations see complex organizations; learning organization
ORX 62
outsourcing 56, 99, 122, 147, 151, 203, 205, 208, 212, 295

P3 risk management 75–93
page guidelines, social media 287
Panjer recursions 59
perception 112–13, 166–70, 207

performance appraisal 158
personal devices (mobile devices) 211, 287
personality 169
personnel (people) 44, 161
   see also employees
place branding 111
Plan-Do-Check-Act (PDCA) 26–27, 146–47, 162
planning
   political risk management 104–05
   strategic 25, 31, 39, 89, 104, 137, 293
   see also action plans; business continuity plans; change management plans; communication plans
PMI (Project Management Institute) 76, 77, 184, 186
Poisson distribution 59
political change 54, 131, 219–20
political risk 96–100, 105
political risk management 94–108
political symbolism 96
political violence 99, 220
portfolio managers 80, 85, 86
portfolio risk 76
portfolios 73–75
   see also P3 risk management
potential exposure 81, 82, 83
PPI mis-selling 53
PPPs (public-private partnerships) 90
presentations 227, 228
principled performance 39–40, 46
prior engagement 228–29
process BIA 150–51
process prioritization 150–51
product and service BIA 148–50
productivity 281–82, 288
professional diversity 169
professionalism 183
profiling 136, 173, 186–87, 223, 286, 292
programme risk 76
programmes 73–75
   see also P3 risk management
project life cycle 75
project management, business impact analysis 154
Project Management Institute (PMI) 76, 77, 184, 186
project managers 79, 82, 85, 86, 92
project risk 76
project risk management 4, 70
   see also P3 risk management
project work breakdown structure (WBS) 79–80
projects 73–75

Index

see also mega-projects; P3 risk management; project risk management
psychology 237–39, 243
psychometric tools 272, 276–77
public service sector 16, 92, 99

qualitative data aggregation 65–66
quality assurance (QA) 158
quantitative risk analysis 82, 87–89, 90–91, 199, 250, 252

rapport talk 170
RBC 111
RCSA (Risk and Control Self-Assessment) 57, 61, 65
Recognition Primed Decision Making (RPDM) 241, 242
recommendation making 170
recovery point objective (RPO) 151, 153, 155–56
recovery time objective (RTO) 150, 155, 156, 157
recruitment 23, 281, 282, 284
regulatory compliance 19–20, 54, 73, 97–98, 282, 288
report talk 169
reporting 28–29, 31, 65–67, 118, 119–20, 221, 277
representativeness 239
reputation 24, 190
reputation capital 280
reputation management 109, *114*
reputation-reality gaps 112, 113
reputation research centres 109
reputational risk 69, 109–21, 127, 281, 286–87
reputational risk evaluation 118
reputational risk management 112–14, 118–20
resilience 50, 142, 158–62, 250, 255–61
resilience healthcheck 259
resilience indicators 256
resources 25, 27–28, 40, 51, 77, 90, 146, 156
responsiveness 40
  see also risk responses
retail industry 98, 135, 137
reviews 7, 25, 82–83, 83–84, 92, 157–58, 176, 251, 284
RIMS (Risk and Insurance Management Society) 20–21, 36–37, 126
risk 2–5, 38, 225, 248, 290–95, 298–99
risk aggregation 53–54, 63–64
risk analysis 51, 61, 78, 81–82, 220–21, 250, 251, 253, 265–66, 276–77

  see also business impact analysis (BIA); quantitative risk analysis; root cause analysis;
  scenario analysis; sensitivity analysis; stakeholder analytics
risk appetite 18, 25, 27, 28, 51, 65, 96, 206
risk aspects culture diagnostic (IRM) 275–77
risk aspects culture model (IRM) 273
risk assessment 6, 57, 86, 89, 153, 160, 225
  see also enterprise risk assessment; in-house risk assessment; national risk assessment;
  self-assessment; supply chain risk assessment
risk attitudes 111–12, 165, 166–67, 180, 206, 264
risk awareness 136, 272–74, 277
risk-based decision making 205, 236–45, 249, 252, 253, 264
risk capacity 19
risk clockspeed 237, 240–41, 243
risk committees 30, 120, 275, 276
risk control 21–22
Risk and Control Self-Assessment (RCSA) 57, 61, 65
risk conversations 136–37
risk culture 36, 37, 44, 269–78
risk disclosure 293
risk-efficient decisions 205
risk evaluation 8, 78, 82, 118, 119
risk exposure 6, 7, 20–21, 25, 31, 51, 53–54, 56, 57, 124
  see also potential exposure
risk identification 6, 8, 9, 78, 79, 80, 266, 267
risk indicators 28, 65, 66–67, 68
Risk and Insurance Management Society (RIMS) 20–21, 36–37, 126
risk inventories 31
risk investment decision 205
risk landscape 123, 131, 294, 295
risk leadership 181–82, 191, 246–54
risk lessons learned 7, 8–9
risk management 3, 4, 5–10, 31, 38, 299–300
  see also disaster risk management (DRM); human fault risk management; major project risk management
risk management function 222
risk management integration 41–43, 51–52, 89–90, 127
risk management process 6–9, 38, 77–83
risk management skills 17–18, 22

risk management standards 5, 7–9, 29
  see also ISO26000; ISO25999; ISO22301; ISO22313; ISO27031; ISO31000; OGC M_o_R
risk managers 58, 66, 189, 191, 222–24
risk mapping 119, 250, 251
risk metrics 52–53, 55, 135
  see also measurement
risk owner 58, 176
risk ratings 65, 221, 248
risk registers (lists) 29, 119, 175, 251, 265–66
risk relationships analysis 251
risk reporting 28–29, 31, 65–67, 118, 119–20, 221, 277
risk responses 6–7, 28, 205, 250
risk reviews 7, 25, 82–83, 92, 157–58, 176, 251, 284
risk scales 65
risk sources 185–86
risk strategy 51, 56–57, 68
risk taking 21–22
risk tolerance 18, 25, 51, 55–56, 57, 65, 66–67, 68, 266
risk treatment 8, 9, 78, 82, 83
risk treatment pattern analysis 251
root cause analysis 61, 62, 69, 187, 200, 253
RPDM (Recognition Primed Decision Making) 241, 242
RPO (recovery point objective) 151, 153, 155–56
RTO (recovery time objective) 150, 155, 156, 157

safety 288, 291–92
sales teams 222
Santa Clara Alternative 185–89
Sarbanes-Oxley Act 20, 42
satisficing 241
scandals 20, 110
scans (scanning) 24
scenario analysis 61–62, 67, 91, 105
scenario testing 20, 23, 132
  see also exercise scenarios; worst case scenarios
schedule uncertainty 87
security 103
security breaches 196, 282, 288
security management systems 126
selectivity, reporting 67
self-assessment 57, 61, 65, 158
Sendai Framework 291
senior management 16, 18, 20–21, 65, 91, 137, 270
sensemaking 167, 298–99

sensitivity analysis 62
severity distribution 59, *60*
shareholders 117–18
Shell 101, 116, 117
silver 17–18
simple decisions 236, *237*
situation awareness 241, 242, *256*, 258
skills 17–18, 22
sleep-walking culture 273, 274
smart devices 210–11
social capital 258
social cyber risks 209
social media 210, 279–89
social media plans 286
social phenomenon risk 290–91, 293–95
societal risk 228
spaghetti plots *229*
specialist risk assessments 89
speed of change, of risk 22–23
SRA (systemic risk analysis) 251, 253
stakeholder abuse 283
stakeholder analytics 171
stakeholder circle methodology 171–74
stakeholder communication plans 79
stakeholder confidence 39, 55
stakeholder engagement 100–01, 172–74, 175, 176–77, 178, 266, 267
stakeholder identification 171–72
stakeholder management 176–77
stakeholder prioritization 172
stakeholder relationships 176, *177*
stakeholder risk 73, 76, 112, 113, 115, 119, 165, 174–77
stakeholder risk management 164–79
Standard Life 111
start-up costs 25
strategic governance 273, 274
strategic level continuity 155
strategic objectives 4, *197*
strategic planning 25, 31, 39, 104, *137*, 293
strategic risks 4, 126–27, 128
strategy 31, 51, 56–57, 68, *89*, 103
stress testing 62, 67
sub-prime mortgage business 24
subsidiary objectives 4
succession planning 23, *270*
supplier performance 158
supply chain disruptions 122–24, 128–31
supply chain risk assessment 124–25, 132–33, *135*
supply chain risk healthcheck *138*
Supply Chain Risk Leadership Council 126, 135
supply chain risk management 122–40, 161
surveys 113, 211, 272, 276–77

Index

sustainability 18, 24, 102, 106, 291, 292
swift trust 181
systematic risk management 51–52
systemic risk analysis (SRA) 251, 253
systemic risk leadership 251–53
systemic risk response registers 251
systems of control 272, 273, 274

talent management 117
Talisman 101
target attitude 173
target times 150
targets 267
technology 15, 37, 73, 111, 190, 196, 198–99
    see also cloud computing; ICT readiness, business continuity; IT operations (systems); mobile (personal) devices
teen attitudes 111
10 Steps to Cyber Security (UK government) 203–04
tendering 86–87
terminology 43–44
terms and conditions 288
terrorist attacks 283
Tesco 117
threats 4, 5, 7, 16, 28
'3 'A's of risk 112
    see also risk appetite; risk attitude
timing 22–23
tollgate reviews 83–86
tone from the top 36, 270
top (level) management 17–18, 20–21, 22, 144, 145–46, 148–49
total risk 185, 186
total risk profiling 70, 135, 136
traceability 283
training 27, 58, 281, 287–88
    see also capacity development
transaction processing 68

trust 110, 111, 115, 180–81, 258, 266
    see also distrust
Turnbull Report on Internal Control 54

UK Corporate Governance Code 54
UK Fire and Rescue Services 242
UN Global Compact 101
UN Principles on Responsible Investment (PRI) 101
uncertainty 2–3, 4, 9, 15–16, 87, 226, 249
'uncertainty that matters' 4, 5, 9, 76
unions 99
United Nations Development Programme (UNDP) 291, 292, 293
unknown known 226
user social media profiles 280, 283, 284

validation, Business Continuity Management 157–58
value-based leadership 181, 182
value creation 182
value drivers 23–24
value flow mapping 125
value uncertainty 87
values 181–82
variability 226
velocity 22–23, 239
vicarious liability 282
Voluntary Principles on Security and Human Rights (VPSHR) 101, 103
vulnerability 292

warnings 170
weak governance 273, 274
weighted risk 186
worst case scenarios 66

Zurich Insurance Group 129–31, 132, 135–36, 140
Zurich Risk Room 131